THE RESHAPING OF FRENCH DEMOCRACY

EUROPE IN THE TWENTIETH CENTURY

GORDON WRIGHT

The Reshaping
of French Democracy

BEACON PRESS   BOSTON

FOR LOUISE

Introduction

by Stephen R. Graubard

Europe in the Twentieth Century

Most historians, until quite recently, looked with suspicion on their professional colleagues who thought to investigate near-contemporary events. Although there was never anything like agreement on the matter, it was generally assumed that the requirements of objective scholarship could not be satisfied by historians who chose to write about their own times. The argument seemed compelling that those who undertook such tasks would always be operating with essentially incomplete archives, particularly in the diplomatic and political fields, but in other areas as well.

When the charge of incomplete documentation was refuted by those who insisted that the historian of twentieth-century happenings was in fact rarely hampered by a lack of materials, but was, on the contrary, generally overwhelmed by their abundance, having at his disposal incomparable documentation of kinds available to the historian for no other period, the argument shifted to a questioning of whether the historian could ever be objective in judging his own times.

The idea that objectivity was possible, but not to be expected of the historian concerned with near-contemporary events, spoke of a bias that owed a great deal to the nineteenth-century German school of history, perhaps best exemplified by von Ranke. The monographic tradition, with its emphasis on facts, supposedly neutral, and with its injunction to avoid judgments, particularly value judgments, still enjoyed currency in the early part of the twentieth century. R. G. Collingwood, in *The Idea of History*, probably did as much as anyone to discredit the notion that the historian was capable of taking himself out of his materials, or that his principal purpose should be the discovery and recording of value-free facts. Once the historian's role in shaping his materials was admitted, it became difficult to argue that what the historian did when he approached the events of the sixteenth century differed significantly from what he did when he set out to study the twentieth. Clearly, the distinction of a particular historical work was the only meaningful criterion for judging its acceptability; there was no intrinsic reason why research on twentieth-century subjects should result in work inferior in any way to what was realized when other periods were investigated.

The acceptance of contemporary history as a legitimate field of inquiry by professional scholars was slow, but once accomplished, it contributed to the creation of a literature that was soon recognized to have distinction and importance. There were, however, marked differences between the reception of these works and of those written by scholars who preferred to concentrate on earlier periods. To put the matter in purely commercial terms, scholarly studies of twentieth-century events competed in a market still dominated by popular books. For almost every imaginable twentieth-century theme, there was generally available a book written by someone who saw the possibility of finding a mass market for his work. The quality of these popular studies was of course uneven: some were original in very important respects; many were well written; a few were scarcely more than popularizations of scholarly works; the greatest number, perhaps, claimed no merit except that they offered amusement for those who wished to be entertained by lively narrative. In any case, because there was a mass market for such books, they were quickly reissued in inexpensive paperback editions and found their way into university course syllabi and onto the shelves of personal libraries.

Happily, Gresham's Law does not always operate, at least not with respect to books. Many publishers resisted the temptation to publish only popular studies of contemporary themes, showing in their selection of books on the twentieth century the same fastidiousness that they demonstrated when they chose a title for some period for which popular taste was less in evidence. The American reading public has been well served in having many excellent scholarly works on twentieth-century subjects issued in paperback editions. Nevertheless, important titles still exist only in hard covers, and one of the principal purposes of the Beacon Press paperback series, *Europe in the Twentieth Century*, is to make such works available.

The Reshaping of French Democracy

The Reshaping of French Democracy, written by Gordon Wright in 1948, is an early account of the framing of the Constitution of the Fourth Republic. The political crises that attended the drafting of an earlier version and its eventual rejection by the French electorate, the efforts of a Second Constituent Assembly to produce an acceptable document, leading to victory by the narrowest of margins in a national plebescite, Charles de Gaulle's opposition notwithstanding, are all fully and ably recounted in this book. Professor Wright completed the work when the institutions of the Fourth Republic were barely in place; he understood the fragility of the Constitution, and did not underestimate the difficulties that would attend a regime that began its life with so narrow a base of political support. Why should such a work, written so soon after the event, be thought worthy of republication today?

Some may think the book important because it captures the essence of postwar political life in France; they will say that the early years prefigured conditions, increasingly hazardous in the 1950's, that culminated in the disintegration of parliamentary forms in 1958. Those who search for early evidences of political and institutional decay will fasten on those parts of the book that dwell on parliamentary wrangling and party rivalry; they will be quick to point out the evidences of a lack of effective and imaginative political leadership. If it is true that the life of a political order is significantly affected by the conditions that prevail at the moment of its birth (a proposition difficult to maintain, given the history of the Third Republic), a close scrutiny into the generative period of the Fourth Republic would seem to require no further defense.

In his conclusions to *The Reshaping of French Democracy,* Wright recognized the possibility that the Fourth Republic would be short-lived; he wrote: "The next generation will know whether the Fourth Republic was destined to be a stormy interlude like that of 1848 or an enduring framework like that of 1875." That verdict is now in; the Fourth Republic was neither the ephemeral Second nor the surprisingly hardy Third. Why, in fact, it survived little more than a decade, however, and whether it ought to be seen as a pale reflection of the Third or as the harbinger of the Fifth, are matters on which opinions differ. The history of the Fourth Republic is not unambiguously clear; neither its weaknesses nor its strengths are as obvious as some pretend. The Fourth Republic remains, a dozen years after its demise, a subject of political controversy. Not the least of the merits of Gordon Wright's work is its dispassionate analysis of the political climate that existed in France after the war. A regime that was called upon to rehabilitate a war-damaged economy, wage war in Indo-China, and put down rebellion in Algeria was not confronted with just the ordinary tasks of government. It is scarcely surprising that the Fourth Republic showed itself incapable of coping with problems of this magnitude. The events of 1952–1958 are in some measure explained by the account the author gives of the problems attending the birth of the Republic.

Charles de Gaulle is by every measure the single most important French political figure of this century. His wartime experiences are fully recounted in his own three-volume autobiography; others have written memoirs and histories to supplement what he has chosen to reveal; as for his achievements as President of France after 1958, they will almost certainly never lack for commentators. One period, however, does lack adequate commentary; we are still without sufficient knowledge of that time after de Gaulle's triumphant return to Paris, when France was obliged to live with make-shift institutions, and efforts proceeded to establish a more permanent form of government. Professor Wright, in his portrait of de Gaulle, both when he is at center stage, but also when he is reduced to playing from the wings, succeeds in recalling how the man captured the imagination of the French, even as he confused them about his intentions and designs, invited their support, but only half-earned their approbation. His sudden resignation of January 1946 was surprising enough; his decision to avoid all commentary on the Constitution framed by the First Constituent Assembly was his way of saying that he remained above party disputes, and that he would not descend into the political arena. He was determined to remain the national symbol.

After the defeat of the Constitution, however, he spoke out at Bayeux, abandoning his earlier reserve. He insisted on a stronger executive than originally provided for; he extolled the virtues of bicameralism and spoke of a new federalism that would create a vital French Union. The presidential idea, so important in later Gaullist pronouncements, was first developed in this so-called "Bayeux Program." The reaction, particularly from the Communists, was instantaneous; they accused de Gaulle of seeking to establish a presidential semidictatorship. The Socialists joined in seeing the proposal as reactionary and authoritarian. De Gaulle returned to his self-imposed isolation at Colombey-les-Deux-Eglises, and was not to speak out again until August 27, when the Second Constituent Assembly seemed hopelessly mired in its work. Then, in a second blast, he criticized what he thought to be the mistaken views of the Assembly, particularly on the matter of the Presidency. The Communists, who until that moment were tending to be hostile to the new draft, swung around in its favor. The M.R.P. was put in an embarrassing position. Would it continue to favor de Gaulle, and thereby split the country, or would it repudiate this latest blast from the wilderness and split the party? In the end, the M.R.P. stood firm in its alliance with the Socialists, and the Assembly proceeded to accept a draft that could be submitted to the people. They, in turn, by the narrowest of margins, with an unprecedented number of abstentions, voted to accept the Constitution. The Fourth Republic was born; de Gaulle's opposition to it was not the least of the factors that had contributed to its creation.

That opposition had been total. Within hours after the Assembly's adoption of the Constitution, de Gaulle indicated that it would not serve France's needs. Against the three principal parties, all urging a "yes" vote, de Gaulle argued for "no" or abstention. His secret hope was that there would be at least a 35 percent negative vote and a number of abstentions sufficiently large to permit the immediate launching of a campaign to revise the Constitution. Just days before the referendum, de Gaulle let it be known that the referendum was "a question of life or death for the country. If this Constitution is adopted," he said, "anarchy and disorder will reign in France." He had done his best, he said, to enlighten the country. To read again of de Gaulle's political activity in 1946 is to be reminded inevitably of later days and later crises, and also, of later Gaullist "calls."

The chief merit of Gordon Wright's work, however, is not that it offers an explanation of why the Fourth Republic failed, or why de Gaulle was obliged to spend so long a time in the wilderness, or even why he finds himself "retired" to that role again today. These are all "bonuses" that come from reading an undeniably brilliant analysis. The major contribution of the work, in my view, is that it emphasizes certain continuities in French political life. France passed through an incomparable moral, political, and military catastrophe during the Second World War. Those who gathered to make a Constitution were in many instances new men. They had no prior political record to defend; they were not the legatees of the defunct Third Republic. Many had received their political educations in the service of the maquis or in equally unconventional circumstances; women were for the first time entitled to vote. Everything suggested the possibility of major innovation. Yet, the results of their labors were not of this kind. The political order was not made over. The Reshaping of French Democracy is a powerful statement not least because it emphasizes so tellingly (and so modestly) the difficulties of political innovation and invention.

Contents

CHAPTER FIVE

False Start: The First Constituent Assembly

CHAPTER SIX

Repeat Performance: The Second Constituent Assembly

CHAPTER SEVEN

From the Provisional to the Precarious: Launching the Fourth Republic

Preface

This volume is a venture onto the thin ice of contemporary history. It is a narrative and analytical account of the making of the new French Constitution; it attempts, without waiting for the perspective which comes from the passage of time, to view that process in its historical setting.

Although the book's central theme is the constitutional problem, it is in a broader sense concerned with the political forces at work in France since liberation. The constitution was not drafted in a vacuum; nothing could be much further from a vacuum than contemporary France. The two years of provisional government from August 1944 to December 1946 brought French politics to a new pitch of complexity, for the revolutionary spirit emerging from the resistance was in conflict with surviving prewar currents, as well as with the remnants of Vichy's pseudo-revolution. Economic stress, international tension, colonial unrest, and personal rivalries sharpened the conflicts among the men who made the constitution. All these elements went into the formation of the Fourth French Republic; none of them can properly be ignored in a study of the constitution-making period.

For many of the details in this book, I am under obligation to men who participated directly in the political affairs of liberated France. Among them were a number of deputies to the two Constituent Assemblies (including members of both the first and second Constitutional Committees); leaders of resistance organizations; party officials; and former associates of General de Gaulle in the latter's provisional government. My debt to them is great, but it seems prudent to leave them anonymous in view of their active present or future roles in politics. I must also express my appreciation to M. Katz-Blamont, Secretary-General of the Assembly, and to many members of his staff. Finally, and most important of all, I am grateful to my former superiors in the American Embassy for furnishing me with a ringside seat at this bit of history in the making. Several of my Embassy colleagues, through their broad associations and their keen perception, have contributed more to this book than they would probably care to admit. They are, however, in no way responsible for the views which I have expressed; nor is the book a reflection of either official or semiofficial attitudes.

G. W.

Eugene, Oregon
October 1947

THE RESHAPING OF FRENCH DEMOCRACY

CHAPTER ONE

From Mystique to Politique

Legend says that Napoleon once asked a group of his courtiers how Frenchmen would react if his death suddenly were to be announced. While the courtiers were groping for a diplomatic reply, Napoleon answered for himself: "They would merely say Ouf! at last!"

France experienced somewhat the same reaction on the morning after the referendum of October 13, 1946, when it learned that the period of constitutional camping out was almost over and that a permanent structure had at last been given to the Fourth French Republic. A great part of the two years since liberation had been spent in the effort to establish a new governmental system which would correct the weaknesses of the prewar regime and would start France on the road to stability and prosperity. There had been a wave of enthusiasm on the morrow of liberation; Frenchmen turned their eyes from the past to the future, and caught the vision of a new, vigorous, rejuvenated *patrie*. The Fourth Republic would be constructed by a people purged of its past errors, unified and tempered by the resistance, guided by the public good alone. Out of collapse and disgrace would emerge a unified and selfless civic spirit, which would find its incarnation in the new constitution.

Two years later, when that constitution finally received the approval of the people at the polls, the most widely shared sentiment was not enthusiasm but relief. The optimism of 1944 had been replaced by frustration and lassitude. Frenchmen were glad that the job was finished, but they were by no means sure that they had gained anything more than a breathing spell. Gone were any illusions that the constitution would serve as a bond of union or would provide the framework for a golden age. Stability and prosperity seemed as far off as before; and even the prospective durability of the new system drew skeptical shrugs. Frenchmen reflected with some bitterness that this was their fifteenth constitution since 1789, and that humorists would probably continue to classify French constitutions in the category of periodical literature. They recalled once more the phrase of the Catholic poet-patriot Charles Péguy: "The *mystique* for which men die becomes the *politique* by which men live."

This cloud of disillusionment showed no sign of dissipating during the months that followed. If anything, it became even more somber. Such an aura of pessimism was not necessarily fatal to the Fourth Republic, but it hardly provided the most favorable atmosphere in which to launch a reconstructed democracy. True, the French could comfort themselves with the recollection that enthusiasm was no prerequisite of success. In 1793 the Jacobin constitution had been deposited in a coffer of precious wood while the citizens of Paris filed by to strew flowers on the holy document; yet that constitution expired before it could even go into effect. Conversely, the most durable written constitution in French history was that of the Third Republic, which, in the words of a royalist historian, was conceived without joy and was certainly no child of love.

If this paradox can be taken as precedent, perhaps the Fourth Republic is off to a healthy start. It seems more likely, however, that the regime will not survive unless it can throw off the initial handicap of general pessimism and *je m'en foutisme*. To do this, economic recovery must come within a reasonable time. It remains to be seen whether the Republic's new political structure and its leadership will be adequate for the task. Certainly the constitution of 1946 will not permit the kind of vigorous and brutal action to which a totalitarian state can resort. The constitution's virtues are more negative than positive; its nature, like that of the prewar system of government, is to reflect the conflicts of social and political forces rather than to resolve those conflicts. Within its framework, the Republic may be able to muddle along toward economic health, political stability, and social justice. If it succeeds, western-style democracy will have scored a major triumph. But whether the outcome is success or collapse, whether the Fourth Republic's life is to be one year or a hundred, the story of how its constitution was made is a necessary and instructive prelude to the new chapter in French history which has now begun.

CHAPTER TWO

The Third Republic:
An Obituary

I. GONE BUT NOT FORGIVEN

The men who make constitutions, like those who plan wars, are often so fascinated by the errors of the past that they misjudge the present and the future. This rear-view approach can be a praiseworthy one, so long as governmental problems remain constant. The difficulty is to know when new conditions have brought new problems, and whether the remedies of yesterday can still meet the needs of today and tomorrow.

Frenchmen have a special penchant for turning over the constitutional rubble of their past, and they have particularly rich ruins in which to dig. The makers of the 1946 constitution indulged in this pastime with enthusiasm. Virtually every topic evoked disputes over the lessons of 1789, of 1793, of 1848, or of the much-abused Third Republic. In their more unrestrained moments, some deputies dipped back even farther into the past, drawing lessons from the Middle Ages or even from ancient Rome. This passion for antiquity was in the true French tradition: in 1793 Hérault de Séchelles, with only a week's leeway to draw up a constitutional project, had begun by studying the laws of ancient Minos.

It was the Third Republic which served as the principal backdrop for the 1946 constitutional debates. Constitutions, when they emerge from serious crises, are usually drafted in the heat of reaction against what went just before. The immediate predecessor in this case was Vichy, but the founders of the Fourth Republic wasted little time in examining Vichy institutions. That regime had never taken hold in France, and the liberation swept its doctrines and much of its structure into the dustbin of history. The constitution-makers leapfrogged over this Vichy interim; they took as their frame of reference the system which had served France for almost three generations, and which they had come to regard as largely responsible for the nation's disasters.

The bitterness of most Frenchmen toward the Third Republic dated in large part from the collapse of France in 1940. They had never been enthusiastic about that governmental structure, and in the decade before 1940 some of them had attacked it with increasing vigor; but the bitterness which gripped them after the defeat was new. Its violence recalled somewhat the reaction of Frenchmen against the Second Empire in 1870.

Vichyites of course had an ax to grind in condemning the Third Republic. Most of them had never become reconciled to parliamentary government, and some of them had never even accepted the idea of a republic. The venom of their attacks was therefore natural enough. As for the mass of anti-Vichy French republicans, however, a repudiation of the Third Republic left them facing a void. The Vichy substitute most of them soon rejected; but what kind of new regime they wanted in its place remained vague. General de Gaulle and his followers in London likewise stigmatized the weakness of the Third Republic, but offered no ready-prepared alternative.

This general revulsion had lost some of its intensity by 1945, but it created an atmosphere of hostility in which the constitution-makers operated. Proof of this hostility was furnished by the referendum of October 1945, when 96 per cent of the voters rejected the idea of a mere revision of the 1875 constitution through the organs provided by that document. A vast majority in France demanded a thoroughgoing new deal, a constituent assembly which would rebuild from the ground up, a Fourth Republic in place of the Third.

In view of this sentiment, it is essential to make a brief excursion into the past, to reappraise the Third Republic, and to isolate those aspects which dominated the minds of the men who made the constitution of 1946.

II. THE REPUBLICAN SYSTEM
AND HOW IT GREW

The Third Republic's constitution was monarchist by birth, republican only by adoption. Its drafters in 1875 had been inspired both by French royalist tradition and by the example of the British parliamentary monarchy; they had designed their makeshift constitution to serve as the framework for a restored monarchy in France. The structure proved flexible enough, however, to adapt itself to republican needs; and so France unintentionally furnished the world with history's first example of the parliamentary republic.

The essence of the parliamentary system lay in the dominant role of the Chamber of Deputies, which could overthrow and replace the executive organ (the cabinet) at will. In contrast to the so-called presidential form of government, there was no attempt at a clear-cut separation of powers, with the executive and legislative branches both stemming directly from the people and kept in equilibrium by a series of checks and balances. At most, there was a separation of functions between the executive and legislative organs. The seat of national sovereignty, the source of executive authority lay in the Chamber of Deputies alone.

Between 1875 and 1940, practice altered certain aspects of the government's operation. The most significant change was a relative weakening of the executive organs in favor of the legislature. Above all, the executive's chief weapon against the legislature—the right to dissolve the Chamber and to order new elections—fell into complete disuse. The dissolution mechanism rusted for two reasons: because it was once utilized for partisan ends by the monarchist President MacMahon in 1877 (so that thereafter it bore an anti-republican odor), and because dissolution required the Senate's consent, which became more and more unlikely as the Senate fell under the control of the same parties which dominated the Chamber.

The decay of dissolution did much to produce that famous French phenomenon, cabinet instability. During the sixty-five-year life of the Third Republic, France had a sequence of 102 cabinets, which scarcely made for executive strength or authority. The changes became increasingly kaleidoscopic as time passed; calculators have figured that from 1875 to 1920, governments lasted an average of less than ten months each; but that from 1920 to 1940, the speed of rotation just about doubled. If the deputies had been faced by the prospect of dissolution and a subsequent campaign for re-election, they might have been much more cautious before putting the skids under a set of ministers.

A second factor which contributed heavily to cabinet instability was the multi-party system. Once the Republic got well under way, no party ever approached a clear majority in the Chamber; a coalition of from two to a half-dozen groups was always necessary in order to form a cabinet, and the life of such a coalition was at the mercy of each component group. Furthermore, the parties themselves were fluid and ill-disciplined, which added to the structural instability of cabinets. The largest single group, the Radical Socialist, was once described as "not a party but only a state of mind"; and the same was true of all groups except the Socialists and Communists, who arrived late on the scene. The average politician, it was sometimes said, felt that an ideal party would be one which included only himself plus enough voters to elect him to office.

A final aspect of executive decline was the creeping paralysis which afflicted the formal head of the state, the president of the republic. A series of presidents beginning with Jules Grévy consciously limited the scope of their office, and parliament helped this process along by usually electing men of distinctly second-rate qualities. Clemenceau was thinking of the presidency when he coined the caustic epigram, "I vote for the most stupid." It was not long before the president became the butt of French witticisms rather than the symbol of governmental authority. His role was sometimes important as a behind-the-scenes adviser, but in general he spent his time receiving ambassadors and presiding at cattle shows. He emerged into the limelight briefly when cabinets fell, for it was his important duty to name a new premier. Critics sometimes compared the president to the pin boy in a bowling alley, whose only function it was to pick up fallen cabinets as the Chamber knocked them down.

Along with executive decline, a second and less important evolution in the functioning of the Third Republic between 1875 and 1940 was a relative increase in the Senate's powers and a change in its political complexion. The Senate, elected indirectly by representatives of the various town, city and departmental (county) councils in France, was designed by its creators to be a conservative check on the popularly elected Chamber of Deputies. It was not specifically authorized to overthrow cabinets, but it absorbed that right as time went by. Many jurists protested at this "usurpation," but there was clearly no way to insure against it so long as the Senate possessed legislative powers equal to those of the Chamber. All the Senate had to do was to reject a bill or an appropriation whose adoption the cabinet regarded as essential to its governmental program. The result of such a rejection could only be the cabinet's resignation, and the Senate acted—rarely, it is true—with full consciousness of what the result would be.

At the same time, the Senate gradually lost its original character of extreme conservatism. Henri Rochefort had remarked in the early days that if the ages of the senators were laid end to end, they would stretch back to Ptolemy. As the decades passed, senatorial beards grew shorter and the upper house came to reflect in a certain degree the political composition of the Chamber. It never caught up with the leftward evolution of the lower house, however. The method by which it was elected assured a heavy overrepresentation to rural areas, so that the Senate remained a somewhat distorted mirror of the political visage of France. Its tendency to bury new legislation sent up from the Chamber of Deputies won it the nickname of "cemetery of laws."

Frenchmen admit that they have an incorrigible passion for tinkering with constitutions. During the course of the Third Republic, there was never a time when some citizens or groups of citizens were not suggesting that the constitution be either junked or altered.

The cry for revision was first taken up by Gambetta and the republican minority before the ink was dry on the constitutional laws of 1875. The republicans had always regarded the parliamentary system as a purely monarchist form of government. Their own century-old tradition rested on the concept of "government by assembly," as typified in the Revolutionary Convention of 1792-95. In some ways the line of distinction between parliamentary government and government by assembly was not easy to draw. Both types subjected the executive to the legislature; but the parliamentary system customarily allowed the cabinet a degree of autonomy, and gave it some kind of counterweight (such as dissolution) against the legislature's control. The formal head of state, too, was normally a king, with the prestige attaching to an hereditary monarch.

Republican tradition, on the other hand, called for fusing the executive and legislative functions in a one-house assembly. There would be neither a president nor a real cabinet; the legislature would choose executive agents who would be mere instruments for carrying out its will. Most republicans had advocated such a system when the Second Republic was set up in 1848; and those heretics who had been temporarily attracted to the idea of an American-style presidency had been quickly cured by the 1851 coup d'état of President Louis Napoleon Bonaparte. "Government by assembly" or "Conventional government" was therefore the quasi-official dogma of republicans in 1875.

It took only a few years, however, for republicans to become reconciled to their "monarchist" system. For one thing, they shortly won control of the Senate and the presidency as well as the Chamber; for another, the system itself gradually evolved in the direction of "government by assembly." Within a generation, it had become a kind of hybrid, half-parliamentary and half-

Conventional, and could therefore be fitted easily into republican tradition of 1793, 1848, and 1875. Left-wing republicans still preached the pure doctrine, notably with respect to the abolition of the Senate, but their attacks took on an increasingly academic air.

When the first real threat to this semi-parliamentary system sprang up suddenly in the Boulanger crisis, it was the republicans who came to its defense against a motley syndicate of monarchists, Bonapartists, superheated Jacobin patriots, and other malcontents. General Boulanger's battle cry—"Dissolution, Constituent Assembly, Revision!"—did not make his reform program very clear; but he certainly aimed at the overthrow of the parliamentary system, and probably at the establishment of a strong, popularly elected president who would govern through the plebiscite. The collapse of the movement in 1889 meant not only that France would continue to be a republic, but that it would be a parliamentary republic for a considerable period at least. During the decade that followed, the regime was solid enough to survive both the Panama scandal and the Dreyfus affair, and at the turn of the century it was accepted by a majority of Frenchmen as an adequate system of government.

The consolidation of the parliamentary republic did not mean that all republicans were satisfied with the way it functioned. Men of a conservative temper were especially discontented with the instability and weakness of the executive. The Boulanger affair, which revived memories of Louis Napoleon, had delivered most of them from the temptation of a president-on-horseback; but they still felt that the executive could be strengthened within the parliamentary system. Their hope was to restore the atrophied powers of the president by placing a man of prestige and determination in the office. To that end, they favored broadening the college of presidential electors in order to free the president from complete dependence on parliament. Such a president, they felt, might be willing to wield the club of dissolution, and thus to reverse the trend toward absolute legislative dominance.

In 1913 an unexpected chance came for the Right-wing republicans to test their strong-executive theory. The critical state of international affairs led parliament to break with precedent and to elect a first-rate leader, Raymond Poincaré, to the presidency. But the "Poincaré experiment," which the Left wing watched with a cold and suspicious eye, ended in failure. At the end of seven years, not a single presidential prerogative had been restored to use. The French executive branch remained weaker than that of any other major democracy; and it seemed likely to stay that way, since the system had stood up under the test of war and had brought France victory.

One other current of reform gained strength after 1900 and carried over into the period between wars. The reform in this case was not strictly constitutional, since it had to do with the electoral law; but in later years (notably after 1944) the close relationship between the electoral system and the constitutional structure became clearly evident.

The established French system of electing the Chamber of Deputies was based on single-member electoral districts, with a run-off ballot if no candidate received a clear majority at the first ballot. The reformers wished to replace this system with the new-fangled plan called proportional representation. The major advantage which they saw in the change was electoral justice. If proportional representation were installed, each segment of French opinion would be fairly represented according to its total popular vote in the country. The votes cast by minority groups would no longer go wasted and unrepresented.

The advocates of electoral reform were mostly political extremists, on the far Left or Right of the spectrum. The Socialists (then the most advanced party) made it a primary plank in their platform, and a considerable number of conservative republicans campaigned vigorously for it too. Both elements stood to gain by the change, for the established voting system favored middle-of-the-road candidates at the expense of extremists. Under the established system, the run-off ballot usually found the field of candidates reduced to two. A center candidate could bid for the support of either the Right or the Left, and could be almost sure of election with the aid of one or the other. Under proportional representation, on the other hand, the extremists could stand on their own feet and could expect their fair share of seats.

The reformers had to admit that their system would be likely to preserve the multi-party system in France, and even to increase the number of parties. At that epoch, however, few Frenchmen had any desire to get rid of the multi-party structure, even though the latter clearly made it hard to form stable and coherent cabinets. The right to choose among a half-dozen different parties seemed normal and necessary to French republicans; and cabinet instability, while it was a serious annoyance, still struck Frenchmen as a problem of marginal importance. The "proportionalists" therefore concentrated on the beauties of electoral justice, adding only that their plan would strengthen party discipline and would make the doctrines of each group stand out more distinctly from those of its rivals. Not until the 1930's, when the number of parties had doubled and when the life of the average cabinet was cut in two, did some Frenchmen begin to toy with schemes designed to develop a two-party system on the British model.

III. THE REPUBLIC IN PERIL

The grinding war of 1914-1918 would have been a severe test for any French regime. The Third Republic survived it intact and, crowned with the halo of military victory, emerged apparently stronger than before. Yet it soon had to meet an even more critical ordeal which seriously shook the confidence of the French people in their system. The financial and economic crisis of the 1930's projected the shortcomings of the Third Republic in crude and perhaps distorted form. From economic stress it was only a short step to latent constitutional crisis. This was the atmosphere in which the Republic passed its declining years.

At bottom, the problems of the inter-war era were doubtless too grave to be solved merely by a change of constitution. Those problems were rooted deep in the social and economic structure of France, and in the minds and prejudices of Frenchmen as well. The growth of large-scale industry produced new social stresses which only the state could properly regulate, and the complexity of economic life demanded positive state action rather than laissez faire. In the face of these conditions (complicated still more by the First World War's drain on French manpower and resources), the Republic's negative political system began to seem plainly inadequate. It was easy, therefore, for critics to trace all of France's difficulties back to that political structure, and to argue that all would be well if the country could only be given a more positive instrument of government. To carry out such a change, however, was next to impossible in a nation which was so deeply divided within. And if the change had been carried out, the question may well be raised whether a positive system with a powerful executive might not have brought civil war rather than stability. That same unanswered question was later to face the builders of the Fourth Republic, still as deeply divided as their predecessors.

At any rate, trouble began with the fall of the franc in the middle 1920's. A series of Left-Center cabinets groped for a solution but were bowled over in rapid succession, largely because they ran up against the *mur d'argent* of powerful financial interests. The Left-wing majority in the Chamber therefore saw no alternative but to accept a cabinet headed by Raymond Poincaré, who had the bankers' confidence and was able to stabilize the franc in 1926. But the Chamber went further: for the first time in the history of the Third Republic, it temporarily transferred some of its own jealously guarded powers to the executive. In order to assure speedier and more effective action in the crisis, it authorized Poincaré to act in the financial sphere by issuing decrees with the force of law. Such "decree-laws" required the Chamber's subsequent approval, but the procedure nevertheless appeared to represent a confession of failure on the part of the legislature. To many Frenchmen, it seemed to indicate that the system which was adequate before 1914 could no longer meet the needs of the postwar era; that parliament was impotent, and was merely trying to patch

over the essential weakness in the system in order to avoid a real
solution. The decree-law experiment of 1926 (loosely and inac-
curately called "full powers") proved an easy precedent during the
1930's; and each use of the procedure encouraged those critics of
the Third Republic who advocated a stronger executive or an outright authoritarian regime.

A short breathing spell was afforded by Poincaré's success, but
the worldwide depression which caught up with France in 1931
provided a second and more serious shock to the regime. Confidence in the system ebbed rapidly as cabinets became increasingly
unstable and showed little ability to take vigorous recovery measures.

The crisis naturally brought to the surface all the latent discontent of Right-wing republicans and of antirepublicans as well.
Constitutional reform projects sprang up in profusion. Most of
them aimed at the same old goal—a stronger, more independent,
and more stable executive. Some of the reformers proposed to remain within the parliamentary framework, and to shift the executive-legislative balance so that the French system would resemble
British cabinet government. Their usual solution was to dust off
the power of dissolution, and in many cases to strip the legislature
of the right to propose public expenditures.

The most noteworthy campaign of this type was the one-man
crusade of former Premier André Tardieu, who retired from active
politics in 1934 so that he might devote himself entirely to preaching his cause. "To save liberty and peace," cried Tardieu, "let us
re-establish authority!" Tardieu's scheme called for the vesting of
full dissolution powers in the hands of the premier, and for various
devices (such as the use of the referendum) to cut down the prerogatives of parliament. Certain powerful financial interests in
France favored the same type of reform; their propaganda agency
was a movement called the *Redressement Français*, founded in
1927.

Constitutional reform within the parliamentary framework early
drew the attention of a tiny new Center party, the Popular Democrats. This "party of Catholic youth and parish priests," forerun-

ner of the post-liberation M.R.P., began to study the problem at
its 1929 congress. It advanced a whole series of specific reforms,
most of which were later taken over by the M.R.P. Like the Right
wing, the Popular Democrats favored stabilizing the executive by
investing the premier with full dissolution powers. But they also
advocated direct democracy in the form of the initiative and the
referendum; obligatory voting; a plural vote for heads of families;
the development of regionalism; and the replacement of the Senate
by an upper house chosen to represent professional and family
groups. Some Popular Democrats also wanted a supreme court on
the American model. The Popular Democrats described their projected system as "pluralistic democracy," and argued that it would
not only make the government more efficient, but would also be
the most effective barrier against totalitarianism. Their plans drew
little serious attention at the time, since the party had only a handful of deputies and gave no promise of future growth.

It was of course easier and more exhilarating to attack the parliamentary system head-on rather than to demand its reform. A whole
series of antiparliamentary movements emerged after 1930 on the
extreme Right wing, seeking their inspiration either in Mussolini's
corporative structure or, less frequently and more equivocally, in
the American presidential system. An example of the latter type
was the Republican Reformist movement headed by Gaston
Henry-Haye (later Vichy ambassador to the United States), which
demanded an American type of separation of powers between the
three branches of government.

Far more powerful agents in the antiparliamentary campaign
were the fascist or semi-fascist mass movements which sprouted
rapidly after 1930. The neo-monarchist *Action Française* of Charles
Maurras now found new listeners; it reviled the Republic as "the
slut," called for the destruction of political parties, and advocated
the establishment of a monarchist state organized on corporative
and regional lines. Colonel de la Rocque's *Croix de Feu*, unlike
the *Action Française*, posed as republican but also demanded a
strong nonparliamentary regime. Much of the *Croix de Feu's* appeal resulted from the vagueness of its program; members could

find in it whatever they wished, provided that they were agreed in damning the parliamentary system. A whole series of smaller movements aped the *Croix de Feu* or else surpassed it in violence.

Further evidence of the strength of the authoritarian appeal, and of the degree of discontent with the Third Republic, was given by the conversion of a minority of Leftists to the doctrine of strong government. In 1933 a group of Socialist dissidents headed by Marcel Déat and Adrien Marquet broke away from the Socialist party over the question of renovating the state structure. These Neo-Socialists, like the Right-wing enemies of the regime, called for a strong and dynamic government based on corporative principles. Keen observers like Léon Blum realized that Déat drew his inspiration from the example of Berlin and Rome. It was logical that most of the Neo-Socialists should rally to Vichy in 1940.

In the face of this varied authoritarian onslaught, the reaction of the major Left-wing parties was at first embarrassed and defensive. They could not approve the Rightist campaign to remodel or destroy the regime, yet they found that few of their voters regarded the constitution of 1875 with much enthusiasm. The Radical Socialist party, for many years the largest in France, naturally did not wish to change the system which had permitted its success. It met the constitutional crisis with a cautious silence, except for some mild remarks about broadening the Senate's electoral base.

Most of the Socialists, who formed the moderate or evolutionary wing of French Marxism, clung to French republican tradition by opposing a stronger executive and by blaming the Senate for the delays and inefficiency of the parliamentary regime. They suggested that if the Senate's wings were clipped at once, the Chamber of Deputies would be free to meet the economic crisis by vigorous legislation. Besides, they pointed out, cabinets would be more stable if they were not forced to please two different legislative chambers at the same time. Generally speaking, the Socialists professed little faith in political remedies; they placed their emphasis on economic "reforms of structure," such as sweeping extensions of state ownership. Léon Blum, the Socialists' leader and theorist, added the sage observation that constitutional reform would be empty without a change in French political morality. Politicians, he insisted, would have to abandon their habit of systematic opposition to every cabinet with the sole purpose of getting cabinet posts for themselves.

Blum vigorously resisted the Rightist campaign to give the executive more independence of legislative control. "Ministry and parliament," he wrote in 1934, "are in no way two autonomous machines . . . , they are two cogs in the same machine whose coordinated movements, whose joint operation, whose isochronal pulsations must work together toward the same end. . . ." The premier, Blum added, must be simultaneously the chief of the executive and the legislative branches; he must constantly "shape the ministerial labors in accordance with the popular will which parliament represents." He believed that the best way to achieve such co-ordination, and to increase the premier's authority at the same time, would be to stabilize and discipline the parties through the use of proportional representation in elections. Blum's 1934 doctrine was essentially that which the Socialists (through André Philip as spokesman) were to uphold against General de Gaulle in 1946.

The Communists far more than the Socialists were contemptuous of the idea of using constitutional surgery to save capitalist democracy. Their attitude was frank enough, as summarized in Maurice Thorez' report to the party's Central Committee in 1934: "We are engaged in the struggle for power. For all power to the soviets [workers' councils]. For the destruction of the bourgeois state and its replacement by the state of workers and peasants." This program obviously left the Communists isolated; at that time they had no more in common with the Left-wing defenders of the Third Republic than with its Right-wing critics. As their organ Humanité put it in 1934, "How could we engage in the struggle for power alongside the Socialist party? The Socialist party wants to save the Republic. The Communist party, on the contrary, fights for all power to the soviets."

The Stavisky scandal which broke late in 1933 came near pushing the Third Republic over the brink. To the semi-fascist leagues, it was a heaven-sent opportunity to stir up hatred against the men in power and against the regime itself. The climax came on February 6, 1934, when Maurras, De la Rocque, and other semi-fascist leaders called on their followers to demonstrate against the "bandits" and "assassins" in the Chamber of Deputies. Several thousand demonstrators attempted to march on the Chamber, and their attack might have destroyed the Republic if the police had not managed to head them off a hundred yards short of the Palais-Bourbon.

In the long run, that crisis served to strengthen the Republic by jarring the Left into a realization that the fascist threat was serious. It consolidated the Left in defense of the regime; the Popular Front, organized in 1935, took an implied stand against either reform or overthrow of the constitution as it stood. For the first time, the Communists abandoned their goal of destruction of the bourgeois state, and joined the Radicals and the Socialists to protect the parliamentary structure of 1875.

In the short run, however, the February sixth affair almost brought about constitutional revision. Public attention was suddenly focused upon the weaknesses of the government, and even some Leftists began to weigh the advantages of reform. Both the Chamber and the Senate set up special committees to study reform proposals and to sound out all parties or private groups with ideas on the subject. But as the idea of revision spread, it became distorted by the intensity of the passions aroused. Constitutional issues could not be studied objectively at a time when the very fundamentals of democracy were under such heavy attack.

The new premier after the February sixth incident was doddering old Gaston Doumergue, called out of retirement to save the republic. In spite of his long years as a Radical Socialist politician, Doumergue decided that it was his mission to give France a stronger executive, and he proceeded in that direction with the utmost lack of good judgment. Instead of trying to persuade the Left that his program was wise, he aroused the suspicion of many republicans by addressing the nation in a series of radio talks, and

by laying plans to dissolve the Chamber if it should prove recalci-
trant. The Left wing, thus led to expect the worst, was not surprised when Doumergue came out with a program similar to that
of Tardieu. He proposed to give the premier three new weapons:
the right to dissolve the Chamber without Senate consent (except
during the first year after an election); the sole right to introduce
appropriation bills; and the right to maintain the past year's budget
if parliament refused to adopt a new one.

Doumergue's declared purpose was to shift the French system in
the direction of British cabinet government, but the Left viewed
his plan as camouflaged authoritarianism. It is barely possible that
a more skillful leader might have pushed through at least part of
the program. But Doumergue was deserted even by his own party;
Edouard Herriot and the other Radical ministers resigned, the
cabinet collapsed, and "Gastounet" went sadly back into obscurity.

The Doumergue fiasco in November 1934 dropped a wet blanket
over the idea of constitutional revision as a practical political issue.
During the subsequent Indian summer of the Republic, partial
economic recovery took off some of the pressure for change; attention turned to the Popular Front's social-economic program and to
the increasingly critical issues of foreign policy. The Senate's overthrow of Léon Blum's cabinet in 1937 briefly revived the old Socialist hostility toward the Senate, and some talk was again heard of
clipping its wings. But the Socialists found absolutely no support
for such a scheme. The Radicals had for many years controlled the
upper house, and the Communists contemptuously brushed aside
the idea of wasting time on Senate reform.

To the extent that revisionism remained active after 1934, it
tended to take either a violent or an academic form. The fascist
cagoulard plot uncovered in 1937 was a sample of the former; Professor Jacques Bardoux's "Technical Committee on State Reform"
was the most publicized example of the latter type. The Bardoux
group, composed primarily of jurists and lawyers, published a
lengthy set of recommendations designed to strengthen both the
president and the premier within the parliamentary framework.
More unusual were its proposals for an American-model supreme

court, and for a three-day cooling-off period prior to the overthrow of a cabinet by the Chamber. The latter scheme, designed to prevent the surprise fall of cabinets on "orange peels," was eventually to be written into the Fourth Republic's constitution.

By the time war came in 1939, the Third Republic seemed to have weathered the worst of its constitutional crisis. Frenchmen still complained of its weaknesses, but most of them no longer considered the problem pressing enough to justify more than a cynical shrug. Only the survivors of the outlawed semi-fascist leagues (reorganized under De la Rocque as the *Parti Social Français* and under Jacques Doriot as the *Parti Populaire Français*) still looked on the parliamentary system with real contempt; but their most favorable moment seemed to have passed in 1934. Although they kept up their propagandist efforts, and in times of crisis plastered Paris with posters calling for a Pétain cabinet, they had little reason to suppose that they would soon achieve their goal.

A few citizens were disturbed at parliament's growing tendency to grant cabinets "full powers." This procedure was invoked six times during the 1930's, and was broadened considerably in scope. To the Right wing, this was further proof that France needed a stronger and more independent executive. To the Left, the grant of "full powers" was a dangerous falsification of the regime, bearing an authoritarian odor; yet Left-wing premiers as well as Rightists reluctantly began to ask for the privilege after 1936. It seemed clear that something was wrong with the system, when the latter could no longer function without continual recourse to an exceptional procedure.

The flaw, however, did not strike most Frenchmen as a fatal one. They recognized vaguely that their regime was more negative than positive; that it reflected the divisions within the country, but did little to resolve them; that it was far from being an effective and efficient instrument with which to attack the problems of the modern era. Perhaps some of them realized the inconsistency between the Left's political doctrine of legislative dominance and the Left's economic program of vigorous governmental action. But few French citizens in September 1939 felt that the system would fail to meet the test of war; and fewer still foresaw its total collapse within a year.

IV. THE STRANGE DEATH OF
THE REPUBLIC

On the Third Republic's tombstone should be carved the date July 10, 1940. Yet it was not till five and a half years later that Charles de Gaulle dared sign its official death certificate—and then only after the French people had spoken in the referendum of October 21, 1945. During that long interim, French jurists and politicians sporadically disputed among themselves as to its fate. Some held that the Republic had been destroyed by its enemies; others argued for suicide; still others asserted that the Republic was not dead at all, but only in a coma. The problem had its tempting juridical aspects, but it was more than purely academic in nature. If the Republic was not legally dead—perhaps even if it had been destroyed by a usurper—it could be argued that France still had a lawful constitution, and that the Third Republic ought to be restored automatically when Pétain fell.

Few Frenchmen even today have more than a vague idea of what happened during the Republic's last days at Vichy in July 1940. Marshal Pétain had been appointed premier at Bordeaux on June 16, on the morrow of the military collapse. Named to the post by President Albert Lebrun, he took office in regular constitutional fashion. On the advice of his vice-premier, Pierre Laval, Pétain then called parliament into special session to consider his proposals for the country's future.

Parliament's last performance in the Vichy Casino was marked primarily by confusion and intrigue. About two-thirds of the senators and deputies managed to reach Vichy on schedule, but few of them had any formulated plans. Almost to a man, however, they were ready to accept some constitutional revision. The shock of collapse had left the country numb, yet sensing vaguely that reform should follow disaster. On July 9 both the Chamber and the

Senate in separate session voted by margins of 393 to 3 and 225 to 1 that "there is reason to revise the constitutional laws." Only Léon Blum and a few other Socialists made an active effort to stem the tide. Blum saw the possible consequences of a vague commitment opening the door to unlimited revision, but he was unable to carry even his own party with him. Most of the Socialists argued that the Left was strong enough to keep revision within republican bounds.

As a result of the July 9 vote, the two houses met in joint session (called the National Assembly) on July 10. A preparatory warm-up session in the morning was faced by two separate proposals. One of these, the so-called Taurines project, was sponsored by a group of senators headed by the independent socialist Joseph Paul-Boncour. This group hoped to postpone the idea of revision and to preserve the Third Republic even though its structure might have to be changed. According to the Taurines project, the constitution of 1875 would be suspended for the duration of the war. During the interim, Pétain would be granted full power to legislate by decree, and would be authorized to set up committees which would draft a new or revised constitution. This draft would be submitted to the nation, presumably by referendum, as soon as conditions made a free vote possible. The Taurines project thus aimed to set up a temporary emergency government, and to put the constitutional question on ice until the end of the war. Pétain himself saw the project in draft form and apparently gave it his sanction. Most Left-wing deputies and senators on July 9 had decided to vote for it the next day.

Laval and his henchmen, however, were determined to seize this opportunity to destroy the Third Republic. "Since parliamentary democracy chose to fight against Nazism and Fascism, and since it lost this struggle, it must disappear," Laval declared. "A new regime, audacious, authoritarian, social, and national, must be substituted for it." Laval persuaded Pétain to sponsor a counterproposal granting "to the government of the republic [i.e., to Pétain] full power to promulgate the new constitution of the French state." During the secret session of the two houses on the morning of July 10, Laval demanded that the counterproposal be accepted.

The backers of the Taurines project were ready to shift over on one condition: that a clause be tacked onto the Laval project transforming its whole nature. They were ready to authorize Pétain to draw up a new constitution, they declared, but only if that constitution were to be ratified afterward "by the National Assembly which drafted it." Such a clause would imply that Pétain might propose but parliament would dispose. The final word on constitutional change would lie with the two houses meeting in joint session as provided by the constitution of 1875. Laval naturally balked, and suggested as a compromise that the new constitution be ratified by the nation rather than by the National Assembly. The idea looked democratic enough, but actually would open the way to the kind of plebiscite which dictators always manage to win. It nevertheless attracted a great many deputies who had been supporting the Taurines project, and increased Laval's chances of success.

That afternoon, in the formal session of the National Assembly, Laval and his backers took their second trick. By resorting to a procedural maneuver, they succeeded in shunting aside the Taurines project. Parliament's rules of order gave precedence to the Taurines project over the one presented by the cabinet. The Laval clique got the floor and jammed through a decision to vote on the Pétain plan first. When the Taurines group tried to protest, they were howled down by Laval's backers. In the midst of great tension and turmoil, the Pétain project was adopted by a margin of 569 to 80. By that gesture, parliament wrote the death warrant of the Third Republic. Blum's fears expressed on the previous day were confirmed; in the showdown, Laval had outsmarted the Left.

It is clear beyond doubt that the proceedings at Vichy on July 9 and 10 were in some ways illegal and irregular. Even though the outward forms for constitutional revision were generally preserved, the fact remains that parliament had no right to hand over its power of revision to Pétain. Pressure and intrigue were used freely, and the burial of the Taurines project by a procedural trick was of doubtful validity. Besides, Pétain in subsequent acts may have exceeded the authority granted him on July 10. In later years, therefore, partisans of a return to the Third Republic could argue that the regime was forcibly overthrown by a Pétainist coup d'état, and that it would be unfair to condemn a system which had been the victim of violence.

What the Third Republic's partisans forgot or overlooked was the fact that nine-tenths of the parliamentarians present at Vichy accepted Laval's demands. The outcome, even though it was falsified by a degree of moral duress, could easily have been different. A majority might have denied to Pétain and Laval the powers which they demanded, and might have adopted the Taurines project instead. Such behavior would probably have saved the Third Republic. If Pétain had then accepted parliament's decision, the constitution would have kept its legal validity until liberation. If, on the other hand, Pétain had rejected the decision and had resorted to violence, the resurrection of the Republic would have been virtually assured. A "martyred" parliament, repudiated and forcibly disbanded by Pétain, could not have been ignored after liberation. Called back into session in 1944, it would have proclaimed the restoration of the Third Republic and would have revised the constitution of 1875 rather than relegating it to the junk heap.

To put the matter bluntly, a heavy majority of the Third Republic's leading politicians abdicated on July 10, either through cowardice, conviction, or mere confusion. Some of those who voted "yes" were at bottom good patriots and sound republicans; but they were not farsighted men. Only eighty parliamentarians were able to understand that Laval was asking them to destroy the Republic, and were ready to speak out in its defense. Not one party stood up solidly against Laval; even the Socialists, who furnished almost half of the eighty anti-Pétain votes, split wide open. That lack of comprehension on the part of so many senators and deputies was a fatal blow to a regime which events had already undermined. Only one conclusion seems possible: the Third Republic was destroyed by its own leaders even more than by its enemies. The most appropriate verdict, then, must be suicide. And since corpses are rarely revived even in politics, the effort of some prewar politicians to breathe life back into the Third Republic after 1944 was foredoomed to failure.

CHAPTER THREE

The Republic Underground
and Overseas

I. THE VICHY INTERLUDE

Of all the regimes under which France has
lived during the past two centuries, Vichy proved to be the most
ephemeral, the least capable of putting down roots in the country.
It could hardly have been otherwise, since the regime rested on the
faulty premise that Germany would win the war. For the first year
or so, when the fallacy of that premise had not yet been proved,
the men of Vichy could properly begin to build a structure of government. But from 1941 onward, it became increasingly clear that
their structure could never be more than a façade; that its total collapse might be postponed, but not finally averted.

Other French regimes of equally brief duration had left behind
them a permanent heritage, a lasting mark on French political
thinking. Vichy might conceivably have done the same, if Pétain
and his closest advisers had been men of a different sort. In the
beginning, Vichy's potential assets were many. Pétain himself was
a symbol of national sentiment and of patriotic unity around whose
person a large share of the population rallied in June 1940. He was
in a position to profit by the widespread revulsion against the Third
Republic and by the current desire for strong government. If he
and the men around him had honestly sought to make a start toward a stronger and healthier republic, they might have survived
long enough to offer France a set of temporary institutions capable

27

of holding the respect and affection of a large bloc of Frenchmen after liberation. No doubt they would have found themselves in German jail cells within a year, but that fate would only have reinforced the influence of their doctrines.

Instead, Pétain frittered away his initial capital by repudiating not only the parliamentary system but the republic itself. His effort to construct a clerico-fascist regime appealed to an extreme Right-wing fringe and to a few maverick Leftists, but it quickly alienated the mass of citizens. His willingness to accept a position in the Nazis' new order cost him much of his remaining support. A good many fence straddlers (known in France as *attentistes*) clung to the belief that Pétain was hoodwinking the Germans and was thus protecting France against a worse fate; that the war would be won "thanks to the Russian soldier, the British fleet, American money, and the *Comédie Française*." But as a form of government, as a set of institutions, Vichy soon lost any hold on French minds. Vichy France came to be not a constructive and fruitful experiment, but a mere interlude between republics.

Only twenty-four hours after parliament abdicated in his favor, Pétain began the piecemeal proclamation of a new constitution. In a series of "constitutional acts" introduced by the medieval phrase "We, Philippe Pétain, Marshal of France," Pétain transferred all power to himself as "Chief of the French State," and repealed the most important sections of the 1875 constitution. He wiped out the office of president of the republic, suspended parliament until further notice (and finally liquidated it), set up a special Supreme Court to try high officials of the Third Republic, and gave himself the right to name his own successor. Pétain never formally abolished the constitution of 1875, but in practice it disappeared along with the trilogy "Liberty, Equality, Fraternity," and the word "Republic" itself. Twelve constitutional acts were issued by Pétain over a period of two years; they merely proclaimed the principles upon which the new constitutional structure would eventually be built.

In January 1941, Pétain created a large and broadly representative constitutional committee to work out the details of the structure. This hand-picked body functioned for more than a year; it was broken down into a series of subcommittees, each of which worked on a prescribed section of the Pétainist constitution. But events moved faster than the committee. On New Year's Day, 1942, Pétain suddenly announced that he had decided to suspend the promulgation of a constitution until French soil should be entirely free of foreign troops. His committee had functioned in the strictest secrecy; none of its recommendations were revealed then or later. When Vichy was swept into the discard in 1944, its constitutional structure remained confined to the narrow limits of the twelve constitutional acts.

In practice, of course, Pétain and his advisers had revealed the general nature of their future state even though they had not issued a formal constitution. The suppression of political parties, of free labor unions, and of farmers' organizations; the attempt to lay the groundwork for a single party, to regiment labor through a government-imposed Labor Charter, to control the farmers through a Peasant Corporation created from the top—all these moves pointed to a corporative structure similar to that of Salazar in Portugal. Pétain's rather abortive attempt to revive the old French provinces of prerevolutionary days showed the influence of Charles Maurras' native variety of fascism. The men of Vichy were by no means united in their attitude toward the problem of government: one Pétainist declared that Vichy reminded him of a café in the Midi which bore the sign "Aux Anciens Romains et aux Nouveaux Cyclistes." But it was easy to see that most of them looked toward a semi-fascist system rather than merely a powerful executive authority within the framework of democracy.

During Vichy's last months, some Pétainists toyed with the idea of trying to bridge the gap between their regime and the provisional government of Charles de Gaulle. Woven into this scheme was the idea of resuscitating the Third Republic by calling the parliament of 1940 back into session. The latter project was noised about so widely that the National Resistance Council felt it necessary late in 1943 to warn the ex-senators and ex-deputies against the temptation to regain their seats. Soon after De Gaulle landed in France in 1944, he was approached by a Vichy agent with the suggestion that the Pétainist and the Gaullist movements join forces in order to re-establish national unity. De Gaulle's answer, naturally enough, was to send the agent packing. The futility of such a proposal revealed Vichy's total disintegration. Its consequence would not have been national unity, but civil war. Fortunately for France, both De Gaulle and the resistance movement had other plans, prepared during the four long years underground and in exile.

II. THEORIZING IN THE MAQUIS

As the mass of Frenchmen recovered from the shock of the collapse, they naturally began to grope for the causes of their disaster. More instinctively than rationally, they agreed that a heavy share of the blame should be loaded on the fallen regime. They seldom asked just how a different system might have turned defeat into victory, but they felt nevertheless that no other system could have failed quite so lamentably. If parliament in its last stand at Vichy had gone down with courage, driven from the Casino by Pétain's troops to the cry of "Vive la république!," good patriots might have had a legend to which they could cling. But parliament's renunciation seemed to be a kind of Wagnerian act of self-immolation, symbolizing the weakness of the regime itself.

It was this sentiment which at first brought Pétain the support of a majority of Frenchmen drawn from all groups except the outlawed Communist party. The most striking aspect of republican thought in 1940 was the general reaction against "parliamentary excesses" and the intense desire for more authority in government. Even after the republicans cut themselves adrift from Pétain—and many had done so by the end of 1940—the sentiment in favor of a stronger executive persisted. Collapse implied weakness at the center; the problem was how to restore authority in the state without at the same time destroying liberty, as Vichy was obviously doing. It almost seemed that an important section of the Left was preparing to accept Right-wing dogma on the issue of executive strength.

Perhaps the most striking phenomenon in this groping search for a new structure of government was the sharp revival of interest in the American type of presidential system. For almost the first time since 1848, a significant number of republicans were attracted to it as a ready-made solution. The system was not a theoretical one; it existed and worked in the United States, where it had proved itself compatible with democracy. The presidential system found its greatest following among young anti-Vichy intellectuals of the Center or the non-Communist Left: Catholics, Socialists, nonparty independents. It had an even more natural appeal to Rightists; but the number of Rightists in the underground was sharply limited by the fact that so many had thrown in their lot with Pétain's variety of strong government.

So powerful was the presidential current that even André Philip, one of the ablest young Socialist leaders (and later the father of the Fourth Republic's constitution), is said to have been drawn to it in 1940-41. Several small resistance groups of the early Vichy period (such as the *Arc*, organized in 1940) proposed its adoption. Catholic resistance sentiment leaned perceptibly in this direction. Their principal underground organ, the *Cahiers du Témoignage Chrétien*, praised the American system as most capable of giving France a strong and stable executive while preserving democracy.

Some of the Third Republic's best-known Leftist leaders also came to be haunted by the feeling that executive weakness had helped to destroy the regime. Jean Zay, a former Radical Socialist minister, mused over the past in his prison cell and noted in his diary that "no regime is in such great need of authority as a regime based on liberty." In another cell, Léon Blum was temporarily attracted to the idea that the American presidential system might save democracy in France. Vincent Auriol, one of the top figures in the Socialist party, moved more cautiously in the same direction. Sitting in seclusion on his rural property near Toulouse, Auriol toyed with a plan by which the lower house of parliament alone would elect a combined president-premier for a three-year term, with the right to overthrow him at will, but only on pain of automatic dissolution.

For a year or more after the 1940 collapse, the anti-Vichy underground was an almost invertebrate organism, split into dozens of small spontaneously formed groups which operated independently. Likewise, the ideas of the underground about the problem of government tended to be invertebrate: they took the form of an emotional reaction against past evils rather than a concrete effort to plan for the future.

Beginning in 1942, the resistance movement and its ideas both began to change character. Efforts to federate the various groups and to co-ordinate their work gradually led to the formation in May 1943 of the National Resistance Council, a kind of board of directors of the underground. The principal artisan of this nineteen-man Council was Jean Moulin, a young career prefect whom De Gaulle had chosen as his personal representative in France. Moulin served as its president until captured and murdered by the Germans late in 1943; his successor was Georges Bidault, Christian Socialist representative on the Council. Before his death, Moulin helped forge a link between the organized underground in France and De Gaulle in London. Many Left-wing resistance leaders had at first doubted De Gaulle's republicanism, but they were finally persuaded by Moulin and by Pierre Brossolette, a prominent Socialist in De Gaulle's entourage, to accept the General's centralizing leadership until and after liberation. In return, De Gaulle adapted his views on the future of France to the wishes of the resistance forces.

Although men of every political color entered the resistance movement, the balance was heavily weighted toward the Left. After June 1941, when Hitler invaded the Soviet Union, it was the Communist party which furnished the largest and most aggressive contingent. The Communists functioned both directly as a party and indirectly through groups like *Front National* which they controlled. Even after they entered the National Resistance Council in 1943, they remained a semi-distinct and unassimilated element within the national movement. The other prewar parties of the Left, which had largely disintegrated after the 1940 collapse, began to pull themselves together by 1941. Many of their individual members had already joined various resistance groups, but it was the Communist example which forced such parties as the Socialists and Radicals to enter the underground as organized entities. There were some patriotic Rightists who chose to join the resistance rather than Vichy; but the bulk of the movement was Socialist, Communist, or nonparty Leftist (especially Christian Socialist) in character; and the underground's attitude toward the future of France was colored accordingly.

The resistance held almost unanimously that the Third Republic was dead; that its leaders had betrayed their trust; and that a totally new regime—both political and economic—should be built after Vichy's fall. Almost the only exceptions to this sentiment were found among the rare Radical Socialists, such as Paul Bastid, who assumed active roles in the resistance. For the Radicals, 1940 had been a worse catastrophe than for any other party. They had been identified with the Third Republic for so long that the collapse of the regime tended to bring the party down with it. Furthermore, a heavy proportion of the Radical senators and deputies had abdicated to Pétain in July 1940, and had branded themselves as unlikely candidates for active underground leadership. Most of the prominent Radicals never went beyond passive resistance to Vichy, and so their voices were scarcely heard until liberation became imminent. Their chief, Edouard Herriot, lived in obscure semiconfinement in the country near Lyon; Edouard Daladier sat in prison, and Pierre Cot in lonely exile.

Although the underground generally agreed that there must be a new Fourth Republic, this unanimity broke down when they began to examine political and constitutional problems concretely. The basic issues were three: (a) should the new regime be of the presidential type, or a streamlined and strengthened parliamentary model? (b) should the new constitution be drafted by a constituent assembly chosen by the people after liberation, or should liberated France be presented with a ready-made constitution drawn up jointly by De Gaulle and the organized underground? (c) should the prewar profusion of parties be replaced by a new pattern, derived from the new unity of the resistance movement?

The presidential system, whose emotional appeal had been great in 1940-41, had lost many of its sympathizers by 1943. A majority of Leftists on second thought drew back before this heresy, and told themselves that a regime which was workable in another country might not be good for France. Vichy's perverted example of the strong executive acted as an effective deterrent. The idea persisted most strongly in certain resistance groups dominated by nonparty intellectuals, notably the *Organisation Civile et Militaire* (O.C.M.) and *Défense de la France*. The O.C.M., founded in 1940 and headed by an economist and former banker named Maxime Blocq-Mascart, leaned further to the Right than most other underground groups. It was accused at times of technocratic tendencies, a charge which had some basis in fact. In a series of clandestine pamphlets circulated in 1942-43, the O.C.M. outlined detailed plans for the rejuvenation of France. It proposed to make the president the active executive, with a cabinet chosen by him and responsible to him alone. In addition, it suggested giving the president the right to dissolve parliament in case of an executive-legislative dispute. This curious adaptation of the American system would have made the chief executive all-powerful. *Défense de la France*, a left-bank student movement in origin, also circulated a series of *cahiers* advocating the presidential system in somewhat less exaggerated form.

The idea of a ready-made constitution drawn up before liberation appealed to all the exponents of a presidential regime. They frankly believed that it would be much easier to get such a regime accepted if it were allowed to take root for a year or so before being put to a vote. In addition, however, many Frenchmen who opposed the presidential form of government were attracted to the idea of a prefabricated constitution. This was true of a considerable share of the Christian Socialists, for example, who wished to retain and strengthen the parliamentary system. The backers of a prepared constitution argued that it would bridge the gap between the fall of Pétain and the definitive establishment of the new regime. It could be put into operation at once during the difficult liberation period, thus permitting France to concentrate on the task of reconstruction without wasting valuable time quibbling over details. A year or two after France had been freed, the constitution could be submitted to the voters for ratification.

Hand in hand with the idea of a prefabricated constitution went the dream of a new grouping of political forces in the Fourth Republic. Many nonparty Frenchmen in the underground felt that the old multi-party system ought to be junked along with the Third Republic. Their goal was the emergence of a broad majority bloc between the Communists on one wing and the die-hard reactionaries on the other, with De Gaulle as symbol and chief. Only thus, they felt, could the beneficent unity born of the anti-German struggle be preserved in part. They admitted that perhaps their plan was less democratic than the idea of an elected constituent assembly and the revival of a multi-party system, but they insisted that its advantages would outweigh its dangers.

De Gaulle, when he first began to negotiate with the underground through his agent Pierre Brossolette, favored the idea of replacing the old party system by a broad political *rassemblement*. A short time later, his views suddenly shifted. Jean Moulin brought instructions from London to encourage the revival of the prewar parties and to offer them a prominent place in the new National Resistance Council. Many "pure resistance" leaders balked at the idea, but they finally had to capitulate. So strong was the London pressure that certain Right-wing parties were resuscitated by a kind of artificial respiration. Those few Rightist leaders who had rejected Pétain were encouraged to set up their parties on a skeleton basis and were offered full membership in the National Resistance Council, in order to give the resistance movement an appearance of broad national unity.

De Gaulle's change of heart was not dictated by any love for the prewar politicians or their system. Rather, he hoped to counteract the sentiment abroad that he was planning a semi-fascist rather than a democratic regime for liberated France. In addition, he may have been disturbed by the prospect that a single political grouping born of the resistance would be likely to fall under the domination of its best organized and most dynamic faction—namely, the Communists. Certainly the Communists themselves after liberation tried hard to prolong resistance unity and to control the movement from within. At any rate, the man who was chiefly responsible for the revival of the multi-party system was Charles de Gaulle himself.

It was obvious that the large prewar Leftist parties would buck the tide toward presidential government and toward a prefabricated constitution. Except for the Communists, they also regarded a new party structure as potentially fascist. Those resistance organizations which were controlled by Leftists (which meant most of the principal ones) early went on record in favor of an elected constituent assembly as the only democratic course. Thus an emergent split within the underground over the nature of the Fourth Republic was beginning to appear in 1943. Only one group, the Christian Socialists, was not quite sure where it stood. These individual forerunners of the M.R.P. still possessed no central organization to bind them together, and their constitutional doctrines had not entirely jelled. The Christian Socialist members of the underground therefore divided, and in many cases waited to follow the lead of Charles de Gaulle.

The most ambitious effort to define the underground's constitutional program—and, incidentally, to turn that program into a ready-made constitution—was made by the *Comité Général d'Etudes* (C.G.E.) in 1943. This body, originally labeled the *Comité Général d'Experts*, was the brain child of two law professors: François de Menthon, a Christian Socialist, and Paul Bastid, an experienced Radical politician. Its eight members were all experts in jurisprudence or in administration, and most of them were eventually to play influential roles in the building of the Fourth Republic. De Menthon and Pierre-Henri Teitgen later helped found the M.R.P., and both became cabinet ministers. Bastid and Robert Lacoste (Socialist) entered the Constituent Assembly; Alexandre Parodi served in the cabinet, and Michel Debré in a high administrative post, under De Gaulle's post-liberation regime. René Courtin and Jacques Charpentier were the only two members who remained out of active politics. All eight members belonged to the political Center, with mild leanings toward the Left.

The original purpose of the C.G.E. when it was organized in 1942 was to study the practical administrative problems which would face France on the morrow of liberation. The C.G.E. gradually took on a kind of quasi-official character in its chosen field; it was closely tied to the National Resistance Council and, through the latter, it furnished recommendations to the Gaullist movement in Algiers. Early in 1943, it decided to tackle the problem of a new constitution, delegating young Michel Debré to handle this task. Debré's Paris apartment forthwith became a clearing-house for the constitutional ideas of the resistance groups throughout France. Draft projects, sometimes anonymous and sometimes identifiable, came in to him by devious routes, marked with the magic letters C.G.E. (which, conveniently, were also the initials of the company which supplied Paris with electricity). On the basis of these projects—or perhaps in spite of them—Debré proceeded to draw up a proposed constitution which was accepted with minor changes by a majority of the C.G.E. members and thus became its official text.

The C.G.E. draft retained the general architecture of the 1875 constitution, but proposed to shift the balance of power heavily toward the executive. In many ways it resembled and even went beyond the reform programs which Tardieu and Doumergue had backed ten years earlier. Its major changes included a broader electoral college to choose the president; the unrestricted right of dissolution for the premier; and narrowed powers for the legislature (notably by limiting the length of parliamentary sessions, forbidding the existence of permanent parliamentary committees, broadening the executive's decree-law powers, and restricting the number of opportunities for parliament to overthrow the cabinet). The draft also contained an electoral system designed to stimulate the growth of a two-party system in France.

Copies of the C.G.E. project were sent out at once to all resistance organizations for their comments and, it was hoped, their
approval. The draft also went to De Gaulle in Algiers. The
C.G.E.'s ambition was to secure such wide general acceptance that
its draft would amount to a ready-made constitution by the time
liberation came. The C.G.E. felt that if it could win the approval
of the resistance movement as a whole, De Gaulle would then feel
justified in accepting the document and putting it into operation
as soon as Vichy fell. De Gaulle could decide whether to have it
ratified eventually by the people or by a Chamber and Senate
elected in the prewar manner.

The C.G.E.'s hopes were quickly wrecked on the hitherto sub-
merged rock of Communist opposition. Until this moment, no one
could say just where the Communists stood on the constitutional
question. Before the war, the party had refused to waste its time
in so un-Marxian a pastime as tinkering with democratic constitutions. The Communists' long-run goal was fairly obvious, assuming that they could some day take power; but their program for
the interim period of bourgeois democracy's survival had never
been made clear.

Early in 1944 the Communist Central Committee brusquely
spoke. The verdict was handed down by the party's leading journalist, Georges Cogniot, in a clandestine issue of the revived party
periodical Les Cahiers du Communisme. Cogniot's article, which
furnished the first detailed exposé of French Communism's constitutional views, created a mild sensation in resistance circles.

Through Cogniot's pen the Communists bluntly repudiated
the C.G.E.'s draft constitution, violently attacked the idea of
creating what they called a "Cromwellian" executive, and demanded that the people be allowed to choose their new regime
with the least possible delay after liberation. They condemned
those groups of resistance intellectuals which had been hatching
constitutional projects. "The re-establishment of democracy," they
proclaimed, "must be achieved by democracy itself, not by technocratic brotherhoods or aristocratic areopagi."

The Communists insisted, therefore, that a constituent assembly be elected as soon as possible after liberation. They warned the people against such schemers as the C.G.E. and the O.C.M., who favored a long provisional period of perhaps two years during which responsible government would be suspended. Plans of this type, they alleged, were designed to let a presidential system take root in France, or else to deprive the people of any part in constitution-drafting except the illusory right of plebiscite.

After dumping this bucket of cold water on the C.G.E., the Communists proceeded to summarize their new constitutional doctrines. They rejected outright the fundamental concepts which had dominated resistance thinking since 1940, and which underlay such plans as those of the O.C.M. and the C.G.E. It was not true, they contended, that executive weakness and legislative encroachment had wrecked the Third Republic. On the contrary: the real trouble was not an excess of democracy but an insufficiency of it; not too much legislative control over the cabinet, but actually a lack of such control. The prewar deputies had lost all sense of responsibility, had abandoned their powers to certain "extra-parliamentary maffias," had forgotten their sacred duty to control the cabinet, simply because they were themselves free of any control by the voters except at elections every four years. Therefore the deputies ignored their party programs and their electoral promises, and abdicated their legislative rights into the hands of the cabinet through the "full-powers" procedure. They let men like Daladier run the country by decree-laws over a period of years, without insisting that the ministers keep the Chamber fully informed concerning their day-to-day stewardship. "Government by assembly" should be the proper goal.

After making this unorthodox diagnosis of the Third Republic's ailments, the Communists proposed an unorthodox remedy. This nostrum would be the recall—the permanent right of the voters to revoke their deputy by petition. Individual deputies would thus be forced to carry out the wishes of their electors; and in addition, parties would become well disciplined, with clear and enduring programs. In consequence, the firmness of majorities would be ensured, and the evil of governmental instability would be corrected not by circumscribing democracy but by broadening it.

Finally, the Communists reproached the self-appointed constitutional planners of other groups for omitting any reference to overseas France. In rather cloudy terms, they demanded a constitutional new deal for the colonial natives, by which the latter would receive citizenship and political rights. They added, however, that this broadening of colonial rights must in no way infringe French sovereignty. This brief comment represented the first reference by any underground group to the empire's future constitutional status, and foreshadowed the Communists' post-liberation activities in the colonies. Although the subject had drawn little attention inside France, it had already assumed real importance in Free French circles in Algiers.

The Communists' startling entry into the constitutional debate blocked any hope of developing a united resistance program on that subject. They had taken a position so clearly contrary to that of resistance circles in general that months of discussion would be required to find any common ground. Furthermore, they had adopted a line which was essentially that of French republican tradition, whereas their rivals who wished to strengthen executive authority found themselves the embarrassed heirs of Right-wing and even of monarchist tradition. Then and later they scrupulously avoided any reference to the Soviet Union as a constitutional model. Other parties might propose to copy parts of the Soviet's fundamental law; but not the party of M. Thorez. From January 1944 the Communist position was unshakably fixed. All through the constitution-making period, it continued to be based on the principles expressed in Cogniot's clandestine article. The issues were at last fairly clear; but the manner of resolving those issues had to be postponed until after liberation.

III. THE ROAD BACK
FROM EXILE

While the constitutional ideas of the French underground were gradually crystallizing and beginning to clash, General Charles de Gaulle's Free French movement in exile likewise found itself forced to consider the question of France's future government.

In the early days at London De Gaulle tried to avoid the problem, partly because he preferred to concentrate on stimulating French resistance to the Germans and preparing a place for France at the peace table, but also because his early adherents were a conglomerate group of men who were deeply divided as to political principles. Since they ranged all the way from Socialists to semifascists, it was not easy to find a common denominator which would not wreck the Free French movement at the start.

Charles de Gaulle himself had no ready-made set of constitutional doctrines. His career had been that of a professional soldier and military theorist, without any admixture of practical politics until June 6, 1940, when he became Undersecretary for War. Even his fundamental sympathies in government were not fully clear. Few Frenchmen in 1940 could have been sure whether De Gaulle was at heart a republican or a monarchist. For that matter, few of them even knew De Gaulle's name, let alone his political ideas. The exceptions were to be found in military circles, and among those politicians who were aware of his unsuccessful ten-year campaign in favor of a mechanized army spearheaded by professional cadres. These men knew De Gaulle as a stiff, unbending nonconformist whose temperament and professional background would naturally incline him toward authoritarian methods.

Although De Gaulle had remained strictly aloof from all political parties and movements, he had revealed something of his political philosophy in two incisive books on military theory published just after 1930. His *Edge of the Sword* (dedicated, by a curious irony, to Pétain) was an especially revealing study of the principles of leadership. Parts of it might well have been entitled "Portrait of Charles de Gaulle by himself."

The temper of the book—and of certain remarks in a companion volume *Toward a Professional Army*—was clearly authoritarian. At bottom, De Gaulle argued, men must be led just as they must eat and drink. By a sort of instinct, they will turn in time of stress to the leader, the man of character and prestige. Such a leader "can scarcely be imagined without a strong element of egoism, pride, toughness, wile." He will consciously reinforce his prestige by creating about himself an aura of mystery, strengthened by a distant demeanor and a sparing use of words and gestures. Subordinates, mediocre men, will complain of his rude and exacting behavior, but let the crisis come and all complaints are forgotten. "A sort of ground swell brings to the forefront the man of character. . . . All that he asks is granted."

De Gaulle was convinced that the ground swell could be heard approaching. "Our age," he wrote, "will not long endure the delays, confusions, and weaknesses which softer times accepted. . . . Every group, party, and leader calls for reconstruction, the new order, authority." He dismissed ordinary politicians with contempt: "Everything that comes from political parties—hypocritical passions, competitive demagogy, political patronage—has had the effect of corrupting the army." This antagonism toward party politicians was to reappear in undiluted form many years later, after De Gaulle had experienced the joys and sorrows of political leadership.

Charles de Gaulle was a man who practiced what he preached. In a sense, his entire life up to June 18, 1940, had been devoted to preparing himself for the burdens of greatness. In later years, in a reminiscent mood, he once told some of his ardent disciples that his childhood had not been like that of other boys in his native Lille. Before the age of twelve, he had reached the conclusion that destiny had chosen him to guide the nation in a future hour of crisis. He had therefore prescribed for himself a thorough program of study in history, philosophy, and various other fields, selected with a view to the responsibilities that would one day be his. Even before he entered St. Cyr to become a career army officer, his serious and austere mind was steeped in the classics and in Cartesian logic. The next twenty years saw him rise to the rank of colonel, and develop a reputation as a brilliant but troublesome rebel against the theories of warfare held by his superiors. His views confirmed by the German breakthrough in 1940, he was catapulted overnight into the Reynaud cabinet. When total collapse came two weeks later, De Gaulle saw opening before him the career which destiny had foreordained.

Never once in prewar years had De Gaulle stooped to tinker with the mechanical details of governmental machinery. His interest lay rather in broad, sweeping principles; and the principles for which he stood were not the liberty, equality, and fraternity of the French Left but rather the order and authority preached by the Right. In later years, his republican supporters were to describe him as "a democrat of the Clemenceau type." The phrase contained a nugget of truth, although his pre-1940 ideas were clearly more authoritarian than those of Clemenceau—perhaps even proto-fascist. As for De Gaulle's ultimate purpose, there could be no uncertainty: he aimed to restore the dynamism and the power of the French Army and the French State.

The normal reaction of a man like De Gaulle after the collapse of 1940 would have been a violent and impassioned condemnation of the Third Republic and all its works. Its ignominious exit at Vichy, the refusal of most of its leaders to follow what he called "the path of honor" into exile, its whole character of much talk and little action, ought to have damned it in his mind. Yet for almost two years De Gaulle studiously refrained from repudiating the Third Republic, and even his criticisms of it were marked by severe restraint.

One source of this inhibition was that De Gaulle was more concerned with rallying the French people against Vichy than with preaching a crusade against the fallen regime. He could scarcely compete with Vichy in vilifying the Republic, and if he had tried to do so, he might have aided Pétain by confusing many Frenchmen. A second restraining factor was De Gaulle's strong aversion for anything which smacked of illegality, and his desire to avert the suspicion that he was a general of *coup d'états* in the Napoleonic tradition. His natural bent toward legality was encouraged by one of his earliest and most influential advisers, René Cassin. This distinguished jurist, whose Jewish descent led him into early exile, was a Radical Socialist in politics and therefore looked on the Third Republic as a generally adequate system of government. Cassin urged De Gaulle to adopt the line that Marshal Pétain had illegally overthrown the Third Republic by a bloodless *coup d'état*, and that Frenchmen therefore owed no allegiance to Vichy. The logical consequence of this premise was that the constitution of 1875 remained the fundamental law of France, and that the purpose of the Free French movement was to put that constitution back in force.

The climax of this conformist period in Gaullism came in November 1940, when De Gaulle issued a kind of manifesto of the Free French movement. This Brazzaville Declaration was obviously drafted by Cassin. After examining all the illegal and unconstitutional aspects of parliament's last meeting in 1940, the Declaration concluded "that in spite of the outrages committed at Vichy, the constitution [of 1875] is still legally in force, and that, in consequence, every Frenchman is freed of any duty toward the pseudo-government of Vichy." The Declaration admitted in passing that "a revision of the constitution might be useful in itself," but repudiated the Pétain revision as totally devoid of legal effect.

The Brazzaville Declaration came back to plague De Gaulle in 1944 and afterward, when the resuscitated partisans of the Third Republic brandished it as a binding commitment. Cassin himself eventually came to feel that perhaps he had been too enthusiastic in urging De Gaulle to cling to the Third Republic. Cassin explained in retrospect that he had meant to build a backfire against any other Gaullist advisers who might later get the General's ear and might push him away from republican legality onto dangerous terrain.

Not until June 1942 did De Gaulle cut himself loose from the dead hulk of the Third Republic. Then, after several months of negotiation, the leaders of the growing resistance movement within France agreed to throw in their lot with De Gaulle. The negotiations had made it abundantly clear that at least ninety per cent of the resistance leaders would have nothing to do with a restoration of the Third Republic, even if the latter were to be remodeled at once. De Gaulle met their wishes in a declaration which the resistance leaders accepted as a binding pact: "A moral, social, political, economic regime abdicated in defeat after having paralyzed itself in license. Another regime, born of a criminal capitulation, now exalts itself on the basis of personal power. The French people condemn them both. While they unify their strength for victory, they assemble for a revolution. . . . Once the enemy has been driven off our soil, all our men and women will elect the National Assembly which will have full power to decide the country's destinies." Doubtless De Gaulle did not regret this repudiation of the old regime. A few months later, the term "Fourth Republic" began to appear for the first time in his public remarks. The breach had become complete.

During the final months of the London period, just before the Free French capital shifted back to French soil at Algiers, an embryonic effort was made to clear the ground for a study of the constitutional problem. A committee was set up under the chairmanship of Félix Gouin, a Socialist deputy who had just escaped from France and found himself temporarily unemployed. The committee's attention was diverted, however, to more immediate problems—notably the organization of an advisory body called the Consultative Assembly, designed to serve as a kind of pre-parliament in exile. Late in 1942 Gouin's committee dipped briefly into the long-run constitutional problem; but at that moment the North African landings interrupted proceedings, and the committee evaporated without leaving a trace of its work.

The long struggle for power between De Gaulle and General Henri Giraud in Algiers left no time for constitutional theorizing. The controversy between the Generals was not directly based on diverging ideas about France's future regime, although had Giraud managed to stay in the saddle in North Africa, events in liberated France after 1944 might have followed another pattern.

De Gaulle by this time was committed to the convocation of a constituent assembly and the creation of a Fourth Republic. His pact with the underground movement was specific on this point; it had wiped off the slate his earlier declaration of fidelity to the Third Republic. Giraud was bound by no such commitment. A typical old-line army officer, honest and patriotic but politically unsophisticated, Giraud had an almost pathological suspicion of "reds." It is said that on one occasion at Algiers he was thoroughly upset when a subordinate entered his office wearing a red flower in his buttonhole. Giraud regarded a constituent assembly as a dangerous dash toward the unknown, for he knew that the principal partisans of a constituent assembly were the Left-wing activists of the resistance. It would be far safer, he felt, to use the constitution of 1875 as a base of operations, and to revise it in accordance with legal forms.

Giraud and his followers, however, neither wished nor dared to risk a revival of the discredited parliament of 1940. As a solution, they sought to exhume the Trévéneuc Law of 1872, which had been gathering dust in the archives for three generations. The Trévéneuc Law was originally designed to operate in emergency conditions. It provided that if parliament were unable to meet, a substitute assembly should be formed by convoking representatives from the various departmental General Councils. Completely forgotten except by a handful of constitutional experts, the law was dragged out into the light of day to serve as a safe and conservative mechanism for restoring democracy.

The gradual victory of De Gaulle over Giraud, which became complete in November 1943, pigeonholed the plans of the conservative republicans. The Free French movement, converted into a kind of interim government called the French Committee of National Liberation, proceeded to consolidate its new position and to plan on Gaullist lines for the post-liberation period.

Two official agencies at Algiers tackled the problem of preparing for the Fourth Republic—one of them from an academic, the other from a practical point of view. The first was the Committee on State Reform, a group of jurists headed by André Philip, which inherited the functions of the embryonic Gouin committee of London days. The second was the Consultative Assembly, which convened in Algiers late in 1943. The work of both agencies was largely bypassed by events after liberation, yet their discussions offered a preview of the constitutional issues which were to arise in 1945-46, and of emerging party attitudes toward those issues. Furthermore, both groups contained many of the men who were later to build the constitution of the Fourth Republic.

Philip's Committee on State Reform included about a dozen specialists drawn from all parties, notably the Christian Socialist law professors François de Menthon and Paul Coste-Floret and the Left-wing Radical Pierre Cot. Its discussions showed that the experts were unanimous only on certain negative points: every member rejected the idea of an American type of presidential system, an American type of supreme court, and a prefabricated constitution to be handed down from above. On the other hand, they could not agree on whether to restore the Third Republic or to replace it by a Fourth; on the character of the Third Republic's flaws; or on the detailed structure of a new parliamentary government.

Perhaps the most significant thing about the Committee's work was the fact that it revealed a common trend of thought linking Socialist intellectuals like Philip with the Christian Socialists who were later to found the M.R.P. Despite differences on many specific points, they looked toward the same kind of stabilized and purified parliamentary system. This evidence encouraged those leaders who were already thinking of a large Left-Center bloc built on resistance foundations, possibly strong enough to dominate the Fourth Republic. De Gaulle's reaction was to ignore the implications of the Committee's work, together with the recommendations which it made. Its final report was unceremoniously pigeonholed.

The other Algiers agency which dealt with constitutional planning was the new Consultative Assembly, established with a view to freeing the De Gaulle regime of its authoritarian appearance. Its members, approximately one hundred in number, were appointed to represent both the underground in France and the Gaullist movement in exile. Here for the first time the two currents in the resistance were brought together to compare ideas.

One of the Assembly's first tasks was to examine a proposed ordinance or law setting up machinery for the restoration of republican government in France. De Gaulle's draft plan rested on the assumption that the total liberation of French soil would be a slow process. It postulated a long period—probably approaching two years—of semi-presidential government, softened only by the presence of an almost powerless interim assembly. By its terms, De Gaulle and his hand-picked cabinet would serve as Provisional Government until two-thirds of France had been freed. A provisional representative assembly would then be elected, and would invest either De Gaulle or some other leader with full power to govern until the election of a constituent assembly, which would follow within twelve months after complete liberation.

In spite of the fact that De Gaulle's plan amounted to a two-year experiment in presidential government, it was approved by the somewhat amorphous Center and Left-Center groups in the Algiers Assembly: the Socialists, Christian Socialists, and many nonparty resistance delegates from both France and the colonies. These elements accepted the need for strong government during the liberation period, and they felt in addition that it would be improper to write a permanent constitution until the two and a half million prisoners of war and deportees could be brought back from Germany. Opposition to the project came from the two extreme wings in the Assembly: the handful of Radical Socialists, nostalgic for the Third Republic, and the vigorous Communist minority, suspicious of a concealed Gaullist desire to give presidential government a permanent foothold in France.

The little Radical contingent took the occasion to proclaim publicly, for almost the first time since 1940, their faith in the Third Republic. "Have you the audacity to abolish the constitution of 1875?" cried former Senator Marcel Astier. "Even Pétain has not dared to go that far." Astier and his colleagues dug out the Brazzaville Declaration, and insisted that its promises be respected. If reforms were necessary, they argued, those reforms should be achieved in a constitutional manner by the parliament of the Third Republic. But the Radicals were fighting a lost cause, and some of them knew it. Men like René Cassin, himself the drafter of the Brazzaville Declaration, realized that De Gaulle and most of the French underground were determined to move on to a Fourth Republic. "Gentlemen," Cassin told his colleagues in the Assembly, "there are certain corpses which need to be killed." No one, he contended, could any longer hope to revive the corpse of the Third Republic, betrayed and destroyed by its own leaders in 1940.

Far more important than the Radical opposition was that of the Communists. They offered a counterproposal reducing the period of irresponsible government to six months. A constituent assembly would then be elected, and would be given a maximum of three more months to draw up a constitution. Communist spokesmen never once mentioned De Gaulle by name, but their suspicion of his motives showed through the seams of their remarks. The Communist position at Algiers faithfully reflected the decisions of the party's central committee in France, which were just then being made public in the *Cahiers du Communisme*.

Support for the Communist position was confined to a few independent resistance delegates and to Pierre Cot, a maverick Radical Socialist who was later to play an exceptionally brilliant, provocative, and—in the eyes of some—equivocal role in the formation of the Fourth Republic. Cot had passed the years of exile in the United States, while Vichy in 1942 tried him *in absentia* for his alleged failure as prewar Air Minister to provide France with planes. He had avoided any close tie with the Gaullist movement, and returned to Algiers in 1943 with his hands apparently free. The Communists seemed to love him no more than the Gaullists: their clandestine *Humanité* in 1940 had applauded Vichy's decision to try Cot before the Riom Court. In the Algiers Assembly, however, Cot argued far more persuasively than the Communists that De Gaulle's project would "involuntarily" lead France into a presidential system; and he called upon history to prove that such a system in France contained the seeds of dictatorship. The only safe way to strengthen the regime, he held, was to give the legislature even more control over the executive through the permanent action of legislative committees. For, Cot argued, the Third Republic's flaw was its failure to be democratic enough. It had not been wrecked by executive weakness, but by the abusive practice of decree-laws and the corrupting influence of the trusts.

The Algiers Assembly's debate showed that party positions on the constitutional issue were taking shape; but it did not seem to deflect De Gaulle's plans for a slow return to responsible government. The ordinance as promulgated on April 21, 1944, scarcely differed from De Gaulle's original draft. It therefore left open the possibility of trouble between De Gaulle and the Communists during the long semi-presidential period. As for the Radicals' hopes, the ordinance seemed to place the tombstone on the Third Republic, for its first article provided that "The French people will decide their future institutions in full sovereignty. To this end, a National Constituent Assembly will be convoked as soon as circumstances make regular elections possible."

Perhaps it was in part the Communists' suspicions, voiced in the Algiers Assembly and in the underground, which after D-Day led De Gaulle to revise his plan and to cut the provisional period as short as possible. As things worked out, the two stages of the plan were telescoped into one, and the Constituent Assembly was elected only six months after the last German troops were driven across the Rhine. Until that Assembly met in November 1945, the revised ordinance of April 21 served as a kind of pre-constitution of the provisional republic. It promised a return to responsible government after a reasonable delay, and without either a resurrection of the old constitution or the promulgation of a ready-made model from above. Whatever De Gaulle's motives, democracy would have its innings: that guarantee at least was carried in the saddlebags of the émigrés when they returned from their long exile in the summer of 1944.

CHAPTER FOUR

Experiment in Presidential Government: The De Gaulle Period

I. THE FIRST CROSSROAD

For fourteen months after Charles de Gaulle's triumphal return to Paris, the government of France was essentially a dictatorship by consent. There were no formal limitations on De Gaulle's authority except those which he himself voluntarily accepted. The cabinet was hand-picked by De Gaulle and was responsible to him alone; he in turn was accountable only to the people. But this latter responsibility was totally without sanctions, and presumably the people could only exercise their powers by an uprising or a threat thereof. Thus the provisional Fourth Republic began its career as a presidential or even an authoritarian regime rather than a parliamentary one. This fourteen-month experiment, serving as immediate background for the constitutional debates, could hardly fail to exert a direct influence —either positive or negative—on the permanent structure of the Fourth Republic.

Four possible paths were open to De Gaulle when he returned to French soil. The first—an unthinkable one except to Pétain and certain Vichyites—would have been to fuse the Free French and the Vichy governments in a futile effort to heal the rupture in

51

French unity. A second would have been to proclaim the restoration of the Third Republic, as some advisers still urged him to do. Third, he might have handed down a provisional constitution, with a promise of later revision by an elected body or else ratification by plebiscite. This course had been suggested to De Gaulle several times during the Algiers period (once by a member of his cabinet), but he had brusquely rejected it as dangerous and illegal. The suggestion was renewed a few days after De Gaulle's arrival in France: this time by M. Blocq-Mascart, the O.C.M. representative on the National Resistance Council. The fourth and final alternative was to stand by his contract with the underground—to enforce the ordinance of April 21, providing for a gradual return to republican forms and finally the election of a constituent assembly.

Two weeks after his arrival in Paris, De Gaulle quieted the vague doubts that were beginning to arise as to his intentions. He announced in a public address that the people alone must decide their future institutions. "As soon as our territory is entirely liberated and our prisoners and deportees have returned," he declared, "the government will call on the nation to elect . . . its representatives who will constitute the National Assembly." To this Assembly, he promised, his government would turn over its authority. De Gaulle's guarantee dampened many hopes and quieted many fears; it implied that he would regard himself as an unprejudiced caretaker, and that he would scrupulously avoid any actions which might serve as precedents and might weigh on the later decisions of the people's representatives. It also meant that the constitutional question would be put in cold storage for a considerable period, for the return of more than two million Frenchmen from Germany would be a major operation.

During the fourteen months that followed, De Gaulle faithfully lived up to his promise (and to most of its implications). Looking back on this period two years later, some Frenchmen of the Center and Right regretted the General's scruples. They argued that France might have been saved long and fruitless controversy, and might have turned much earlier to the material problems of recovery and reconstruction, if De Gaulle had either restored the Third Republic outright, had issued a provisional constitution, or had summoned a constituent assembly without delay. They complained that postponing vital decisions had grown to be a habit by the end of 1946, with the result that recovery efforts had almost bogged down. Some of them felt that France had wasted two years in stalking and then wrestling with the constitutional problem, only to end with a system not much different from the execrated Third Republic. Certain critics, partisans of a stronger executive, resented the fact that De Gaulle had failed to use his opportunity in 1944-45 to guide France in that direction, either through consciously establishing precedents or through openly preaching the gospel before the voters. They felt that by waiting until 1946 to intervene in the constitutional debate, De Gaulle had left his mission unfulfilled.

It can scarcely be doubted that De Gaulle's decision was a vital one, and that a different choice by him in 1944 might have given the Fourth Republic another kind of constitution. Whether France would have been better off as a result is for history to judge. At any rate, De Gaulle's reserved attitude was beyond doubt the most democratic one, for it left to the people alone the right to choose their new structure of government.

II. SURGERY OR REST CURE?

One may debate the wisdom of De Gaulle's hands-off policy on the constitution. It is much less possible to question the fact that in the economic field the first winter after liberation was a period of lost opportunities, and that De Gaulle's failure to seize these opportunities had an indirect but real effect on the constitution of the Fourth Republic.

The economic and financial state of France in August 1944 was, naturally enough, chaotic. Industrial and agricultural production had fallen to one-third of the 1938 figure. The transportation system was shattered; one-eighth of the working population was in foreign captivity; currency in circulation had quadrupled since 1939; all reserves of food and raw materials had been drained off by the Germans; huge sums had found their way into the hands of a small group of profiteers; real wages had fallen to an unhealthy level because of Vichy controls. There was obviously no quick or fool-proof remedy for such grave economic ills. Men like André Philip declared that the nation would have to face an austerity program of ten or even twenty years' duration in order to bring back prosperity. But the time to start was the autumn of 1944. It would have been possible to hasten the process of convalescence if the government had dared to adopt drastic measures.

The Belgian and the Dutch governments in exile, foreseeing a somewhat similar situation, had formulated sweeping plans before D-Day. At the earliest possible moment their governments called in the inflated currency, replaced it with new, and blocked all bank accounts in order to restore the stability of the monetary system and to permit the skimming off of illegal wartime profits. Many Frenchmen favored vigorous steps of the same type, even though they knew that the problem would be more difficult in France than in the Low Countries. The Socialists in particular urged a program similar to that of the Belgians, with certain aspects borrowed from the wartime controls of the British.

Instead, General de Gaulle landed in France with absolutely no economic plan prepared; and during the first winter, he simply let the monetary problem slide. As a temporary palliative, wage increases were authorized, but they were soon absorbed by the rising cost of living. Socialist complaints in the newly broadened Consultative Assembly had little effect, nor did the protests of the Minister of National Economy, Pierre Mendès-France. The latter, a prewar Radical Socialist deputy, was regarded as a financial expert among politicians. Of humble Jewish extraction, wealthy by marriage, he had escaped from a Vichy prison in 1941 after having served in the French Air Force during the war, and had joined the Free French in exile. Mendès-France urged De Gaulle to give convalescent France a set of integrated controls similar to those

which the United States had set up for the war period. He advocated a bold program of price and wage stabilization, heavy taxa-
tion of illicit profits, tight rationing, and the mobilization of all
French resources in order to speed up recovery. Failure to adopt
such a plan, Mendès-France held, would bring hyper-inflation and
economic disaster.

Mendès-France's chief opponent in the cabinet was Minister of
Finance René Pleven, an able but conservative former businessman and one of the most fervent of the Gaullists. A Breton by
birth, Pleven had been a representative of French industrial con-
cerns in London before the war, and had become one of De
Gaulle's first converts in 1940. By 1945 his loyalty to the General
had brought him into the small inner circle of influential advisers.
Pleven operated on the liberal theory that deflation would come
by natural processes as soon as production could be expanded; that
a rest cure was preferable to surgery. He proposed to allow price
rises in order to encourage production, and to go slowly in taxing
illicit profits.

Friction between these two Gaullist advisers reached a crisis in
January 1945, when Mendès-France threatened to leave the cabinet. He withdrew his threat only after an eight-hour showdown
session with De Gaulle and Pleven, during which De Gaulle promised to take into account the views of both men. Such a promise
could hardly be kept, and in April Mendès-France resigned in disgust. Pleven took over the Ministry of National Economy as well
as that of Finance, thus effectively burying any prospect of a
vigorous policy. When Pleven finally got around to calling in the
old currency, the damage had already been done. Holders of huge
illicit profits had sunk their cash in anything tangible—real property, foreign money, or perhaps one of the luxurious new bars
which sprang up in profusion all over Paris during that icy winter
when thousands of bombed-out Frenchmen could still get no
building materials. In addition, Pleven refused to block bank accounts or to institute heavy extraordinary taxes, and therefore introduced no real brake on the amount of currency in circulation.
The inflationary process continued without pause, chasing the

will-o'-the-wisp of revived production but never quite catching up.

Hindsight suggests that De Gaulle missed a major opportunity in the autumn of 1944. Most Frenchmen would have accepted almost any sacrifice at that moment, during the flush of post-liberation enthusiasm. A year later, the moment for action had already passed. Why De Gaulle failed to act is not easy to determine. Pleven's personal influence, far stronger than that of Mendès-France, must have been one factor. Another was De Gaulle's fear that a bold policy might split the country and throw part of the population into a panic. It may be, too, that he was not yet fully confident that his authority in France could survive unpopular measures. In this connection, the strong antagonism of the Communists to any currency-exchange scheme in the fall of 1944 may have had some effect. This surprising attitude on the part of the Communists was generally explained by their alleged possession of several billion francs in "hot money," seized by them during the active liberation period. The Communists never offered any satisfactory explanation of their stand, but their opposition may have added to De Gaulle's hesitation.

Perhaps the principal factor, however, was De Gaulle's own lack of interest in the prosaic question of finance. His major concern —perhaps his sole concern—was to restore the greatness of France. By greatness the General meant prestige, military power, national spirit, morale. Two years later, one of De Gaulle's confidants described him as the only living Frenchman capable of raising himself above even such issues as republic versus monarchy so as to see France in the framework of centuries. "He was completely indifferent," said this former minister admiringly, "to whether or not the French people ate nothing but turnips for six months." De Gaulle believed that if Frenchmen wished to rebuild a France in the tradition of the great days of Richelieu, Napoleon, and Foch, they should be ready to endure hardships with a soldier's cheerfulness and fortitude. No doubt most Frenchmen in 1944 needed an injection of national pride and morale (although those who had actively participated in the underground had developed it for themselves). At the same time, De Gaulle's exalted approach made him by-pass concrete opportunities which might have changed the course of post-liberation France. If his provisional government had met the immediate crisis with vigor, efficiency, and foresight, Frenchmen one year later might have been strongly tempted to retain both the framework of the governmental system and the leadership which had met their needs. Instead, they elected two Constituent Assemblies in an atmosphere of growing gloom and discontent, and cynically repeated their time-worn phrase on government: *Plus ça change, plus c'est la même chose.*

III. CLEARING THE VICHY DEBRIS

Charles de Gaulle's promise to his countrymen when he returned to France was that his government would *"faire du neuf et du raisonnable."* Although the phrase struck a responsive chord, many Leftists were in a mood to stress the new and let the reasonable go. Instead, the General's tendency during his year in power was to reverse the emphasis. Moderation and caution rather than vigorous reform guided his government, not only in the economic sphere but in other fields as well.

It is easy to criticize the government's record during that first post-liberation year. Perhaps it would have been wiser to turn at once, as the newspaper *Combat* recommended, *"de la résistance à la révolution."* Certainly the cabinet's effectiveness might have been greater if De Gaulle had chosen his ministers on the basis of ability alone. Instead, considerations of personal loyalty weighed heavily in the selection, so that the national union cabinet was a motley collection of first-, second-, and third-rate men drawn both from the underground and from the Free French returning from exile. Some reports suggested that De Gaulle himself was contemptuous of the men who helped him govern. While still at Algiers he had remarked to a critic of his cabinet in exile, "You don't take my Commissioners for ministers, do you?" And he is alleged to have said enviously to a Communist leader in November

1945: "At least, you have men around you; *moi, je n'ai que des c——.*"

It would be unjust, however, to write off De Gaulle's first government as a collection of incompetents and bunglers. The problems which it faced were immense in their scope and complexity, yet the government managed to carry the republic through these critical months, and to handle its task with moderate if spotty success.

One of the most pressing problems was the purge of Vichyites and collaborators. During the days of the German retreat, local vigilantes often took the purge into their own hands, arresting or executing offenders without benefit of formal justice. The number of rough-and-ready liquidations can never be determined; Rightists later inflated the figure to 80,000 (and added that a million persons had been arrested), whereas Minister of Justice Teitgen insisted that not more than three or four thousand summary executions had occurred. In any event, the period of vigilante justice ended within a few weeks, by which time De Gaulle's agents had reached every liberated department and had taken over authority from the local Liberation Committees.

A hierarchy of special courts was quickly established to handle the accusations—more than 100,000 in all—which poured into the Ministry of Justice. At the top, the High Court of Justice assumed jurisdiction over leading Vichy officials, including Pétain himself; at the bottom, *chambres civiques* in each department dealt with petty offenders ranging from women conspicuously guilty of "horizontal collaboration" up to members of the Vichy *milice.*

A special body called the Jury of Honor was later added to study the records of those parliamentarians who had voted for Pétain in 1940. These "yes men" were ruled automatically unfit for public office in the Fourth Republic unless they could show proof of active participation in the underground. When the Jury of Honor finally disbanded in 1946, it had blacklisted two-thirds of the almost 600 "yes men," thus guaranteeing that the politicians of the Fourth Republic would mostly be new men rather than survivors of the prewar regime. Of the approximately 200 ex-parliamentarians reinstated by the Jury, only a handful succeeded in re-entering public life. Among them were, notably, Robert Schuman and André Maroselli (both destined to become cabinet ministers), René Coty, Jacques Bardoux, Frédéric-Dupont, Henri Meck, Joseph Laniel, and Raymond Laurent. The most curious record of all was that of Schuman, the future Minister of Finance. Not only had he been born on foreign soil (though of Lorraine parents) and educated in German universities, but in addition he had allegedly been conscripted into the German Army after 1914, had voted full powers to Pétain in 1940, and had even served for a few weeks as an undersecretary in Pétain's first Vichy cabinet. Such a record would have damned any ordinary politician, but Schuman's forthright honesty and intense Lorraine patriotism elevated him above attacks even from the Communists. And if Schuman needed absolution for his political errors, he could point to an active career in the underground which earned him seven months of imprisonment in a German fortress.

The purge policy of De Gaulle and his Ministers of Justice (successively François de Menthon and Pierre-Henri Teitgen, both Christian Socialists), was conciliatory rather than vindictive, cautious rather than brusque. Little Belgium, by way of contrast, had three times as many collaboration cases brought up for judicial inquiry. De Gaulle keynoted the policy just after liberation: "France," he declared, "has need of all her children." The government's attitude drew periodic but vehement attacks from the Left, especially the Communists. The latter complained that important offenders were still at large or in comfortable confinement, or even continued to hold official posts, while the government pursued a "purge of concierges." Teitgen later admitted that he had consciously aimed to keep the purge within bounds and to prevent it from becoming what he called "an instrument of revolution."

By the end of 1945, the load borne by the courts began to lighten. Teitgen reported that 112,000 cases had been investigated and that two-thirds of those accused had been brought to trial. Forty thousand Frenchmen had received the mildest penalty of national unworthiness (involving loss of civil rights and confiscation of property); about 20,000 had been given long prison terms; and over 3,000 had been condemned to death (although only about 600 had actually been executed). Thus the Fourth Republic's origins were not marked by a spirit of Jacobin vengeance, and only a small minority of Frenchmen was excluded from the body politic. Whether this lax policy benefited or undermined the Fourth Republic will long remain controversial. Most Frenchmen felt that there had been too many loopholes and inconsistencies; they knew that some unscrupulous schemers and doubtful democrats had slipped through the leaky net of justice. Such cases deepened the atmosphere of cynicism which gradually tarnished the bright hopes of the resistance period. Yet where could the line have been drawn in order to ensure perfect justice? Perhaps it was wiser to err on the side of generosity rather than to risk deepening the multiple divisions among Frenchmen.

The problem of replacing or reconverting the bulky, inefficient administrative bureaucracy of Vichy was also a puzzling one. Since it was impossible to return at once to a peacetime economy, most of the Vichy machinery was retained with a partial replacement of personnel and sometimes with a change of name and structure. Thus the Vichyite "committees of organization," entrusted with allotting raw materials and markets in each industry, were replaced by "professional offices" with similar duties but with representatives of the government and the consumers added to those of the industrialists. This change meant an end to the corporative doctrines of Vichy, patterned after fascism, and a return to democratic government control during the crisis period. The De Gaulle regime found it impossible to cut down the sprawling bureaucracy which burdened the budget and reduced productive capacity; but a worse shortcoming was its inability to rationalize that bureaucracy and to make it more honest and efficient.

Vichy's ambitious mechanisms for regimenting labor and the farmers (the Labor Charter and the Peasant Corporation) collapsed of their own weight in 1944. In the labor field, the Socialist and Communist C.G.T. and the Catholic C.F.T.C. had kept tight-knit organizations underground and were able to resume their prewar roles at once. In agriculture, however, hothouse methods were needed in order to grow a new and healthy plant. De Gaulle gave his Minister of Agriculture, Pierre Tanguy-Prigent, a free hand in this respect. Tanguy-Prigent, the boy wonder of the Socialist party, had entered parliament in 1936 at the age of 26. During the occupation he had retired to his farm in Brittany, and in 1943 had helped to organize an underground peasant group called the *Confédération Générale d'Agriculture* (C.G.A.). Despite two brief periods of arrest by the Germans, he had managed to keep up his activity and to be on the scene when De Gaulle was selecting his cabinet. As Minister, Tanguy-Prigent turned the struggling C.G.A. into a semiofficial body, and for more than a year gave it a complete monopoly. He refused to authorize the formation of competing groups on the ground that the prewar farmers had dissipated their strength by splitting into several weak and antagonistic associations. The Minister's political enemies, especially in the M.R.P., charged that his real purpose was to give the Socialist party a strangle hold in the countryside. If so, his strategy was only a half-success; for when the C.G.A. was finally cut loose from the government's apron strings in January 1946, control spread out to the M.R.P. and Right as well as the Socialists. Whatever his aim, Tanguy-Prigent did force the farmers to channel their strength into a far more powerful pressure group than they had ever had in the past.

When the De Gaulle government faced the issue of limiting capitalism and broadening the rights of labor, it did little more than mark time. A few mines and factories were partially or completely expropriated by the state, but no consistent program of nationalization was followed. Social insurance was reorganized into a single co-ordinated system. Factory workers were given a voice in plant management through the creation of plant production committees in all large enterprises. These boards received full authority in matters of social welfare, and the right to advise the management with respect to plant organization and production methods. The government stopped considerably short of labor's full desires; for example, it denied the committees access to corporate board meetings and to certain "trade secrets." During subsequent months French labor leaders were to find that their new rose had its thorns. Most workmen showed little enthusiasm for the idea of devoting part of their spare time to committee meetings, and in many plants it was impossible to find candidates who understood the problems which the committees had to face. The C.G.T. was finally forced to set up training classes so that labor could make use of the rights which it had long demanded.

Reconstruction of war damage lagged badly during the De Gaulle period. In part, the explanation was a severe shortage of building materials; in part, it was the priority granted to restoring the transportation system; but in addition, there was a degree of sheer inefficiency and injustice involved. By the end of 1945, few of the 1,888,000 destroyed or damaged buildings in France (twenty per cent of the country's prewar total) had been rebuilt, and even temporary housing for the bombed-out population was sadly insufficient. Worse, there did not seem to be any adequate plan for future reconstruction, and even the clearing of debris had not been carried out with the speed and vigor shown by the British or even the Germans. On the other hand, the railroads—greatest key to an economic revival and eventual reconstruction—had been put into operating shape again and were ready to carry their prewar burden of traffic. The record in reconstruction was therefore not entirely black, even though it seemed inadequate to the thousands of *sinistrés*.

De Gaulle's personal attention was concentrated mainly on foreign affairs and on the military problem; domestic matters he left to his ministers. He sought by his foreign policy to make France a bridge or a balance wheel between the Anglo-Saxons and the Russians, and thus to restore his country to a front-rank role in world affairs. One of his first acts as Provisional President was to visit Moscow and to sign a treaty of alliance with the Soviet Union; but the counterbalancing pact with Britain was postponed until Franco-British differences over Germany could be resolved.

That treaty finally had to wait until more than a year after De Gaulle had left office.

De Gaulle's "bridge" policy necessitated preserving the French Empire and strengthening its bonds. Therefore he attempted to maintain some French prerogatives in Syria and the Lebanon when the latter states demanded their promised independence in 1945; and he tried to persuade the Americans and British to arm and transport a French force to Indo-China before Japan surrendered there. Neither of these ambitions was fulfilled. The French had to clear out of the Levant entirely, and to let the British and Chinese occupy Indo-China temporarily, thus giving the nationalist Viet Minh movement a chance to get a powerful foothold in the Chinese zone. De Gaulle's "bridge" theory, like his imperial policy, failed to pay dividends. A year after liberation, De Gaulle had to admit privately (although not yet openly) that his choice had been made between Moscow and the Western Powers.

In the military sphere, De Gaulle did see to it that France took an active part in the closing months of the German war. Whether the resultant gain in prestige balanced the drain in men and resources may be open to question. At least it seems doubtful that the incessant military parades staged in Paris by De Gaulle raised morale high enough to offset their economic waste. While the war continued, few Frenchmen objected to the maintenance of more than a million men in uniform or to the large share of the budget allotted to the military. But after Germany's collapse, that aspect of De Gaulle's policy drew rising protest from the Left. Even the M.R.P., despite its chauvinistic leanings and its Gaullist sympathies, complained in September 1945 that 2,700,000 Frenchmen were still in the armed forces or in government offices while only 2,318,000 were engaged in reconstruction. Eventually the military question was to contribute much to the crisis which brought De Gaulle's retirement to private life.

IV. AGE OF THE MONOLITHS

While the constitutional issue lay dormant during the first post-liberation winter, the blurred features of the Fourth Republic's political countenance began to take shape.

Only a month after the liberation of Paris, De Gaulle's *chef de cabinet* and closest confidant, Gaston Palewski, surveyed the French scene and concluded that the political parties of prewar days were extinct. Palewski observed nothing beyond a persistent Communist nucleus, a profound nationwide enthusiasm for De Gaulle, and a healthy republican sentiment which was waiting to be channeled. He expressed the hope that out of this vague mass there might crystallize two new parties: one moderately socialist, the other Catholic and conservative. Isolated on the extreme Left fringe would be the Communist party, whose strength Palewski estimated at about its 1936 level of fifteen per cent of the country's vote. The basis for government in the Fourth Republic would be a coalition agreement between the two major parties.

Palewski's estimate was a curious blend of shrewdness and wishful thinking. Except for the Communists and possibly the Socialists, the prewar parties did seem to be in an almost hopeless plight. De Gaulle's wartime instructions to encourage party activity had kept their heads above water, but how long they could keep afloat in the uncharted sea of the Fourth Republic was uncertain.

The underground's ideas on future party structure were diverse and often nebulous. Some resistance leaders, like Palewski, hoped for a new two- or three-party system. Others still clung to the idea of a single broad Gaullist *rassemblement*, excluding only the Communists on the one hand and the die-hard reactionaries on the other. Still others (notably the Communists) demanded that De Gaulle govern through the National Resistance Council and the local Committees of Liberation; that the resistance movement preserve its wartime unity and be given a monopoly of political power.

President de Gaulle disappointed all these hopes. He immediately sidetracked the National Resistance Council, and made it clear that the resistance movement could expect no political monopoly. The Communists complained bitterly of De Gaulle's cavalier treatment of the organized resistance; they charged that when De Gaulle arrived in Paris on liberation day, he had first gone to the Arc de Triomphe, the Prefecture of Police, and Notre Dame, and only then to the City Hall to say *"un petit bon jour"* to the National Resistance Council. The story circulated that when he visited Lyon and was greeted by a motley crowd of resistance leaders, he asked with some asperity, *"Où sont les corps constitués?"* *"Mais, mon général,"* replied Regional Commissioner Yves Farge, "they are all in jail." These anecdotes, whether true or not, were suggestive. De Gaulle's intention was to rest his government on the broadest possible base, excluding only the small minority of active Vichyites.

As for the notion of a broad Gaullist bloc, its formation depended on De Gaulle's willingness to become its symbol and its active chief. De Gaulle chose instead the role of national symbol above all party conflicts, and left French political opinion to find its own channels. No course could have been more democratic; and aspiring politicians took full advantage of that freedom during the year that followed.

The Communists alone among the prewar parties entered the Fourth Republic with a guaranteed future before them. By their all-out activity in the underground since 1941, they had almost succeeded in making Frenchmen forget their record of "revolutionary defeatism" before Russia entered the war. After all, they could prove that they had condemned the Vichy regime from its very inception; the files of their underground *Humanité* showed that they had greeted Vichy as "a government of rotters," no better than such "crooks, traitors, and thieves" as Daladier, Reynaud, and Blum. True, their line toward the German conquerors of France had been somewhat more embarrassed. In June 1940, just before Paris fell, the party had demanded that the people be armed to fight off the invaders. But during the month that followed, *Humanité* carried several curious items such as the one headlined "Franco-German Fraternity": "Friendly conversations between Parisian workers and German soldiers are spreading. We are glad of it. Let us learn to know each other, and when we tell the German soldiers that the Communist deputies were thrown in jail for defending the cause of peace . . . , we are working for Franco-German fraternity." Items of this sort were soon discontinued, however; and by October 1946 *Humanité* had become righteous enough to condemn those "lewd vipers" the Trotskyites as "traitors who, in the midst of the occupation, called for fraternization between the French and the Nazi invaders."

In spite of zigzags and jail sentences, the Communist organization and leadership had remained almost intact; only a few second-rank figures had left the party in 1939. After 1941 the party had become the spearhead of the resistance movement and had furnished the largest number of militants to the maquis; it had organized and dominated the group known as *Front National* and its military arm, the *Francs-Tireurs et Partisans*, and had sent its members into other groups as well. The self-styled "party of 75,000 martyrs" emerged from the Vichy period with its reputation enhanced, its ranks thinned but in no sense broken, its leadership faithful to the cause, and its monolithic unity and discipline unimpaired. It possessed a long lead over any rival party when liberation came, and its strategists wasted no time in taking advantage of their opportunities.

Some Gaullists feared that the Communists might try to seize power during the chaotic interim between the departure of the Germans and the arrival of De Gaulle. The fear proved groundless; even in those parts of France where the Communist underground did take over temporarily, it readily surrendered its authority when De Gaulle's agents arrived. The Communists even capitulated—although with loud protests—when De Gaulle disarmed the Patriotic Militia which they had organized to police France after liberation, and when De Gaulle left the army under the control of old-line career officers. Their pressure did lead the government to absorb some 5000 maquis officers into the regular army, but the victory was an almost empty one; within a few months 3000 of the new officers had been retired to the reserve. The armed forces (with the exception of the air force) remained almost impervious to Communist penetration.

The Communists' aim after liberation was not to prepare a coup d'état. Rather, it was to work through legal methods; to assume the role of a great republican party, heir to a long and honorable French tradition. They campaigned for new members, going so far as to print application blanks in certain provincial papers; and within a year, the number of party-card holders had risen from the 1944 figure of 385,000 to an all-time high of a million. They gained control of a flood of publications, beaming their propaganda not only toward the proletariat but also toward farmers, women, intellectuals, and every segment of the population. They adapted that propaganda to each group: for the peasants it was higher prices for farm products; for the bourgeoisie, the best brand of rose-water reform; for the workers, destruction of the trusts; and for all groups, the promise of "a strong, free, and happy France." They broadened their network throughout the country until almost every rural village had its party organizer. Above all, they gradually built up their hold on the Confédération Générale du Travail until, by 1946, eighty per cent of the C.G.T.'s top positions were in Communist hands.

No other party possessed such a galaxy of leaders from prewar days. They included specialists in all types of party work and propaganda, many of them trained at the Marxist-Leninist Institute in Moscow. A few, like Maurice Thorez and André Marty, had lived through the Vichy years in exile. "Handsome Maurice," the Communists' chief and long-range strategist, had deserted from his army unit in 1939 on orders from the party and had turned up in Russia during the war. How and when he got there remained a subject of bitter controversy; his enemies charged that he had accepted German aid. Thorez was an authentic proletarian; the son and grandson of miners, he himself had entered the northern coal mines at the age of twelve, and had soon become a union organizer there. The road to the top of the party had been rough but rapid, and there were few who disputed his capacity to be the

French Stalin. Marty, the man of the Black Sea mutiny and the Spanish Civil War, had been caught in Moscow on Comintern business at the outbreak of the war and had returned via Algiers. A fiery revolutionary with deep contempt for parliamentary methods, he might have passed in a crowd for a small-town grocer.

Another set of front-rank Communists, like Jacques Duclos, Benoit Frachon, Charles Tillon, Raymond Guyot, and Léon Mauvais, had lived underground in France for five long years. Duclos, who left school at twelve to become a pastry-cook's apprentice in the Pyrenees, was the party's tactician and master of parliamentary debate. Squat and barrel-shaped, resembling a bald-headed kewpie in blue serge and horn-rimmed glasses, his appearance belied his remarkable qualities of leadership. Frachon, a self-educated and tough-minded miner's son, was destined to become the postwar boss of organized labor. Still a third group of almost thirty prewar deputies had been jailed by Daladier's government and then by Vichy, and had thus been preserved to renew their fiight for power. Among them were men like François Billoux, Etienne Fajon, and Waldeck-Rochet, all members of the party's Political Bureau.

Leadership, discipline, faith, tight organization—all these the Communists alone possessed in quantity. The result was a powerful magnetic attraction exerted upon many non-Communists, and especially upon the Left wing of the Socialist party. Many impatient young Socialists were beginning to believe that French Communism, to borrow Charles Rappoport's phrase, was "only Socialism with a touch of Tartar sauce," and not Stalinism with French dressing. And yet some doubt persisted in French minds: had the Communists become a thoroughly French party, or were they still, in Léon Blum's phrase, a party of "foreign nationalists"? Had they given their lives in the underground because Hitler was France's enemy, or because he was Russia's enemy? Once this "moment of dialectical necessity" was over, would not the French Communists be guided onto a new course by what they called "the infallible compass of Marxist-Leninist theory"?

The current party line was above reproach. No other group beat its breast quite so violently in protesting its patriotism, or in condemning foreign interference in French affairs. None could boast of so many martyrs who had died for *la patrie*. The *Marseillaise* competed with the *Internationale* at Communist mass meetings, and the clenched-fist salute became rare. The party's hagiology was broadened to bring in such irreproachable figures as Descartes, Rabelais, General Hoche, Robespierre. French patriots' demands for a powerful army, for the pitiless punishment of Germany, for the preservation of the French Empire, became Communist dogma. It was natural for many Frenchmen to feel that the Communists had really changed their spots. Skeptics, however, preferred to wait for the moment when Soviet policy might diverge from French national interests, as interpreted by a majority of Frenchmen. Such skeptics were ready to admit that if one accepted all the premises of Marxist-Leninist-Stalinist theory, then the Communists were the only real patriots in France. They merely wished to be sure that the Communists were not hiding that kind of patriotism behind a façade of the old-fashioned variety.

Late in 1944 Maurice Thorez returned from his wartime haven in Moscow. De Gaulle himself authorized the military deserter of 1939 to enter France without threat of arrest. Perhaps in later years De Gaulle came to regret that leniency, but the act illustrated the truce then in effect between the General and the Communists. The party continued to accept a minor role in the De Gaulle cabinet, scrupulously avoided any direct criticism of the Provisional President, and loudly proclaimed its desire to contribute to French recovery. That contribution was a considerable one; through Communist efforts, strikes and labor strife were stifled and production was stimulated wherever party organizers were active. Surprised Frenchmen remarked ironically that "the Communists are becoming the new Radical Socialists." Whatever the motives behind the party line may have been, the Communist bid for leadership in the Fourth Republic was skillfully planned and executed.

The Communists' next-door political neighbors, the Socialists, were seriously shaken and divided by the collapse in 1940. More than half their parliamentarians had voted for Pétain, and the party had lost its guide and prophet Léon Blum shortly thereafter. Some Socialists had begun to pick up the pieces as early as 1941. Many militant members entered the first resistance groups, and a number of them joined with trade-union elements to found the movement known as *Libération-Nord*. The latter was intended by some of its organizers to serve as the nucleus for an eventual *union travailliste*, a kind of broad Left-Center bloc along the lines of the British Labor Party.

A few weeks after Paris was liberated, those Socialist leaders who had worked in the underground met in family council to consider the future. Their organization was still shaky and their tactics uncertain. Léon Blum, deported to Buchenwald, was not to return until 1945. At the head of the party in 1944 was frail, sardonic Daniel Mayer, a youthful product of the resistance. In prewar days Mayer had been an obscure journalist and party official in his native Paris, with little or no prospect of future prominence. After 1940 he had made his way up to the top post of secretary-general of the underground party, and that post he was to hold for two years after liberation in spite of the jealousy, the personal antipathy, and the subsurface anti-Semitism of some of his fellow Socialists.

The Socialists struck out on their new career by purging two-thirds of their prewar deputies and senators, including such prominent figures as Paul Faure, former Secretary-General, and Georges Monnet, presumptive heir to party leadership. They thus indicated their intention to start afresh, and to present themselves as a purified and reconstructed party worthy of the resistance. Despite the purge, they still possessed a number of able and shrewd leaders, some of them with prewar reputations, others barely emerging from obscurity. Among the former were Vincent Auriol (classed as the party's financial expert by everyone except other financial experts); former professor André Philip and former school teacher Eugène Thomas (the latter still in a German concentration camp); Léon Blum's brilliant cousin Jules Moch; irascible André

Le Troquer and jovial Félix Gouin. The newcomers to national politics included such men as Robert Lacoste, Albert Gazier, and Henri Ribière (all former trade union or co-operative officials); Edouard Depreux and Gaston Defferre, lawyers from Paris and Marseille respectively; Marcel Naegelen, Guy Mollet, and Raymond Badiou, all school teachers; the eminent anthropologist Paul Rivet; and a long list of others who had risen from the prewar rank and file. Although most of these leaders were still largely untested, they seemed to provide the Socialists with an adequate if not brilliant vanguard.

Many of the party's new chiefs, including Daniel Mayer himself, leaned toward the *union travailliste* idea, provided that the Socialists could dominate it. They wished to broaden the party's base by taking in fresh and vigorous new elements from the underground, and to replace the fallen Radical Socialists as the great Left-Center party of France.

But the *union travailliste* program stuck in the craw of many Socialist militants. Marxist dogma was still a powerful force in the party, and doctrinaire believers feared that if the back door were opened to bourgeois elements, the working class would simultaneously flood out the front entrance into Communist ranks. Even men like Mayer himself were good enough Marxists to hesitate at the implications of their program. The party therefore straddled. It announced that unity of action between the two proletarian parties, the Socialists and the Communists, was a desirable goal because it would solidify the working class and would assure the victory of Marxism. At the same time, it attached enough strings to this suggestion to show that the Socialists were still skeptical of the "brother party's" aims and methods. The Communists, who had scorned a similar proposal during the underground period, now grabbed the ball and ran off with it. Outright fusion became their major aim, for it would inevitably allow them to dominate the smaller, less vigorous and less tightly organized Socialists. The idea of fusion was to keep the Socialists divided against themselves during the months that followed, seriously hindering their attempt to make a political comeback.

A few Socialists felt at the time—and many more came to believe later—that the party missed its greatest opportunity during the six months after liberation. A vast mass of French voters of mildly leftist sympathies were floating aimlessly in search of political leadership. In addition, a number of young French intellectuals or non-Communist workingmen had developed leadership qualities in the underground; they dreamed of a rejuvenated and purified France, and were ready to enter politics if they could find a party willing to accept their aid. In that early post-liberation period, the ideals and principles of the Socialist party seemed to offer the kind of democratic new deal which millions of Frenchmen wanted.

The occasion was made to order, but the chance was muffed. Long-time Socialist militants, jealous of their prerogatives in the party, looked down their noses at newcomers from the resistance. Some candidates for admission they rejected outright; others were let in, but were quickly discouraged by being pushed down in the party hierarchy in favor of old-timers. Meanwhile, the party's doctrinaire Marxism and its straddling tactics prevented any consistent campaign to win a following among the Left-Center drifters. The latter gradually turned away from the Socialists and looked elsewhere for leadership.

In preserving themselves from the bourgeois menace, the Socialists not only lost their chance to become the largest party in France, but condemned themselves to gradual decline. They refused to expand on their Right, but found it impossible to expand on their Left and to compete successfully with the more dynamic Communist movement. The best that can be said of their choice is that it left the Socialist party as a buffer between the Communists and the Center, and perhaps postponed an open division of France into Communist and anti-Communist camps. It also preserved the party's Marxian foundation, and made Socialism a potential refuge for disillusioned Communists who might some day refuse to zigzag along with Moscow.

Of all the large prewar parties, the Radical Socialists' organization was hardest hit by the collapse. A heavy proportion of its parliamentarians had voted the wrong way in 1940, and the party's resistance record had been considerably short of brilliant. Edouard Herriot, the Radicals' principal figure, had been deported to Germany in 1944 and did not return until mid-1945. Without Herriot the Radicals were woefully lacking in leadership and in self-confidence. Their first party congress late in 1944 offered neither inspiration nor encouragement; Frenchmen looked on them as a band of bearded elders with eyes turned to the past and voices raised in quavering indignation at having been forgotten. Their determination to start afresh seemed even more doubtful when the Radicals purged only a few of their "yes men." Nevertheless, the Radicals had old and presumably deep roots in many parts of France, and there were few observers yet willing to dismiss them as mere fossils of the Third Republic.

The fate of the old Right-wing parties such as the Republican Federation and the Democratic Alliance was highly uncertain in 1944. They had never possessed either unity or tight organization, and now they were badly discredited by the fact that so many of their leaders had rallied to Vichy. A few prominent figures like Louis Marin, the grand old man of Lorraine, and Joseph Laniel, the Norman industrialist-politician, were untouched by the Vichy tarbrush; but they stood out in splendid isolation, almost without followers. A few of them toyed with the idea of fusing or federating the Right groups and the Radicals into a loose-knit "Republican" party, which they hoped might eventually attract the Christian Socialists and become a massive counterweight to the Marxian parties. Some of Colonel de la Rocque's old lieutenants in the semi-fascist *Parti Social Français* made persistent efforts to revive the P.S.F., pointing out that De la Rocque had finally broken with Vichy and had been deported to Germany. In general, however, the Right lay low during the first post-liberation year, hoping against hope that better days might return.

In the great political vacuum between the Socialists and the far Right, a new force began to appear in the autumn of 1944. Both Frenchmen and foreigners had noted that De Gaulle's revised cabinet contained a disproportionate number of Left-wing Catholics loosely called Christian Socialists. Several of them in prewar days had belonged to the tiny Left-Center Catholic party called the Popular Democrats. Georges Bidault, one of that group, had emerged during the later stages of the occupation as president of the National Resistance Council; in a sense, therefore, he ranked second only to De Gaulle in liberated France. A professor of medieval history at the Lycée Louis-le-Grand, a 45-year-old bachelor, a veteran of two wars (corporal in the first, infantry sergeant in the second), Bidault had been his party's expert on foreign affairs before 1939. Although a political career had always been his goal, his only venture into politics had been in 1936 when he ran unsuccessfully for the Chamber. During the Vichy period his temporary classroom at Lyon had been a principal headquarters of the underground movement.

Another Christian Socialist was perhaps more generally known in France just after liberation—by ear, if not by name and by sight. For four years Maurice Schumann, correspondent of the Havas Agency by profession, had served as the Voice of Free France at the London radio, and his dramatic, deep-purple appeals had made a widespread impression. Schumann, born in 1911 of an Alsatian Jewish family, had been converted to Catholicism in 1939. His fervent faith, his ascetic personal life, and his tendency to sermonize had given him a unique status in the London Free French group; he was privately labeled "Savonarola," or sometimes "the mad virgin of Carlton Gardens." His personal devotion to De Gaulle approached the level of worship, and his patriotism was of the spread-eagle variety. Less prominent but more effective than Schumann was André Colin, a handsome and deliberate young law professor from Brittany. Colin had once been national president of the Catholic youth association, and in 1944 he had risen to the very top in the underground, becoming a member of the National Resistance Council. Francisque Gay, sparse-bearded patriarch of the Popular Democrats, owner of a publishing firm on the Left Bank, lent a touch of age and experience. François de Menthon, a mild professor of law from the University of Nancy, and P. H. Teitgen, an acrid one from the same place, fitted nicely into this group of intellectuals who had scattered out among various resistance groups after 1940.

The future course of this little Catholic nucleus was completely uncertain when liberation arrived. Some of them expected the resurrection of the Popular Democratic party as an enlarged but still second-rank political force. Others nursed varying schemes for expanding one or another of the resistance groups into a new party. A few were tempted to try for an *union travailliste* with the Socialists. The Socialists made a half-hearted bid in their direction in November 1944; they invited individual Christian Socialists to apply for membership in the Socialist party, but the offer found few takers. As for the idea of a mushrooming Catholic party, destined to become Communism's only serious rival for pre-eminence in postwar France, scarcely any Frenchman imagined such a development in August 1944.

Not many of the M.R.P.'s future leaders foresaw it either. During the occupation a few of them had thought of trying to build a mass party, but when Vichy fell they had no definite plans, no skeleton organization throughout the country, no certainty even that the church hierarchy would favor them over a clerical party of the far Right. In prewar days, most of the upper hierarchy had viewed even the Popular Democrats with alarm; and the new crop of Christian Socialists was considerably more Leftist-minded than the Popular Democrats had been. However, they did possess some real assets: a small group of well-known and vigorous leaders, a solid resistance reputation, and—according to rumor—the silent blessing of General de Gaulle. For cadres they could fall back on the prewar Popular Democratic organization, but even more on the two youth movements known as the Jocistes and the Jacistes—the *Jeunesses Ouvrières Chrétiennes* and the *Jeunesses Agricoles Chrétiennes*. There was also the Catholic trade union organization, the C.F.T.C., relatively small in size but intact at the end of the occupation. Finally, their number one asset was their realization that a huge gap existed in the center of the French political spectrum, and that one or several parties would shortly attempt to fill that gap.

The decision to play for high stakes was taken soon after liberation, and with that decision the *Mouvement Républicain Populaire* was born. The name indicated an intent to break with the past and to give the new party flexible boundaries. Far more important, however, was the leaders' selection of the Communist party as their organizational model. They consciously set out to build a monolithic, highly centralized machine, with local units in every town and village, but with instructions going out from Paris. They established training schools to prepare party workers for the arduous tasks of modern politics. In propaganda methods too—notably in the use of posters—they imitated the Communists. Never before had a French republican party abandoned the French tradition that a party should be a collection of individuals loosely grouped together around a common ideal. If the M.R.P.'s strategy proved successful, it would mean the beginning of a new era in French politics—the age of the monoliths.

During the early months of the M.R.P.'s existence, its leaders were optimistic but by no means overconfident. In April 1945, five months after getting under way, they privately estimated that they could poll only about 180,000 votes; and in August their paid-up membership still amounted to little more than 100,000. In comparison, the Socialists had 250,000, and the Communists 1,000,000. Their organizers were active in only about half the territory of France; their reception by the clergy varied considerably in warmth; their future remained highly uncertain. Conservatives scoffed at them as "*poissons rouges dans un bénitier*," or as "a party with a red head and a white tail"; Communists proclaimed that M.R.P. really stood for "*Machine pour Ramasser les Pétainistes*" or "*Mensonge, Réaction, Perfidie*."

The nationwide municipal elections of April and May 1945 saw them win control of fewer than 500 of the 35,000 town councils in France. Yet six months later, in October 1945, they were to poll the remarkable total of four and a half million popular votes, and in 1946 they were to run neck and neck with the Communists for leadership in France. Their overnight success, a combination of method and moment, was unprecedented in French history. It was natural that their internal unity should leave something to be desired, and that the party's leftward-looking leadership should find itself burdened with a great many unsympathetic converts. The M.R.P. was by no means so perfect a monolith as its Communist rival, but it was solid enough to justify the strategy of its founders.

Part of the M.R.P.'s success was no doubt due to the admission of women to French political life. The role played by women in the underground, along with the weakening of the chief anti-feminist party, the Radical Socialists, ensured them of political equality in the Fourth Republic. One of the most striking novelties of that first post-liberation year was the inclusion in every public meeting of one female orator, who with a combination of justifiable pride and mechanical regularity recited the feminine record in the resistance movement. Only the Radicals refused to bow before the storm. Like the courtly senator of prewar days, they held that "women's hands were made for kisses, not for the sordid task of voting." Their real fear was that clerical influence might be far stronger among women than among men voters, since far more of the former are practicing Catholics. That fear was in considerable part justified, for most of the female vote eventually tended to divide between the Communists and the M.R.P. In Edouard Herriot's ironic phrase, French women voted either for paradise on earth or for paradise in heaven.

By the end of De Gaulle's first year in power, the outlines of the Fourth Republic's party structure were pretty well established. That structure represented a kind of amalgamation of the old and the new. Again France had a multi-party system, and most of the party labels were familiar; but the number of groups was smaller, and the rigidity of party organization was on the increase. The multiple resistance groups, some of which had hoped to develop into new parties, had been largely absorbed by the Communists, the Socialists, or the M.R.P. Almost the only underground remnants to enter politics separately were the M.U.R.F. (*Mouvement Unifiée de la Renaissance Française*), a Communist affiliate, and the U.D.S.R. (*Union Démocratique et Socialiste de la Résist-*

ance), which first flirted with the Socialists but in 1946 swung into alliance with the Radicals. Whether for good or ill, political power was on the way to becoming concentrated in the central offices of three or four party machines.

V. THE CONSTITUENT ASSEMBLY: CORSETED OR UNCONSTRAINED?

In the late spring of 1945, nine months after Paris was liberated, the constitutional question brusquely emerged from hibernation. Hitler's armies had collapsed in April and May. French prisoners and deportees were pouring home with unexpected speed. At a cabinet meeting on May 31, President de Gaulle suddenly announced that the return of the absent French voters would remove the last obstacle to the election of a constituent assembly. He added that the election ought to take place not later than the end of the year.

De Gaulle spoke none too soon to forestall a Communist-led campaign for an early end to the period of quasi-dictatorship. The Communists had long been suspicious of a possible Gaullist attempt to stretch out the provisional period in an effort to make it permanent. They had swallowed their suspicions during the winter because they dared not urge an election while more than two million voters were still captives in Germany. They had to admit that such an election would have been dominated by women and old men. But in May they began to show signs of restiveness, and so did other political leaders, especially those in the frustrated Consultative Assembly. Complaints against "dictatorship" began to be heard in public meetings, and on June 5 the Assembly vociferously applauded a speaker who described De Gaulle as "restorer of our *future* liberties."

All the parties were caught somewhat off guard by De Gaulle's pronouncement. As late as April 1, a member of De Gaulle's cabinet had privately remarked that he did not expect regular elections for at least another eighteen months. Not a single party had given the constitutional question any serious attention since liberation; no study committees had been set up to clear the ground. Even the Consultative Assembly's Committee on State Reform had dodged the issue, much to De Gaulle's irritation. De Gaulle's statement therefore caused some hasty scrambling to find just where party doctrine lay.

But before the politicians could come to grips with the problem of what kind of constitution to give France, De Gaulle again stepped in to divert their attention to a preliminary issue: how and by whom should the constitution be drafted? It was this question which came to dominate the summer of 1945.

De Gaulle remarked in an early June press conference that Frenchmen seemed to be split into three different groups. One element insisted that the 1875 constitution was still valid, and that a Chamber and Senate must be chosen to consider its revision. A second group called for a completely sovereign constituent assembly to rebuild from the ground up. A third school of thought proposed a "corseted" assembly with restricted powers and a fixed term, these limitations to be suggested by the De Gaulle cabinet and ratified by means of a referendum. De Gaulle implied that he himself was still undecided in face of the three alternatives.

These impromptu remarks brought two unexpected factors into the problem. That De Gaulle should still consider the possibility of reviving the Third Republic was a shock to almost everyone, for he had openly abandoned such an idea after his pact with the underground in 1942. At the root of his sudden hesitation was the return of Edouard Herriot from German captivity a few days before. De Gaulle was profoundly impressed by the case which Herriot made for retaining the old framework, and he suddenly wondered whether he had not overstepped the bounds of legality by discarding the 1875 constitution.

The second new factor in De Gaulle's statement, the referendum, appeared to spring from nowhere. The paternity of the idea seems to have been shared by two leading constitutional lawyers in De Gaulle's entourage: René Capitant, Minister of

Education, and René Cassin, newly appointed head of the Council of State. These advisers argued that a constituent assembly unlimited in its powers or its duration would be a dangerous mechanism; that it might carry France to an unknown and redoubtable destination before consenting to disband.

But how, they asked, could the prerogatives of the people's chosen representatives be limited in advance? Obviously the Provisional Government had no authority to limit them by fiat. The only possible safeguards would be either to restore the constitution of 1875, or to request the sovereign electorate to ratify a set of limitations.

De Gaulle's remarks brought a quick and hostile reaction from the Left. The Communists led off with a double-barreled blast against either a return to the 1875 constitution or a referendum; and for good measure they threw in an attack on the general idea of a presidential regime. The Socialists, the C.G.T., and the principal resistance groups all swung into line; and after three weeks of hesitation, the M.R.P. finally followed. Most of the M.R.P. leaders sympathized with the idea of a stronger executive and were proud to describe the M.R.P. as "the party of fidelity" (to De Gaulle). But since the General had not yet announced his preference, the M.R.P. had to choose; and a single sovereign assembly seemed most consistent with the program of the wartime underground.

Bucking this heavy current toward a sovereign assembly were the Radicals, the Right wing, and a few "technocratic" elements in the resistance movement. The Radicals naturally demanded that "republican institutions" (i.e., the constitution of 1875) be respected; they insisted that there was no need for a referendum on an issue which they considered above dispute. The far Right-wing leaders who were still in active politics went along with the Radicals in order to avert what they called "dangerous adventures." On the other hand, in certain resistance circles there reappeared the idea of a prefabricated constitution to be drafted not by an elected assembly but by an appointed committee, with eventual ratification by popular referendum. A variety of other schemes, mostly proposed by individual Gaullists or conservatives, called for limiting the powers of the future constituent assembly to the single task of constitution-drafting, in order to deprive it of the right to overthrow the government or to adopt sweeping economic reforms.

President de Gaulle, by withdrawing into total silence for a month, encouraged this pullulation of theories. He conferred privately with leaders of various political groups, including the National Resistance Council (which informed him that it had voted 13 to 3 for a sovereign constituent assembly). On July 1, during a brief visit to central France, he let fall some cryptic remarks which were pounced upon exultantly by the partisans of the Third Republic. "We must build a new France," De Gaulle declared, "but a France which remains solidly attached to the one which preceded it. . . . Even though we must create anew, that does not mean that we must sweep away everything old." The report quickly spread that De Gaulle had finally succumbed to Herriot's persuasion and was about to resuscitate the Third Republic. The Left parties were so shaken that some Socialists talked of withdrawing their ministers from the cabinet in protest.

But the report was premature. On July 7, De Gaulle put the whole question before the cabinet, and informed the ministers that his sole aim was to block at all costs the election of a fully sovereign constituent assembly. He had at last reached the conclusion that such a body might lead to anarchy and disorder from which, in his words, "democracy might not emerge alive." His own choice would be a constituent assembly limited by the verdict of a referendum; but if the people should prefer to use the 1875 machinery, he would not stand in their way. The decision between the Third and the Fourth Republic would have to be made by the people, he contended; the Provisional Government could not take so grave a responsibility. But the Government could decide to deny the people the dangerous right to choose an "omnipotent" assembly.

De Gaulle thus set himself squarely against the three leading parties, the organized resistance movement, and a majority of his own cabinet ministers. It required two full days of what the press politely called "an exchange of views" before he could browbeat the cabinet into accepting his plan. The project offered the voters only two choices: either a return to the 1875 constitution, or a constituent assembly with its powers and tenure specifically limited in advance. The latter alternative would restrict the assembly's term to seven months, and would deny it the right to overthrow the cabinet during that period. It would elect the new provisional president, but would not be able to get rid of him thereafter. The plan therefore amounted to a curious hybrid of the parliamentary and the presidential systems during the short but vital interim period of constitution-making. It might easily serve as a model for the permanent structure of the Fourth Republic: certainly its authors, De Gaulle and Capitant, hoped for such a result.

The De Gaulle plan was published with the formal approval of the whole cabinet, even the Communist and Socialist ministers. Faced with a choice between preserving cabinet solidarity and resigning, they chose the former course, but the Left wing felt in no way bound by the decision. Cries of "plebiscite" and "Bonapartism" went up at once. "The people are neither provisional nor consultative—they are sovereign!" cried the Communist leader Auguste Gillot at a mass meeting held that night. Through the Left's outcry the fear was discernible that the temporary expedient of a semi-presidential system might be able to take root even in the short period of seven months. Just as bitter as the Left were the Radicals, who had counted their chickens a bit prematurely after De Gaulle's apparent conversion by Herriot.

In the face of this almost unanimous hostility, De Gaulle first stiffened and then beat a retreat. His initial reaction was to appeal to the nation by radio, evoking the danger of an "omnipotent" assembly. The report spread that De Gaulle was considering a brusque resignation if the country failed to follow him. A day later, however, he gave in before the threat of a cabinet crisis. The cabinet met again and revised the project so as to introduce a third referendum choice—a fully sovereign assembly. This tactical withdrawal spared De Gaulle his first head-on clash with the Left, and kept the door ajar for an eventual compromise.

The Left parties were somewhat mollified by this concession, but they feared that the voters' right to choose a sovereign assembly would be an empty one if De Gaulle should proceed to throw his personal weight into the scales in favor of "corseting" the future assembly. De Gaulle was obviously determined to do exactly that. In a speech at Brest on July 21, he repudiated both a return to the Third Republic and an assembly "without brake or time limit," and announced that he would campaign in favor of his temporary semi-presidential system.

When debate on the De Gaulle project opened in the moribund Consultative Assembly, it was evident that only a few ultra-Gaullist delegates were ready to take it straight. Some groups—the Communists, Radicals, and Right—were determined to reject it bag and baggage because they opposed the referendum procedure as either dangerous or unnecessary. Between these two extreme wings of the Assembly, however, the notion of compromise began to grow. Contained in the Center groups—Socialists, M.R.P., and nonparty resistance—were most of De Gaulle's loyal personal supporters. Even in the Socialist party, the strain of Gaullism was still strong at that epoch. The Center groups were therefore willing to meet De Gaulle halfway if he in turn would take a step or two in their direction. But when they approached him privately, De Gaulle adamantly refused to descend from his cold and lofty pinnacle.

In spite of this rebuff, the Center leaders proceeded to seek a solution on their own, and finally found one in a compromise suggested by Vincent Auriol. This veteran Socialist, a long-time friend and close associate of Léon Blum, was regarded as the warmest admirer of De Gaulle in the party. His plan accepted the three-pronged referendum, but proposed that the "corset" alternative be made flexible rather than rigid. Above all—and this was the key to the Auriol plan—the president would not be guaranteed seven months of independence; he would be responsible to the assembly at all times. His only protection against overthrow by the assembly would be a "cooling-off" clause, which would require a delay of two days before the assembly could vote nonconfidence. The Auriol plan thus aimed to ensure an immediate return to the parliamentary principle, and at the same time to correct one of the prewar abuses of that principle—the overthrow of cabinets on impulse, without mature reflection.

The Auriol project seemed to be the best bet for a compromise between De Gaulle and the Consultative Assembly. In the showdown vote, however, the Communists, the extreme Right, and the Radicals all remained adamant, and it was rejected by a margin of 108 to 101. Thus the Assembly confessed its impotence: it turned down the De Gaulle plan, yet could not agree on any alternative. De Gaulle might therefore draw such conclusions as he wished from this hopeless deadlock of the politicians.

De Gaulle's decision a few days later was a surprising one. Instead of maintaining his original project, as might have been expected, he scrapped it in favor of the defeated Auriol plan. This startling concession grew out of De Gaulle's belief that a new political bloc was at last in process of crystallization, and that the 101 Socialist, M.R.P., and pure resistance delegates who had backed the Auriol plan might represent the foundation for a future governmental majority. Furthermore, De Gaulle reasoned, this same coalition might be willing to draft a new constitution in general harmony with his own concepts of government. His only immediate alternative would be to align himself with a Right-wing bloc against the solid Left. The gamble seemed worth the sacrifice of his interim semi-presidential scheme. That the gamble eventually failed to pay returns does not condemn it as naïve and futile. De Gaulle's error did not lie in his choice of strategy, but in the fact that he chose it halfheartedly and was incapable of following it up. Conciliation and compromise, unfortunately, were not in his nature. Subsequent months were to show that a more supple political leader with equal prestige might have made the gamble pay, and might have spared France a year of bickering and wasted effort.

VI. PROGRAMS IN EMBRYO

The election of a constituent assembly is a rare and momentous occasion in the life of any nation. Three-fourths of a century had passed in France since the voters had been called upon to choose such a body. Careful preparation and clear, well-understood issues would seem to be essential in such circumstances. Instead, when the voters went to the polls on October 21, 1945, the keynote was confusion. Except for the Communists, all the new or revived parties were barely emerging from an invertebrate state; their doctines and their leadership were still more or less obscure. Few citizens had more than the haziest notion of the kind of constitution for or against which they were voting when they chose deputies. The campaign was not fought on that issue; it centered around the accompanying triple-barreled referendum by which the character and the powers of the assembly would be determined. Of all the parties, only the M.R.P. cluttered its electoral posters with any precise constitutional proposals.

Conscientious readers of the political press, however, were aware that the major groups had begun to survey the problem. The Communists were better prepared than any of their rivals; they possessed a complete constitutional text ready for presentation to the new assembly. The Socialists in their August national congress approved without debate (and without the least show of interest) a set of basic principles drawn up by Vincent Auriol and André Philip. As for the M.R.P., its high command had called on all local units of the party to submit suggestions, and was examining these grass-roots contributions before drafting a kind of constitutional catechism for the use of their future deputies. The Radicals and the Right-wing factions were more reticent. They offered no precise programs of reform, but made it plain that they intended to salvage as much as possible of the prewar system.

On two basic issues, the Communists, Socialists, and M.R.P. were in complete agreement from the start. All of them insisted that France needed a new constitution rather than a revision of the old one; all of them joined to reject the American-style presidential system of government, whatever its theoretical merits might be. Acceptance of these two points seemed to mean that half the battle of constitution-making was won in advance.

Descending from broad principles, however, the seeds of dissension began to appear. Most critical of all was the question of how much power and independence could be given to the executive branch without abandoning the parliamentary system. In Communist eyes, "government by assembly" was the proper form for the next stage on the road to sovietized democracy. Their constitutional draft, for example, would not even allow the cabinet to transfer a military unit in time of peace without the consent of the assembly's steering committee. The premier himself would be elected by the legislature, and would possess no recourse such as a threat to dissolve the assembly.

The M.R.P. objected to this concentration of power. Their theorists agreed with the historian Michelet—and with De Gaulle —that a collective dictatorship is the worst of all forms of oppression. They pointed to the Convention of 1792-95 as a horrible example of the evils of government by assembly. Authority, they felt, must be distributed among various organs of government, although without going so far as the American separation of powers. Therefore they proposed a system resembling that of the Third Republic, except that the cabinet would be relatively stronger than before. The premier would again be chosen by the president of the republic, but he and the president together would in future have the right to dissolve the lower legislative house at will. The cabinet would also be protected against spur-of-the-moment crises by the requirement of a cooling-off period prior to any vote of confidence.

The Socialists took a position halfway between those of their two neighbors. They agreed with the Communists that a one-house assembly should elect the premier, but they wished to stop short of government by assembly. They agreed with the M.R.P. that a cooling-off period would be useful in order to cut down the number of cabinet crises, but they did not want to give the premier so powerful a weapon as free dissolution. Their remedy

for cabinet instability, the heart of their compromise system, was
the idea of automatic dissolution. This scheme would work as a
kind of political boomerang. It would confirm the assembly's right
to overthrow a cabinet, but in exercising that right the assembly
would automatically dissolve itself. The Socialists believed that the
threat of having to face a new election would discourage most
deputies from bringing on cabinet crises, and would therefore correct the worst weakness of French parliamentary government.
André Philip, its chief exponent, argued that dissolution must not
be a club which the premier could swing over the assembly's head.
Rather, it should be a safety valve for getting rid of an assembly
which could not produce a workable and stable cabinet majority.
This, Philip insisted, was the way in which dissolution really
worked in Great Britain, whereas the M.R.P.'s plan smacked of
the Weimar Republic, in which the executive dissolved parliament
so often that the regime itself was undermined.

On this all-important issue of executive-legislative relationships,
the Communist, Socialist, and M.R.P. programs overlapped each
other. On other disputed points there was a similar overlapping,
with the Socialists agreeing now with one side and now with the
other. Always, however, the Communists opposed any mechanism
which would force the assembly to share its power. Thus the Communists demanded a one-house legislature, while the M.R.P. urged
a modified form of bicameralism in which the upper house would
have a purely suspensive veto. Many individual Socialists, including Auriol and Philip, looked on this M.R.P. plan with a degree
of sympathy, but the Socialists officially stuck to their traditional
doctrine of unicameralism. With respect to a president of the republic, the M.R.P. wished to use the constitution of 1875 as a
model. The president would be a formal and fairly weak official,
but would retain the single important right to name the premier.
The Communists favored depriving the president of even that
right, thus turning him into a kind of fancy-dress dummy; and the
Socialists, with much more logic, proposed to abolish the presidency completely as a useless and expensive cog in the machine.
Still another check on the assembly which the M.R.P. favored was

an American type of supreme court, with authority to act as watchdog over the new constitution. Both the Marxian parties opposed any such body.

A second broad aspect of the Communists' constitutional program was the expansion of certain aspects of direct democracy. Their principal cure-all, suggested by them already during the underground period, was the right of voters to recall their deputies. But they also advocated the direct election of all judges, and the transfer of local administration from the hands of the prefects to the presidents of locally elected councils. They proposed to abolish outright the Paris-appointed prefects, who had made France one of the most highly centralized states in the world ever since Napoleon's day. On the other hand, the Communists rejected one mechanism of direct democracy, the referendum, with horror. In their ideal system, it would be an improper infringement on the assembly's all-embracing power.

The Socialists were ready to go along partway with the Communists' program of direct democracy. They approved the recall of unfaithful deputies—but by the party machine rather than by the voters. They accepted the idea of electing judges—but only in the lower brackets. They agreed that local government might be transferred to elected councils—but felt that the prefects should be preserved with shorn powers. The M.R.P., however, rejected both the election of judges and the idea of decentralization as dangerous to French unity and to governmental efficiency. They hinted that the Communists' real aim was to weaken the republic's authority in every possible way, rather than to bring government closer to the people. The M.R.P.'s only gesture toward direct democracy was its sponsorship of the referendum procedure.

One novelty proposed by both the Socialists and the M.R.P. was bound to bring them into conflict with the Communists. This was the idea of inserting in the constitution a "party statute." Its sponsors argued that political parties had become such vital and direct organs of government that they could no longer be treated as private associations of citizens. They ought, therefore, to be regulated by the fundamental law of the land. The "party statute"

would consist of a series of budgetary and organizational rules designed to keep any party from falling under the domination of the
trusts, of foreign powers, or of undemocratic leadership within the
party. The Communists remained tight-lipped with respect to this
suggestion, but they could scarcely fail to see that it might be
turned against them as well as against fascist parties.

Those rare Frenchmen who took the trouble to compare the
parties' constitutional plans in the fall of 1945 could draw two
main conclusions. First, the Communist program fitted better
than any other into the 150-year-old current of French Left-wing
republican tradition. Mere consistency with tradition, however,
was no guarantee that their program would meet the needs of a
modern republic. Second, the doctrinal differences separating the
three major parties did not seem great enough to preclude a satisfactory compromise, assuming a reasonable degree of good will on
all sides. The prospect of compromise appeared even brighter because party doctrines (except those of the Communists) had not
yet hardened into rigid, inflexible molds. Most citizens still did not
know just what kind of constitution they desired, but they saw no
reason why the approaching assembly would be unable to offer
them an acceptable one. Events were to prove them over-
optimistic.

VII. CHOOSING THE ARCHITECTS

The character of the assembly which would
draw the blueprints of the Fourth Republic depended in large
part on the system used to elect it. France had experimented with
seventeen different electoral laws in a little over a century. A heavy
majority of political leaders was determined to move on to an
eighteenth plan—"pure" proportional representation. The Socialists had long preached its virtues; the Communists were committed to it; and the M.R.P. swung into line as well.

There persisted two nests of opposition to the heavy proportionalist current. One, concentrated in the Radical party, preferred a

return to the Third Republic's customary system of small electoral districts with a single deputy each, and with a run-off ballot provided in case no candidate received a clear majority in the first day's voting. Edouard Herriot once likened such electoral tests to "gladiatorial combats," although Aristide Briand had preferred to use the more pungent phrase "stagnant pools." The system had assured the Radicals of their past successes, and they hoped that it would preserve their foothold in the new France. It allowed a variety of parties or individuals to try their luck in the first ballot, with coalitions forming around compromise candidates in the run-off.

A second and smaller opposition group, growing mainly out of the intellectual resistance, preferred to experiment with a plan which might help to develop a two-party system in France. Its chief exponents were De Gaulle's Minister of Education, René Capitant, who had preached it in the desert for some years before the war, and Michel Debré, who had written the scheme into the constitution which he had drafted for the underground *Comité Général d'Etudes* in 1943. These men contended that no modern democracy could function efficiently on a coalition basis, and that the only way to force a dozen parties to fuse into two blocs would be to adopt the Anglo-Saxon system of election by a mere plurality. Proportional representation they condemned as the worst of all evils, for it would assure minority groups of representation and would thus encourage a further splintering of parties. They pointed darkly to the fate of the Weimar Republic, where the proportional system had helped keep alive a half-dozen or more competing groups and had led to permanent instability.

De Gaulle was impressed by Capitant's arguments, but he ended by accepting the wishes of the proportionalist majority. In spite of proportionalism's weaknesses, he felt that a constituent assembly was a special kind of body which ought to reflect as faithfully as possible all the main currents of opinion in the country. The chief immediate problem was not to secure a coherent majority on which to base a government; rather, it was to work out a constitution which would so far as possible meet the wishes of all Frenchmen. Besides, both he and Capitant felt that the question posed in the referendum would begin to sort the voters out into two large blocs, and that one of these blocs could serve as a governmental majority. De Gaulle therefore handed down an electoral law based on the proportional principle, but with certain peculiar clauses which somewhat denatured its purity.

De Gaulle's decision won him no friends. The "pure" proportionalists damned his plan as "bastard, unjust, and ridiculous"; they felt that his left hand had taken away what his right hand had given. The plan, instead of totaling each party's votes throughout the nation and assuring to each party its exact ratio of seats, provided for proportionalism within each electoral district (usually the department). As a result, parties with strong local influence would be favored; a fair number of minority votes would be wasted in each department; and a premium would be offered to the formation of coalition tickets on a departmental scale. Such coalitions would be "immoral," cried the purists; they would falsify the real purpose of proportionalism. Hidden behind these moralistic protests was the practical fear that the badly disorganized Radicals and Rightists would be able to build on their strong local influence in many regions to compete successfully against the three large nationally organized parties.

The outcry failed to budge De Gaulle an inch; it merely embittered his relationships with the party leaders. His plan was not only put into effect in October 1945, but it was used again in June 1946 and, with only slight changes, in November 1946. Thus it tended to become a semipermanent institution in the Fourth Republic. Its general effect was to slow up any trend toward either a two-party system or a further increase in the number of parties. It therefore contributed to the growth of a new political pattern, with four or five strong party machines replacing the undisciplined and flexible formations of prewar days. It also dealt a severe blow to the ambitions of certain resistance groups which had hoped to have a try at politics under their own labels. They were usually forced to ally themselves with established parties, and to accept secondary positions on the latters' tickets. Their almost complete absorption followed as a matter of course. As for the eccentric individual candidates of prewar days (like the one who used to label himself *Mécontent National*), they became virtually extinct. A lone survivor was Ferdinand Lop, perennial candidate of the Latin Quarter students, with his program of extending the rue Cujas in both directions to the sea and abolishing poverty after 6:00 P.M.

De Gaulle's time schedule left the parties less than three weeks to map their campaign strategy and to scrape together lists of candidates. Coalitions, whether moral or immoral, offered so clear a premium that they became almost a political necessity. The Communists bid first and highest; they invited all "republican and laic groups" to form joint tickets. Their proposal excommunicated only the M.R.P. and the Right. Many Left-wing Socialists were tempted by this offer, but the party finally rejected it in favor of a Socialist alliance with the U.D.S.R. (the anti-Communist wing of the underground).

Curiously enough, the Radicals were more strongly attracted by the Communists' siren song. These two parties had been indulging in a mild flirtation ever since July, when they voted together in the Consultative Assembly against the Auriol compromise. Edouard Herriot himself had begun to smile benignly and opportunistically upon M. Thorez; he had been liberated from German captivity by the Russians, and had returned to France via Moscow. In the end, however, Radical-Communist joint tickets could not be worked out except in one small district; but a tacit truce between them was in effect during the electoral period.

The only group which wholeheartedly accepted the Communist offer was the M.U.R.F., the fellow-traveling wing of the underground. Nevertheless, the Communists cut their party label off the ballot and substituted the jawbreaking title "Patriotic Republican and Anti-Fascist Union." Under this tricolored umbrella, they hoped to win many non-Communist voters who admired their resistance record and their dynamic demands for a "French renaissance." A marginal illustration of the catholicity of their appeal was a circular letter sent to female voters in the most bourgeois section of Paris. It concluded: "We have the honor of soliciting your vote in the coming elections. Accept, dear Madame, the assurance of our respectfully devoted sentiments."

On the Right wing, old personal and doctrinal rivalries stood in the way of coalition tactics. The prewar groups painfully collected enough candidates in most electoral districts, but they offered the voters meager fare. Besides, in a number of districts prewar habits could not be broken, and two or three Right-wing lists engaged in civil war for the same votes.

Alone among the parties, the newborn M.R.P. chose to test its strength without allies. The choice was not hard to make, for the only offers received by the M.R.P. came from the extreme Right. Far more difficult was the task of locating enough presentable candidates. The party machine was new, almost nonexistent in many departments, and it possessed only a handful of well-known leaders. By working till the very deadline, the M.R.P. Executive Committee finally managed to enter lists in all but ten departments. Some of their candidates had not been members of the party until they accepted places on the ticket; many had never resided in their electoral districts, and a few had never even set foot in those districts until they arrived for the campaign. An apocryphal story of the period illustrated the M.R.P.'s problems. In one district the leaders hoped to include a woman among their candidates—preferably a war widow with several children. As the deadline approached, a party official suggested that his housekeeper possessed those qualifications. She was given a presumably innocuous position on the ticket and, to her employer's consternation, was elected a deputy on October 21.

One of the M.R.P.'s major victories was its last-minute absorption of the largest Alsatian party of prewar days, the Popular Republican Union. Until 1940 this group had been loosely affiliated with the old Popular Democrats, but its strongly clerical and semi-autonomist doctrines had kept it from being annexed outright. In 1945 the M.R.P.'s mushrooming growth broke down the diffidence of the Alsatians, and gave the M.R.P. direct control over this fervently Catholic region.

Hovering above the parties was the figure of Charles de Gaulle, who dominated the campaign even though he undertook no overt political activity. He showed no sign of favoritism or hostility toward any party. It was widely believed, however, that a vote for the M.R.P. would be the nearest thing to a vote for De Gaulle. Some presumptive evidence was offered by the fact that Gaston Palewski's brother and De Gaulle's brother-in-law were both M.R.P. candidates. Certainly the M.R.P. itself did nothing to weaken that supposition. Maurice Schumann, the party's loudest and most superheated spokesman, trumpeted the M.R.P.'s claim to be "the party of fidelity." The M.P.R. also campaigned vigorously for De Gaulle's known choice in the referendum, which accompanied the election of an assembly. They and the Socialists (who showed a bit more hesitation) urged that the voters choose a constituent assembly limited in powers and duration. The Communists pulled out every stop in demanding a fully sovereign assembly; they confidently expected to attract enough Socialists and nonparty voters to win their fight. Radicals and Right advocated a return to the Third Republic, but their cause began to seem so hopeless that some Rightist leaders switched at the last moment and called for a corseted assembly as the best way to head off the Communists.

Election day brought out a record total of over twenty million voters. For the first time in a national election, Frenchwomen cast their ballots; also for the first time, every overseas French possession except Indo-China had the right to choose deputies.

The result seemed at first sight to be a triumph for De Gaulle. Over ninety-six per cent of the voters followed his advice to reject a return to the Third Republic; two-thirds ratified his plan for putting hobbles on the Constituent Assembly. Evidently many Radicals as well as Rightists had given up their fight for the old constitution in advance; and the Communists had been able to persuade only about one-third of the Socialists to bolt in favor of a fully sovereign assembly.

The composition of the new Assembly could also be regarded as a vindication of De Gaulle's hopes, for the M.R.P. and the Socialists together captured a slight majority of the seats. In coalition, therefore, they could serve as the foundation for De Gaulle's new cabinet, and could jointly draft a constitution. The only disquieting factor for De Gaulle and his advisers was the emergence of the Communists as France's first party. They had polled twenty-six per cent of the popular vote, a healthy increase from the last prewar elections in 1936 when their share had been fifteen per cent. Amateur statisticians could easily calculate that just as the Socialists and M.R.P. together possessed a clear majority, so the Communists and Socialists would have an even larger margin if they should decide to work together. Everything would depend, therefore, on the Socialists' choice.

The two most striking aspects of the balloting were the meteoric rise of the M.R.P. and the complete collapse of the Radicals. Not even the most optimistic M.R.P. leader had predicted more than 100 seats for his party. Instead, the figure reached 150. Clearly, a new force had entered French politics; but the stability and permanence of that force were still uncertain. In one southern department (Vaucluse) the party polled 26,000 votes even though it had only 100 dues-paying members. Could a monolithic party absorb such a mass of unorganized and undisciplined converts? Among the M.R.P.'s new backers, too, were thousands of Rightists who had come over out of desperation rather than faith. Therefore the M.R.P. leaders might have to choose between holding to their progressive policies and losing these voters, or watering down their program in order to maintain their new strength.

If the M.R.P. had to face problems born of success, the Radicals were confronted with those born of failure. Their fiasco was so complete that even Edouard Herriot barely missed defeat in his home city of Lyon. The remains of prominent Radicals such as Edouard Daladier, Paul Bastid, and Pierre Mendès-France littered the political landscape. No one had foreseen such an atomic disintegration of the group which had long dominated French politics. "The Radicals," remarked one observer, "are paying their war debts." And another callously added, "*Spurlos versenkt.*"

Out of these first postwar elections there began to emerge the new political map of France. In fundamentals it differed little from the prewar map; this and subsequent elections were to prove again the stability of French political opinions. Those areas which had traditionally voted Left—notably the south, parts of the Central Plateau, the Paris suburbs, and the industrial area adjoining Belgium—continued to vote Left, and the old strongholds of the Right—Normandy, most of Brittany, Alsace-Lorraine, parts of the Rhone-Alpine region, and Paris itself—generally remained faithful to their heritage.

Within the areas of Left and Right dominance, however, a shift had taken place. The Socialists continued their prewar inroads on the Radical party, and took over many of the old Radical fiefs in the southwest, such as the Bordeaux region. Meanwhile the Communists pushed into Socialist areas, particularly the northeastern coal and textile region and industrial cities like Limoges. The M.R.P. held the old Popular Democratic centers in Brittany and Lorraine, but also poached heavily on former Right-wing preserves throughout the northern half of France (notably within the Paris city limits). The Right, however, resisted M.R.P. encroachment more effectively than the Radicals were able to stand off the Socialists. Seventeen departments chose "unreconstructed" Right-wing candidates, whereas only a single department returned the Radicals as the largest party. This meant that the Right had become a regional rather than a national force in politics, but that it would cling tenaciously to its well-anchored positions. The Radicals, conversely, were now spread so thinly over most of France that they might be easily dislodged.

It was the Communist party which could boast of being the most widely distributed group. In only ten of the eighty-nine departments did they fail to elect at least one deputy. Their successes in rural areas were startling. They led the field in a large contiguous bloc of nine departments in the Central Plateau, and made a strong showing all along the Mediterranean and Breton coasts. They continued their prewar control over the "red belt" surrounding Paris, but made no serious progress there. It seemed that they had reached a kind of saturation point in Paris and its suburbs, and that their future expansion would be in smaller cities and agricultural regions. In the last prewar elections, 33 of their 72 seats had been won in the department of the Seine; in 1945, only 22 of their 152 seats came from that Parisian department, and only 8 more from Seine-et-Oise and Seine-et-Marne. In more ways than one, the Communists could claim that they had become a truly national party.

One set of almost unnoticed election returns which dribbled in during October and November were the results from the empire. Few Frenchmen realized the future implications of De Gaulle's revolutionary decision to give every colony and protectorate a voice in constitution-making. Once granted, that privilege could in practice never be taken away, and it might even be extended. The sixty-four overseas deputies might some day become one, two, or three hundred; but even if they should remain sixty-four, their votes might at times hold the balance of political power in Paris.

De Gaulle's electoral law gave the suffrage not only to all French citizens in the empire, but also to limited categories of noncitizen natives. Because the latter usually outnumbered the citizen colonists, even when restricted to a few categories, the law divided the voters into two separate colleges throughout "Black Africa," Madagascar, and Algeria. In the older colonies where citizenship was almost universal, all voters were lumped into single colleges; while in the protectorates of Morocco and Tunisia, French citizens alone could vote.

Hastily announced, hastily organized, these first elections could reveal no clear pattern in most of the overseas areas. A lopsided proportion of nonparty "resistance" deputies were chosen: men who had early joined De Gaulle, and who had built up reputations in various colonies as Gaullist representatives. In a few areas—notably Senegal and the West Indies—the Socialist party had gotten a firm foothold before the war, and maintained its advantage. The Communists had made only slight progress overseas, and the M.R.P. of course had no roots there at all.

Nor was there much evidence of vigorous native nationalist movements demanding either autonomy or independence. The Viet Minh in Indo-China was potentially the strongest of such movements; but Indo-China was barely emerging from Japanese occupation, and conditions were still too unsettled to schedule elections there. In Algeria, which was assigned twenty-six of the sixty-four overseas deputies, leaders of the two strongest Arab nationalist organizations had been in jail for periods ranging from six months to seven years, and were therefore *hors de combat*. In both Morocco and Tunisia there were dangerously strong Arab movements—the Istiqlal party of Ahmed Balafrej and the Neo-Destour group of exiled Habib Bourguiba—but the natives in both areas were technically subjects of their native rulers and could not take part in a French election. Only in Madagascar did a feeble flicker of native nationalism show itself on October 21. The two native deputies elected to represent that island, Drs. Ravoahangy and Raseta, aimed at autonomy and perhaps full independence; Ravoahangy had once been condemned to life imprisonment for anti-French agitation. Two Hova voices, however, scarcely seemed potent enough to shake the empire.

With the October elections, the first period of the provisional Fourth Republic neared an end. Fourteen months of quasi-dictatorship were over; a temporary pre-constitution had been adopted in the referendum, and a responsible regime was about to reappear for the first time since 1940. De Gaulle had kept his promise to the French people. The architects of the future had been freely chosen; France waited to see them in action, and to judge the result.

CHAPTER FIVE

False Start:
The First Constituent Assembly

I. THE FACE OF REBORN DEMOCRACY

The atmosphere of the Palais-Bourbon seemed charged with electricity on the afternoon of November 6, 1945, when the newly chosen Constituent Assembly convened. Visitors who jammed into the galleries sensed a latent tension, a spontaneous but suppressed enthusiasm, which emanated from the crowded benches of the deputies. Here, it seemed, was democracy being reborn before their eyes. For the first time since Hitler's armies overran Europe, the people of a great continental nation had spoken. For the first time in more than five years, a freely elected assembly was gathering with power to determine the destinies of France. Gone was the atmosphere of rancorous frustration which had pervaded the ineffectual Consultative Assembly. The deputies felt their new authority and their responsibility; deeply imbued with a sense of the past, they realized that they themselves were about to make history.

The physical setting itself seemed to be a kind of symbol. The historic Palais-Bourbon, which had been the legislative heart of France for more than a century, suddenly came back to life. Five years of German occupation had left it unchanged, save for the pockmarks on its façade from machine-gun bursts during the lib-

99

eration of Paris, and the burned-out wing housing the library. Outside, guarding the main entrance, Sully and Colbert still gazed in granite majesty out over the Seine, bearing on their pedestals the traditional Gallic legend *Défense d'uriner*. Within, officials who came to set the place in order found the calendar in the legislative hall still turned to June 1940. The semicircle of red plush benches, mounting rapidly from the speaker's rostrum; the ornate presidential desk installed by the Duc de Morny, and the presidential chair first used by Lucien Bonaparte in the Council of Five Hundred; the rostrum itself, which had served as pulpit for every modern French statesman (and from which Alfred Rosenberg had more recently harangued an assemblage of Nazi officers)—all carried an aura of history and tradition.

Most of the deputies who took their places on November 6 were new, inexperienced, and unknown. Of the 586 men and women who finally made up the Assembly, only 121 had served in the prewar Chamber or Senate, and only 65 others in the Consultative Assembly. The remaining 400 were mostly products of the resistance movement. A fair number had returned not long since from German prisoner-of-war or concentration camps. Many others had lost close relatives, shot or deported for underground activity.

The Assembly's professional makeup differed noticeably from that of the prewar Chamber. The Leftward trend of the elections brought in a far larger number of workingmen and teachers, and cut the ratio of lawyers, businessmen, and farmers. Heading the list were laborers and white-collar workers with 113, followed by 88 teachers, 73 lawyers, 52 farmers, 52 journalists or writers, 39 businessmen, and 105 of miscellaneous background (mostly professional men). The low prewar salary paid to the deputies was raised to 20,000 francs a month, but the Communists were required to turn in all but 8500 francs to the party treasury.

Of the prewar political veterans who returned to public life, almost all were men who had voted against Pétain in 1940, or who had been absent from Vichy at the time of that vote. A mere handful of "yes men," twenty-two in all, managed to make the grade.

Twelve of these forgiven sinners were Rightists, seven joined the M.R.P., two were Radicals, and one a Socialist. The largest bloc of holdovers from the Third Republic was to be found in the Communist group, thirty-eight of whose deputies had served in the prewar parliament.

The Communists also led all other groups in the representation of women and youth. Sixteen of the thirty-three female deputies who for the first time in history invaded the Palais-Bourbon took places on the Communist benches. Their leader was Jeannette Vermeersch, listed as a textile worker by trade, and described in the Communist press as the "companion" of Maurice Thorez. A strapping woman full of vitality and zeal, "Jeannette" looked and dressed the part of a daughter of the people. By way of contrast, there was frail, blond Marie-Claude Vaillant-Couturier, still wearing the pallor of a German concentration camp, and with it the most luxurious fur coat in the Assembly. Indeed, this contrast symbolized the variety of social status within this most monolithic of French parties. Certainly most of the 152 Communists could justly claim proletarian origin, but there were enough exceptions to give the group something more than a straight working-class basis. It ranged from Guy de Boysson, son of a French railway magnate (who had been described on election posters as "fils de cheminot"), through Marcel Prenant, renowned biologist of the Sorbonne, to Marcel Paul, a foundling raised in a public orphanage. But variety of personnel in no way marred the unity of the group in action. Like a well-trained orchestra, the Communists arose, sat down, cheered, jeered, almost as if their leader Jacques Duclos had stood before them with a conductor's baton. It was an impressive and in some ways a disturbing sight to see Professor Prenant on the edge of his seat, applauding Duclos' oratorical thrusts with all the enthusiasm of a small boy at the circus.

The Communists chose to put a special accent on youth. Their benches held an extraordinary number of political benjamins in their twenties or early thirties. For that matter, the general age level for the entire Assembly had dropped by about ten years in comparison with prewar days. The luxuriant beards of senatorial tradition survived in quantity only on the Right wing; even the Radicals had abandoned that mark of distinction, and betrayed their vanished youth by a prevalence of bald heads. In a sense, the status of the Radicals was symbolized by aging Edouard Herriot as he painfully hoisted his massive bulk up the narrow stairway to the Radical benches, and as he wandered about the corridors like the Ancient Mariner, buttonholing unwary deputies to talk of better days. Time had reserved a higher destiny than this for Herriot, and by the end of the session he was to recover most of his shattered prestige.

An exotic note was added by the sprinkling of Arab, Negro, Malagasy, and Hindu deputies from every corner of the empire. The red fez of Amar Ouzegane, Algerian Communist, and the Senegalese features of M. Lamine-Gueye, Socialist mayor of Dakar, stood out among the Assembly's secretaries who sat flanking the president's chair. As the native deputies straggled in from their distant electoral districts, they scattered out in various parts of the chamber and showed no real tendency to form a cohesive bloc. Eventually all sixty-four colonial representatives organized an Intergroup of Overseas Deputies, but internal division between the white colonist and the native deputies made it totally ineffective. Most of the natives were totally without experience in legislative matters and were somewhat awed by their sudden elevation to such prominence. The only well-knit native group consisted of seven Algerian Arabs headed by Dr. Mohamed Bendjelloul, a professional politician of pro-French tendencies. The Arabs formed a little oasis in the center of the semicircle and soon distinguished themselves by long and dull harangues on the Algerian question. One of their number, M. Benchennouf, a picturesque figure complete with flowing beard and burnoose, was an object of special attention and sympathy except when he occupied the speakers' tribune.

Following old tradition, the various parties were seated from left to right of the president's chair in accordance with the radicalism or the conservatism of their views. This practice created a thorny problem in connection with the seating of the M.R.P. Its leaders insisted that the party was a progressive and advanced movement which belonged to the Left in spirit and program, and that it must adjoin the Socialists. But the Radicals demanded that their ancient Leftist prerogative be respected, and refused to be pushed far over to the Right by the huge bulk of the M.R.P. Assembly officials finally came forward with a successful compromise; the M.R.P. was placed next to the Socialists, while the tiny Radical remnant received a kind of enclave carved out of the topmost Socialist and M.R.P. benches. In an adjoining enclave, by a curious bit of foresight, were placed their future allies, the nonparty resistance deputies of the U.D.S.R.

Some political regrouping was inevitable when the Assembly met, for the elections had been marked by a great deal of confusion and many candidates had borne no clear party labels. The membership of the Communist delegation presented no serious problem; there remained only the question of those M.U.R.F. deputies who had run on joint tickets with the Communists. A number of these men were at once absorbed outright by the Communist parliamentary group, but a handful of M.U.R.F. leaders chose to form a small separate group labeled "Republican and Resistance Union" (U.R.R.), which sat next to the Communists and was tied closely to it. The M.U.R.F.'s leader, Emmanuel d'Astier de la Vigerie, a onetime naval officer and prewar journalist, was the political black sheep of a prominent royalist family. Handsome, aquiline, aristocratic, he was a consistent and bitter critic of General de Gaulle, whom he had once served in Algiers as Commissioner of Interior. His two older brothers meanwhile remained impassioned Gaullists. The M.U.R.F. offered a convenient refuge for nonparty fellow-travelers; Pierre Cot was eventually to find a haven there, and in later assemblies it attracted a number of colonial deputies from Black Africa.

A larger question mark was the future of the U.D.S.R., the non-Communist wing of the resistance movement which had in most cases formed electoral coalitions with the Socialists. It was generally assumed that these deputies would unite or affiliate closely with their Socialist allies. Instead, their leaders chose to gamble for high stakes. They retained their identity as a separate Center group in the hope that around the U.D.S.R. might form a loosely organized federation of Center deputies. Such a federation, they felt, might become the fulcrum of politics in the Fourth Republic, much as the Radicals had been before the war; its strategic position might enable it to serve as a bridge between the Socialists on the one hand and the M.R.P. and Radicals on the other.

Of the forty-odd deputies who rallied to the U.D.S.R. standard, one-third represented French colonists in overseas areas, and a large proportion were fervent personal supporters of De Gaulle. This Gaullist strain was later strengthened when the General left office; several of his former ministers (René Pleven, Jacques Soustelle, and Paul Giacobbi) took seats there alongside René Capitant. Contained in the U.D.S.R. group was the surviving remnant of that element which, before 1944, had dreamed of a great new political bloc between the two extreme wings. Only a few U.D.S.R. doubters felt that such plans were empty ones in an age of political monoliths, and this minority shortly deserted to the Socialist party.

The Socialists, who had fully expected to emerge from the elections as France's first party, looked with the bitterness of disappointment at their unfaithful U.D.S.R. allies and their two overgrown neighbors. Their group was a kind of microcosm of the petty bourgeoisie—the class which the Socialists had come to represent in spite of themselves. School teachers, impecunious lawyers, and journalists predominated, many of them in worn and unpressed suits, with hand-knitted sweaters as comfortable substitutes for vests. Only the young former schoolmaster Max Lejeune still sported the flowing black tie of Socialist tradition. Léon Blum's leadership was lacking, for health and age had kept him off the list of candidates. Since his return from Buchenwald, Blum had become the party's elder statesman rather than its active chief. Seated sagely and benevolently above the battle, dispensing wisdom in a philosophic Old Testament vein, Blum's influence remained deservedly great. Time had taken away none of his intellectual vigor and subtlety, his intense idealism or his love of

France. His socialism was "humanist" rather than narrowly doctrinaire; he preached co-operation with any group which aimed at social justice through democratic methods. Many Frenchmen who had once regarded Blum as a weak and dangerous utopian now openly confessed their admiration for both the man and his ideas. But a leader whose doctor limited him to four hours of work a day could not descend into the political arena. No single individual took his place; a kind of general staff guided the party's course in the Assembly.

The M.R.P. kept within striking distance of the Communists by winning over a few nonparty deputies after election day. In at least one sense, the group presented a more homogeneous appearance than the Communists: its members were a cross section of the bourgeoisie rather than of the French people as a whole. Professors, lawyers, and small businessmen abounded on the M.R.P. benches; and those workingmen to whom the M.R.P. proudly pointed were mostly of the white-collar variety.

The M.R.P. also announced with satisfaction that its group practiced as well as preached the gospel of large families (a gospel which one irreverent Socialist described as *lapinisme intégrale*). Its statisticians proved that the M.R.P. deputies averaged 2.8 children apiece, whereas the Socialists could boast only a 1.6 average and the Communists 1.3. No other party, observed the M.R.P., included a deputy with thirteen children and four others with ten each. The embarrassing fact that several of their front-rank leaders were bachelors was well on the way to being corrected. Maurice Schumann had already taken a bride (after deciding to enter politics rather than a monastery); Georges Bidault was shortly to follow; and only André Colin was to remain a rugged individualist at the top of a party of *pères de famille*.

Scattered through the M.R.P. ranks were more female deputies than any party except the Communists could boast. Germaine Peyroles, a husky-voiced Paris lawyer who specialized in social problems, drew particular attention, both because of her poise at the speakers' tribune and because she was the Assembly's only platinum blonde. Old habitués of the galleries wagged their heads a bit and concluded that the Fourth Republic really had its revolutionary aspects. Two of the Assembly's three priests also sat among the M.R.P. On the cassock of one of them, the Abbé Pierre-Grouès, were the ribbons of the Resistance Medal and the Croix de Guerre, won for his share in founding the famous Vercors maquis group.

Because the M.R.P. had swallowed so many latter-day converts, there remained some doubt as to the party's ability to digest them. More than once during the Assembly's life, dissent appeared within the M.R.P. group on the floor, and it was evident that the party still fell considerably short of the monolithic ideal. The angular and agitated figure of the M.R.P.'s president, Maurice Schumann, "missionary of the Christian faith in the regions of daily politics," was often seen mounting to the back benches in order to plead or reason with potential bolters. Several months were required before M.R.P. unity could be assured beyond serious danger; and even then the possibility of schism was always latent.

To the right of the M.R.P., squeezed into a narrow slice of the semicircle, there existed a kind of primeval chaos. Between sixty and seventy deputies took places there, but they were without organization and were heavily burdened by their varied prewar affiliations. White-haired Louis Marin, aged president of the old Republican Federation, had hopes of grouping the amorphous Right around his standard; Joseph Laniel and other adherents of the moribund Democratic Alliance (prewar party of Paul Reynaud and P.-E. Flandin) were less hopeful of reviving their prewar label. There was even one prominent survivor of Colonel de la Rocque's semi-fascist *Parti Social Français*: André Mutter, a provincial lawyer with a foghorn voice, a bitter hatred of Communists, and an active resistance record.

Several weeks of internal maneuvering on the Right finally led to the formation of a new group which labeled itself the Republican Liberty Party (P.R.L.). For lack of a first-rate leader, it chose a symbol as president—the son of Georges Clemenceau. Its organizers hoped that it might become the nucleus for a single

Right-wing bloc, solid enough to win back many voters who had deserted to the M.R.P. Slightly more than half the Rightist deputies adhered to the P.R.L., but the remainder clung to French tradition and refused the temptation of monolithic strength. Most of the holdouts loosely coalesced as the Independent Republican group, which possessed no national organization or structural solidity, but joined together in order to secure representation on committees. A tiny fraction re-established the prewar Peasant Action Party, with a rigidly conservative program stressing the interests of independent farmers; and a few rebels of the extreme variety refused to join any group at all.

Thus split into four segments, the shattered Right wing sacrificed what little effectiveness it might have had as an opposition force in the First Constituent Assembly. P.R.L. leaders, who could draw on the bank accounts of many well-heeled industrialists, had to postpone their hopes of unity and expansion until a future election; and when those hopes eventually failed of fulfillment, they concluded that their fault had been to organize too late. Perhaps it was; but perhaps also their program of economic liberalism and the defense of big business lacked any wide appeal in a country like post-liberation France.

II. END OF A POLITICAL
HONEYMOON

By the weight of long tradition, no man may appear on the floor of the French legislature in military uniform. When Charles de Gaulle stalked into the Assembly on November 6, stiff and awkward in unaccustomed blue serge, a new phase seemed to be opening in his career. During the preceding five and a half years he had been transmuted step by step from soldier to symbol of the resistance spirit, then to head of a government-in-exile, and finally to nonresponsible president of a crisis regime. In November 1945 he prepared to assume the thoroughly civilian role of political leader of a peacetime government.

The structure of the seven-month interim government was defined by the pre-constitution which the voters had adopted in the October referendum. A brief and flexible document, it contained the outline of a somewhat modified parliamentary regime. Two notable innovations were included in the system. First, the president of the Provisional Government combined the prewar functions of both president and premier. He would owe his election to the Constituent Assembly, but the latter's right to get rid of him again was slightly limited by the cooling-off clause. Second, the pre-constitution placed two restrictions on the Assembly's legislative powers. The deputies were denied the right to introduce appropriation bills, and the president was given a suspensive veto, over which the Assembly might re-enact laws by an absolute majority. Neither of these restrictions seriously hobbled the Assembly. It was an essentially sovereign body, with the power to change the executive or to adopt a sweeping legislative program in addition to its fundamental right to draft a constitution. The precise functioning relationship between the president and the Assembly was left for practice to determine.

De Gaulle's letter of resignation lay before the Assembly on November 6, ready to be accepted as soon as the latter should choose its officers. Few Frenchmen could imagine any other successor to De Gaulle than the General himself. He had no rival as to national stature; his triumphal re-election seemed foreordained. Yet it was not until after a near-record crisis of seventeen days that De Gaulle was able to set up a new cabinet acceptable to the Assembly. The severity of that crisis showed how far removed France was from political unity, and it foreshadowed the difficulties France would have to face in returning to responsible government.

The only potential threat to De Gaulle's renomination came from the Communists. They had never regarded him with any enthusiasm, but they had nevertheless entered his cabinet in 1944 and had carefully refrained ever since from criticizing him personally. Even during the referendum campaign, they had vigorously fought

De Gaulle's ideas but had professed to maintain his person above controversy. It was nonetheless evident that the character of their relations with the General amounted to no more than a truce. November produced the rupture, and while it was finally patched up temporarily, it never really healed thereafter.

Whether the Communists aimed from the start to push De Gaulle out of office in November is a moot question. They certainly considered him a major barrier to their development in France, for in the long run, it was around his person that an anti-Communist bloc might form. In the immediate future, his renomination as president would tend to slow down any drastic program of social-economic reform which the Communist-Socialist majority might decide to push, and it might keep the Communists out of key positions in the government and the armed forces. Furthermore, the character of the new constitution might be shaped in part by De Gaulle's presence at the helm during the seven-month interim period. True, the law adopted in the October referendum denied the executive any right to interfere in the constitutional debate, which was reserved for the Assembly alone. Nevertheless, De Gaulle's continuance in office for seven more months would strengthen the executive during this final "laboratory" period, and would make it harder to establish the Communist ideal of government by assembly. The impending experiment of a strong executive alongside a sovereign Assembly might, if it proved workable and efficient, shape the future even more than the experience of quasi-dictatorship during the abnormal year after liberation. Thus the ousting of De Gaulle, if it could be achieved without alienating too many Frenchmen, would benefit the Communists from every point of view.

Their attack on the Gaullist positions was delivered from the rear, and was designed to break up in advance the Socialist-M.R.P. coalition upon which De Gaulle had pinned his faith. The Communist scheme was to bring together the "republican and laic" parties (Communists, Socialists, and Radicals, but not the M.R.P.) on a seven-month program of legislative action, and to require the provisional president to endorse it in advance. The president would thus be forced to base his cabinet on a revived Popular Front, with the M.R.P. either tailing along in support or going into the opposition. At the same time, the Communists refused to present Maurice Thorez as a candidate for the Gaullist succession; they broadly implied that the referendum had really amounted to a Gaullist plebiscite, and that the Communists must bow to this perverted evidence of the popular will.

The success of the Communist plan depended on the Socialists' reaction. That response was cautious; most of the Socialist leaders had no desire to be caught alone with the Communists in a cabinet. They refused to draw up a pre-election program unless the M.R.P. was admitted to the agreement. It took a week of high-pressure maneuvering before the Communists and the M.R.P. could be brought together on a program. This Socialist success meant that the quasi-unanimous election of De Gaulle as President was assured.

No sooner did the crisis seem to be resolved than it rebounded. The Communists informed De Gaulle that while they were prepared to enter his new cabinet, they would demand their just share of the important posts. As France's first party, they insisted on one of the three key ministries: Foreign Affairs, Interior, or National Defense. De Gaulle rejected their demand, and in a stormy personal conference with Thorez, made it plain that he regarded the Communists as agents of a foreign power. He raised the temperature even further by reminding Thorez that the latter would be in jail except for De Gaulle's personal decision not to press charges of military desertion. After Thorez stormed out with only this rebuff to show for his visit, De Gaulle drew up a peculiarly worded letter in which he "returned his mandate to the Assembly."

A tense week followed, during which minor Gaullist demonstrations occurred in the Latin Quarter and heavy police cordons appeared at strategic points in Paris. The Communists flatly declared that they would have nothing more to do with the General, and after some hesitation, formally demanded the presidency for Thorez. The M.R.P. insisted just as strongly that it would enter no cabinet except one headed by De Gaulle. Further confusion was caused by doubt as to whether De Gaulle had really resigned as President. He himself took to the radio and interpreted his letter to mean that he had only asked the Assembly to choose between himself and the Communists. This radio appeal to the nation seemed to lend finality to the breach.

Beneath the surface, however, the crisis shook the monolithic unity of all the major parties. Some Communists were disturbed over a possible pro-Gaullist reaction in the provinces; they knew that thousands of their voters were still under the General's spell, and they wanted no national crisis at the moment. A few M.R.P. leaders—prominent men such as Georges Bidault and Francisque Gay—favored entering a cabinet without De Gaulle if necessary, in order, as they put it, to keep the M.R.P. from becoming identified with the forces of reaction. Out of the apparent impasse, therefore, came a compromise. The Assembly called on De Gaulle to make one more try, specifying that the cabinet posts should be "equitably distributed" (in other words, that the Communists should get their just share). Only the Communists fought the idea of giving De Gaulle another chance; Jacques Duclos almost broke up the meeting with a venomous attack on the General from the tribune.

Once this compromise was voted, tempers suddenly cooled. The Communists, having spoken their piece, dropped their attitude of injured innocence and accepted a compromise plan concocted by De Gaulle. The National Defense ministry was split into two parts called Armaments and Armies, and the Armaments half alone was handed over to a Communist. In addition, De Gaulle assumed the supervisory title of Minister of National Defense along with his presidential functions. The other cabinet posts were parceled out four ways among the three major parties and certain faithful Gaullist "technicians" like Pleven, Soustelle, and Raoul Dautry. The new government thus became a forerunner of the three-party coalition structure which was to be the typical formula of the Fourth Republic's early years. It was a solution built neither on a coherent majority nor on a complete national union concept; in the long run, its effect was not to eliminate the opposition but to bring most of it inside the cabinet. The potential weakness of such a formula was obvious from the start.

In appearance, the Communists had suffered a setback. They had neither kept De Gaulle out of the presidency nor gotten one of the three key ministries. In fact, however, they had won the first round of their contest with De Gaulle. They had driven a partial wedge between the Socialists and the M.R.P., and they had brought De Gaulle down from his ethereal perch into the realm of party politics. The General still seemed to be the indispensable man, yet he had lost face, and the country had for the first time been forced to consider an alternative to his leadership. The honeymoon at last was over. De Gaulle, if he wished to remain in politics, would have to change both his temperament and his tactics. The time had come when he needed the support of a party coalition, and that support would never be won by casting down occasional thunderbolts from Mount Olympus. The next two months were to prove that the habits of a Jupiter cannot be altered overnight.

III. FORTY-TWO MEN
AND A CONSTITUTION

After the long prelude devoted to forming a cabinet, the Assembly at last could turn to its primary task. Both tradition and common sense dictated that the constitution should be drafted by a special committee rather than by the Assembly as a whole. A sharp controversy occurred over the size and character of the committee, but it was finally decided that the standard figure of forty-two members would be adequate. The seats were assigned, not to the forty-two outstanding deputies in the Assembly, but to the various parties in accordance with the latter-day gospel of proportional representation. This procedure gave the Communists and the M.R.P. twelve places each, the Socialists eleven, and the minor groups the remaining seven. Here again the

Socialists had the key position; there existed either a Socialist-Communist or a Socialist-M.R.P. majority of one. Much of the Assembly's top-drawer talent (including such men as Edouard Herriot and Jacques Duclos) was kept out of the Constitutional Committee by the provision that its members could not simultaneously sit in other committees. The major parties naturally wished to spread their strength, and so each one delegated only two or three prominent spokesmen. As a result, the Constitutional Committee never took on the character of a brain trust. It hammered out detailed provisions, but only after each party's delegation had sought instructions from the inner circle of party leaders.

It was perhaps normal (although some deputies found it deplorable) that the Committee should be dominated by lawyers, jurists, and professors. Twenty-six of the members fell into one of those categories; eight others described themselves as journalists, and three were career civil servants. Lost in this professional crowd were two office workers, a publicist, a mechanic, and a type-setter. Such a group was naturally tempted by the joys of abstruse academic debate. Before the Committee had finished its first business meeting, the chairman found it necessary to suggest that "certain members stifle the professor of law within them," and that they stick to concrete issues.

Leader and spokesman for the Communist delegation was Etienne Fajon, one of the ablest men in the party. Fajon had begun his career as an elementary-school teacher, but had been retired at the age of twenty-four for spending more time in party activity than in teaching. Since then he had been occupied with the more congenial task of educating party members to be better Communists. Elected to the Chamber in 1936, he had been expelled from parliament in 1940 along with all the other Communist deputies who clung to the Moscow line, and had been imprisoned in Algeria until 1943. Fajon's rasping voice was one of those most frequently raised in Committee sessions; he carried weight both because of his forensic talents and because, with a monolithic bloc of committeemen behind him, his strength was as the strength of twelve. Fajon's understudy was Pierre Hervé,

thirty-two-year-old *enfant terrible* of the party, a brilliant philosophy professor of Byronic appearance and Breton origin, with a
long record of Communist student leadership before the war and of
active resistance to Vichy after 1940. Arrested once by the Gestapo,
he had escaped in mystery-thriller fashion, but his wife had been
deported to Germany. Hervé's underground pseudonym "Char-
don" (Thistle) was in some ways symbolic of his character. His
chief talent was not constitutional theorizing but newspaper
polemics; in *Humanité* his sharp pen and his dialectical skill
showed to special advantage. Some politicians considered him
more than a mere polemicist and "priest-eater"; they spoke of him
as potential heir apparent to Thorez as head of the party.

The brightest star of the Socialist delegation was André Philip,
whom the Constitutional Committee unanimously chose as its
chairman. Philip, a forty-three-year-old ex-professor of political
economy at the University of Lyon, combined in his person a belief in Marxian principles and a devout Protestant faith. In his
student days (when he had been an outspoken pacifist), he had
spent two years studying labor conditions in the United States,
followed by a year in India at the feet of Gandhi. Elected to the
Chamber in 1936, he had voted against Pétain at Vichy, had
played a front-rank role in the underground, and had finally escaped to join De Gaulle in exile. Brilliant, attractive, energetic,
but considered somewhat erratic and utopian, Philip was to place
his personal imprint strongly on the Committee's work until he
departed in January to enter the Gouin cabinet. None of the other
Socialist committeemen approached Philip in talent or prestige.
Next in rank was Guy Mollet, a highschool teacher from Arras, a
newcomer to politics by way of the resistance. A more unusual
figure was Lithuanian-born Gilbert Zaksas, an irrepressible young
lawyer from Toulouse.

The M.R.P.'s delegation, studded with lawyers and jurists, was
headed by François de Menthon, who was elected to the Committee's number two post of Reporter-General. De Menthon was a
professor of political science who had been boosted into active
politics somewhat by accident. A quiet and rather retiring pure

intellectual, sprung from the petty provincial aristocracy, he had been active in the Left-wing Catholic movement before the war, and in 1940 had naturally gravitated into resistance work. After some harrowing experiences (his M.R.P. friends claimed that the Germans had tied him in a sack and thrown him in the Lac d'Annecy to drown), he had escaped to Algiers in 1943. After liberation, he had served for a time as De Gaulle's Minister of Justice, where he had come under heavy fire from the Communists for his failure to carry out a sufficiently vigorous purge.

De Menthon was backed in the Committee by Paul Coste-Floret and P.-E. Viard, two law professors from the University of Algiers; by Jacques Fonlupt-Esperaber, elderly, walrus-mustached member of the Council of State; and by Henri Teitgen, father of the Minister of Justice and himself one of the outstanding provincial lawyers in France. Teitgen had spent sixteen months in Buchenwald, and his six sons had all been arrested by the Germans. These may have been secondary qualifications, but they lent him added distinction. Of the M.R.P. group it was Coste-Floret who was to rise most rapidly from obscurity to prominence. Born and raised in Montpellier, his effervescent Midi temperament sometimes erupted through the crust of the cool and correct professional jurist. He had served in 1939-40 as a Zouave officer, and had then helped found a Gaullist movement in Algiers. Only thirty-four years old, his keen juridical mind expanded his influence until, in the Second Constituent Assembly, he attained the post of Reporter-General. He was regarded as belonging to the more conservative wing of the M.R.P.

Outside the big three parties, the most commanding voices were those of Pierre Cot (Radical Socialist) and René Capitant (U.D.S.R.). Cot's stormy course in prewar politics showed no tendency to abate after 1944. No one could be quite sure where Cot stood politically when he returned to liberated Paris. On the way from his wartime refuge in America, he had managed to spend several weeks mending fences in Moscow. The shattered Radical Socialist organization had welcomed his arrival and had nominated him to the Consultative Assembly in 1944. There, by sheer brilliance of oratory, he had reconquered the admiration if not the confidence of virtually every politician in France. Acquaintances felt that Cot's future would be shaped in large part by two of his personal qualities: his genuine desire to be agreeable and accommodating, and his intense, burning ambition. Since Cot had once been a professor of constitutional law, he was a natural choice for the Constitutional Committee. The Radicals named him to carry their colors, but Cot was already showing clear signs of an inclination to migrate further to the Left. His impossible attempt to speak for a party of old-school liberals while voting along with the Communists was eventually to end in his resignation from the Committee.

René Capitant became a member of the Committee rather in spite of himself. Until November 1945 he had been one of De Gaulle's ministers, but the cabinet reshuffle had pushed him down into the position of an ordinary deputy. Capitant was another product of the resistance, a professor turned politician by accident. For many years a specialist in constitutional law at Strasbourg University, son of another eminent constitutional lawyer, he had won a reputation as one of the leading French authorities in his field. After the 1940 collapse he had left in disgust for Algiers, where he had taught in the University and had founded a strongly Gaullist resistance group. Capitant's devotion to De Gaulle was almost religious in its fervor; few leading politicians except René Pleven could compete with him in that respect. In the Constitutional Committee, his caustic tongue and his scholarly contempt for the "mediocrity" of most of his colleagues acted as a constant irritant; but his technical competence could not be ignored.

The Right wing's most assiduous spokesman was Jacques Bardoux, a tiny, wizened figure with a piping voice and a brief case stuffed with plans. By a strange irony, Bardoux represented the Peasant party, even though no one could possibly have mistaken him for a dirt farmer. In prewar days he had been a professor at the famed Ecole Libre des Sciences Politiques, and he once reminded his Committee colleagues that he was the author of twenty-two books. He had long been one of the most persistent propagandists for the Right-wing doctrine of a strengthened executive. Bardoux's background had a number of paradoxical aspects. He was the only second-generation constitution-maker in the Assembly: in 1875 his father had helped to put through the constitution of the Third Republic. Stranger still, Bardoux had served on Pétain's Constitutional Committee in 1941. An old friend of the Marshal, elected to the Senate in 1938 with the aid of Pierre Laval, he had been one of the parliamentary "yes men" in July 1940 and had gone so far as to write an introduction to a collection of Pétain's writings published in 1941. This rather equivocal record had been offset by his later activities in the intellectual resistance. The Left scoffed at his underground record (confined, they claimed, to a few meetings with other senators at the Brasserie Lipp), but they tolerated Bardoux as a harmless theorist without a following, and regularly steam-rollered his prolific suggestions.

It would be wrong to suppose that the remaining members of the Committee were all nonentities. Several of the younger delegates were men of above-average talent, but party discipline usually kept them in the background. The fact remains, however, that a considerable share of the members were mere rubber stamps whose sole function was to register the decisions of their party leaders. The Communist delegates in particular sat silently alongside Fajon and Hervé, seldom emerging from their monastic reserve except when matters were put to a vote. On days when both their spokesmen happened to be absent, these delegates drifted like a ship without a rudder. Although the Constitutional Committee contained forty-two members, in practice that figure might as well have been cut to a dozen. Some cynics went even further, and suggested that three men bearing the proper number of proxy votes could have achieved the same results without wasting so many man hours. The thrust was both unkind and unjust, yet it contained a grain of the kind of truth that hurts.

The Committee's most serious personnel weakness lay in its underrepresentation of the colonies, if the Assembly really meant to revolutionize the status of the empire. Only four overseas deputies were included, and only one of them—Paul Valentino, colored

Socialist from Guadeloupe—was not of French colonist stock. Midway through the Assembly's session, the Socialists replaced Valentino by another colored deputy, Léopold Sédar Senghor of Senegal. Senghor's views on the empire were less unorthodox than Valentino's, and besides, the Socialists were proud of his reputation as a poet and professor of French literature in a Paris lycée. It was to Senghor that the Committee turned when the new Declaration of Rights came under fire for its faulty literary style. "M. Senghor's grammatical competence and literary virtuosity," declaimed an M.R.P. committeeman on that occasion, "are highly necessary for the perfecting of this new monument of political literature." The men of 1789 could scarcely have foreseen that their successors would call upon a Senegalese to polish their phrases dealing with human rights. The idea undoubtedly would have pleased them, just as it appealed to the men of 1946.

IV. THE SOCIALISTS' CHOICE

The Assembly's brief seven-month term had six months to run when the Constitutional Committee at last chose its officers and got down to work. Chairman André Philip wasted no further time. With a professor's thoroughness and a politician's foresight, he immediately proposed a plan of action which would divide the Committee's operations into two stages. First would come a general discussion of basic principles, during which tentative rather than binding decisions would be taken. Then, the basic philosophy and major outlines of the new constitution having been determined, the Committee would turn to the actual process of drafting a text. Philip's plan, logical enough to suit the most Cartesian Frenchman, was accepted unanimously.

Philip also reverted to academic practice by collecting a small reference library for the use of the Committee. It eventually grew to include some forty volumes—most of them basic works on French or comparative constitutional law, plus several studies of the British and American systems. But the Committee members drank sparingly at Philip's trough of knowledge, as the former professor should have expected. Perhaps it was just as well that practical politics rather than textbook theories came more and more to guide the Committee's course.

The Committee set bravely off on December 4 under a self-imposed rule of strict secrecy. By the end of its first week, readers of the Communist press could guess that all was not well; one more week, and the Communists' anger boiled over in the columns of *Humanité*. Violent daily accounts of the Committee's misguided decisions poured from the pen of Pierre Hervé, and with them, the secrecy rule collapsed. The press of all parties leaped into the controversy, and the constitutional debate, distorted and twisted by partisan passion, became semipublic property.

Those first two weeks had been enough to show that the Socialists would decide the nature of the new constitution, and that the Socialists more often than not were inclined to vote along with the M.R.P. Certainly there was no solid coalition between them, for the Socialists swung to the Communist side on several of the most fundamental issues. Notably, the two Marxian parties agreed that the legislature should be unicameral; that the premier should be elected by the assembly; and that the president of the republic should be stripped of all effective powers. But these important decisions were offset by a whole series of defeats for the Communists in their attempt to vest all power in the future assembly. Twenty-five Socialist, M.R.P., and U.D.S.R. delegates repeatedly brushed aside Communist protests to fasten a variety of restrictions on the powers of the legislature.

This Socialist-M.R.P. team first of all voted to ration the future assembly's consumption of cabinets. It endorsed the Socialists' automatic-dissolution plan, to apply if two cabinets should be overthrown during the legislature's five-year term. To André Philip, this clause would be the keystone of the new parliamentary structure; it would preserve the assembly's fundamental sover-

eignty, yet would correct the chief flaw of such sovereignty—
cabinet instability.

The Socialist-M.R.P. coalition also proposed to restrict the
assembly's legislative powers proper. They agreed that the assembly should be required to adopt any bill twice in order to make it
law. Between the two readings, a juridical committee would examine each bill for errors in form. Second, the assembly would be
required to submit certain bills to one or more new "technical
advisory bodies" (such as an Economic Council, for example), for
a preliminary opinion. Third, the assembly would be deprived of
the right to amend the constitution; it would only be allowed to
propose amendments for ratification by popular referendum.
Fourth, the assembly's laws could be declared unconstitutional,
not by judicial review but by referendum. Doubtful laws would be
referred to the people by a special committee of experts on constitutional law. Fifth, the assembly would be stripped of the traditional right to validate the election of its own members. This
power to seat or unseat new deputies had sometimes been made a
political football in prewar years. The majority voted to turn it
over to a newly created semijudicial committee, which would presumably view the problem from an objective and nonpolitical
angle.

Each of the foregoing decisions ran counter to the Communists'
constitutional doctrine of an assembly without strings on its
authority. Their irritation was natural; but it was a second conflict
between them and the Socialist-M.R.P. majority which roused the
Communists to even greater fury. This was the majority's desire to
write into the constitution a "party statute," together with various
other devices designed to regulate the activities and strengthen
the discipline of French political parties.

The prewar party system, in the opinion of the majority, had
been one of the worst flaws of the Third Republic. In the first
place, only the Communist and Socialist parties had possessed any
real structural form or discipline. The others had been amorphous
and shifting groups whose members had wandered from one to
another in an effort to improve their personal fortunes. Frequently

deputies had been elected on one ticket, then joined a different group in the Chamber or started a new one of their own. The invertebrate nature of the prewar parties had added to the difficulty of maintaining stable cabinets or putting through consistent programs of legislation. Second, the Socialists and M.R.P. argued that prewar democracy had been falsified by the influence of money in elections. Rich parties with fat campaign funds had possessed a heavy advantage over parties that were poorer and perhaps more honest. Third, Marianne in the past had been excessively tolerant toward "fifth column" fascist groups. The Socialists and the M.R.P. felt that constitutional barriers ought to be set up against the reappearance of anti-democratic parties, which might again take advantage of democratic liberties in an effort to destroy the new republic.

The Socialist-M.R.P. majority proposed a whole series of correctives for these abuses. The lack of party discipline would be corrected in three ways: (a) every deputy elected on a party ticket would be required to join that party's group in parliament; (b) any maverick deputy who might refuse to follow party directives or who might resign from the party would lose his seat and would be replaced by a more faithful follower selected by the party organization; (c) voting would be made not only a privilege but an obligation: voters failing to perform their civic duty would be warned and eventually fined. This "obligatory vote" procedure would tend to discipline the mass of party followers rather than the active militants. It would serve as a substitute for a tight organization capable of getting the voters out on election day—a type of organization which only the Communists possessed. All these provisions would encourage the growth of monolithic parties where none had grown before. Most notably, it would aid those parties which were already aspiring to monolithic status but had not yet attained it.

The majority further proposed that the electoral chances of all parties, both rich and poor, be equalized. This aim would be achieved by limiting and standardizing the electoral propaganda of all parties, and by providing that these limited campaign costs

would be paid by the state. Finally, the resurgence of antidemocratic parties would be blocked by the so-called party statute. This
section of the constitution would require every party to make
public the source of its funds, to organize itself on democratic lines
with real control of its leaders from below, to subscribe to a new
Declaration of Rights, and to repudiate the idea of a one-party
state.

As this novel structure of government-regulated parties took
shape in Committee, the Communists' irritation grew in direct
proportion. M. Fajon and his twelve-man phalanx were pushed
into a highly embarrassing corner. They knew that every measure
to regulate or stabilize parties would injure the Communists either
directly or indirectly; yet they found it painful to confess this fact.
Thus, for example, they had to fight the party statute without
admitting that under the statute their own party might be accused
of certain antidemocratic practices and principles. They had to
oppose the equalization and state financing of campaign expenses
without admitting that the Communists had graduated from the
ranks of the poor and underprivileged parties. They had to reject
the idea of disciplining the voters and deputies of each party, even
though they themselves thoroughly believed in and regularly practiced the most rigorous self-discipline.

The Communist committeemen and their friends therefore fell
back on arguments which seemed to be drawn from John Stuart
Mill rather than Karl Marx. They branded as a dangerous threat
to liberty any state intervention in party affairs, and sought to
argue that the result would be a kind of multi-party fascism. Pierre
Cot warned that public opinion abroad, especially in the Anglo-
Saxon democracies, would be horrified. Besides, Cot added, there
would be no limit to the infamous party statute. The state would
soon be poking its nose into every rod-and-gun club or musical
society on the ground that the group was engaging i. politics and
ought to be regulated. As for the obligatory vote, the next step
might be to declare parenthood a civic duty and to require every
citizen to procreate. During one whole Committee session, several
Socialist and M.R.P. delegates sadistically needled the Commu-

nists into an impassioned defense of the cause of personal liberty against the encroaching state.

The Communists' proposed substitute for all this machinery of party regulation was their recently discovered cure-all—the recall of deputies by the voters. This mechanism, they held, would achieve the same purposes in a more democratic way; it would force the deputies to remain faithful to their promises, and would therefore strengthen party discipline and stabilize cabinets. Besides, it had been proposed by Robespierre in 1793, so that its republican pedigree was above question. The recall, however, got short shrift before the Committee. Etienne Fajon was repeatedly asked to explain how recall by the voters could work within an electoral system of proportional representation. The critics pointed out that if, for example, a Communist deputy were elected with 20,000 votes out of a total of 100,000, he might be recalled by petition of 20,001 Rightist voters. Fajon could find no answer because there was no answer; and soon no more was heard from the Communists of their pet scheme. The Socialist-M.R.P. bloc proceeded to substitute the idea of recall by the party organization, which the Communists disliked because it might keep maverick Socialist deputies from adopting a fellow-traveler line.

The Communists' decision to bring the constitutional debate out of the Committee room into the open was a transparent and well-planned bit of strategy. Originally they had hoped that the Socialists might go along with them consistently in Committee. Defeated in this hope, they turned at once to a public campaign with a view to putting heavy pressure on the Socialists to mend their ways. The M.R.P., they charged, secretly aimed to set up a corporative state inspired by Salazar's Portuguese system, and the Socialists had become their unsuspecting tools. Rumors of Léon Blum's imminent conversion to Catholicism began to circulate, buttressed by anonymous reports that Blum had been seen emerging from the back door of Notre Dame just at dusk. The Communists knew that most Socialist leaders feared nothing so much as the bourgeois-clerical tarbrush. They knew too that the Socialists were alarmed at the possible effect of such accusations on the

Socialist rank and file. Socialist deputies who visited their districts over the week end began to return to Paris each Monday with ears burning. The Communist strategy quickly began to pay dividends.

At the same time, the unhappy Socialists began to realize that their middle position was not only advantageous but also uncomfortable. While the Communists delivered their daily blasts, the M.R.P. also moved to the attack against those Committee decisions which had found the Socialists voting with the Communists. The M.R.P.'s National Council in mid-December denounced the idea of a unicameral assembly, of a premier elected by that assembly, and of a deaf-mute president of the republic. M.R.P. leaders also assailed a Socialist-Communist decision to decentralize France somewhat by broadening local self-government. A weak president, a subservient premier, and a relaxed central authority, they charged, would weaken democracy against its enemies and would amount to nothing better than a camouflage of government by assembly. The M.R.P. made it plain that they did not aim at a clear separation of powers in the American sense; like every other party except the Right wing, they felt that the goal should be collaboration rather than separation between the executive, legislative, and judicial branches. They were ready to admit that an American type of president would be too powerful in a centralized state like France, and that the American system was likely to produce insoluble executive-legislative deadlocks. What they did demand was a separation of functions, permitting the executive branch a fair degree of independence within the parliamentary system. M.R.P. leaders began to hint that unless the Socialists accepted their version of parliamentary government, the M.R.P. might have to reject the whole constitutional draft.

Attacked thus on both flanks, the Socialists began to waver. Left-wing Socialists in the executive committee—notably Dr. Paul Rivet, well-known anthropologist and head of the *Musée de l'Homme* in Paris—increased their pressure on Secretary-General Daniel Mayer and his fellow party officials. Mayer himself began to experience qualms: could a good Marxian cohabit with a set of bourgeois clericals without losing his virtue?

Sensing their advantage, the Communists stepped up their campaign. On January 4 they proposed that the two Marxian parties short-circuit the Constitutional Committee. They suggested that the moribund Socialist-Communist *comité d'entente* (set up in 1944 to prepare unity of action between the two parties) be brought back to life, and that it draft a constitution which could then be jammed through the Constitutional Committee by the Left-wing majority. The Socialists, after some hesitation, finally agreed to talk things over with the Communists on January 16. Out of that session of the *comité d'entente* came a decision to modify the tactics of the preceding six weeks, and to work more closely with the "brother party." Arrangements were made for Mayer, Duclos, and a few other top-ranking Socialists and Communists to meet regularly henceforth to shape a common constitutional policy. No joint draft would be drawn up, but each problem would be examined as it arose.

The Socialists' about-face on January 16 was a far-reaching decision. It meant that De Gaulle's hope of a coherent Center bloc had suffered another severe setback. During the November cabinet crisis De Gaulle had lost the first round to the Communists; now he had lost the second as well, this time in the constitutional field. Barring another change of heart by the Socialists, the Communists were sure to get a constitution in general harmony with their ideal. But the January 16 decision also meant that the Assembly's work might be done in vain. Out of it might come an open split between Right and Left, leading perhaps to a constitutional stillbirth. After January 16, France faced the prospect of either a Left-wing constitution or no constitution at all. Few politicians, however, yet realized the full import of the Socialists' choice.

V. DROPPING THE PILOT

While the Consitutional Committee jerked along toward either a compromise or a crisis, the figure of General de Gaulle began to cast its shadow across the constitutional question.

By the terms of the October pre-constitution (which had been drafted with De Gaulle's approval), the president and cabinet were denied the right to intervene in the constitutional debate. It was nonetheless almost inevitable that De Gaulle's opinions should become known, and that they should cause reverberations both within and outside the Assembly. Not only De Gaulle's views, but also his actions as provisional president, were likely to exert a kind of prenatal influence on the embryo constitution. Much would depend on the spirit in which De Gaulle chose to govern, for the pre-constitution did not define precisely the relationship between president and Assembly.

Less than two months were needed to show that De Gaulle and the Left parties differed widely on their interpretation of the executive's proper role. The first clash came at the very start, during the long November cabinet crisis. De Gaulle took the position that he alone as head of the executive branch should select the individual ministers and should shape the governmental program. The Communists and Socialists, however, contended that the parties entering the cabinet should recommend both personnel and program, and that the president should subordinate his personal wishes to their recommendations. The outcome of this dispute was an uneasy compromise, with neither De Gaulle nor the Left willing to back down completely.

Two weeks later came a second flare-up, this time over the executive's role in legislation. The cabinet introduced a bill to nationalize the major deposit banks and to give the government control over credit. This bill was the first positive step to apply the program of economic reform drawn up by the National Resistance Council in March 1944. Almost everyone agreed on the principle of such a measure; the only controversial issues were its scope and the question of compensating shareholders in the expropriated banks.

The cabinet's bill steered a middle course between Left and Right doctrines. It went beyond mere state supervision of banks, but it proposed to limit nationalization to the four largest banks, and to compensate the former owners more generously than the Left desired. The measure most nearly approached the M.R.P.'s ideal of progressive reform through cautious, conservative methods. But the thing which irritated the Left most was De Gaulle's use of the big-stick technique to jam the bill through. They were determined to amend the bill, but De Gaulle arose from the government bench and warned that if the measure were "deformed," he would throw his personal influence into the scales and would use his suspensive veto for the first time. The Left capitulated, but the cry of "personal power" went up in the next day's press. The Socialists even more than the Communists were shaken by De Gaulle's abruptness. Along with their natural resentment at such domineering tactics went a sudden revival of the old Leftist fear of authoritarianism.

The estrangement reached a brusque climax in the early morning hours of New Year's Day, 1946. Debate on the 1946 budget had reached its concluding stages in the Assembly. Arriving at the chapter on military credits, the Socialists proposed a flat twenty-per-cent cut in De Gaulle's requests. This proposal mushroomed into a major crisis, and brought out starkly for the first time the conflicting constitutional doctrines of De Gaulle and the Socialists. To De Gaulle, any reduction in the military credits would amount to a vote of nonconfidence, and he warned bluntly that he would resign if they were cut down. He accepted the Assembly's sovereign right to force the cabinet out of office, if it should so desire. But, as a counterpoise, he insisted that so long as the cabinet possessed the Assembly's confidence, it should have full and unlimited freedom to govern, and to decide what measures must be adopted by the Assembly to allow it to govern effectively.

The Socialists delegated no less a figure than André Philip to refute De Gaulle's arguments. Philip took the position that the De Gaulle thesis would result either in frequent cabinet crises or else in a kind of quasi-abdication by the assembly in favor of the executive. Either alternative, said Philip, would be a distortion of the parliamentary system. He argued that the assembly should have the right to influence and guide the cabinet's action from day to day, with only rare recourse to a showdown vote of confidence. Drawing heavily on Léon Blum's doctrines, Philip insisted that the goal should not be greater independence for the executive. Instead, the premier should co-ordinate the efforts of the cabinet and the legislature. He should not be the chief of one branch of government against the other, but the chief of both at once; and he should shape cabinet policy according to the will of the people, as represented by the majority in parliament.

Philip and the Socialists felt that during the preceding weeks De Gaulle had succeeded in forcing the Assembly to abdicate again and again, through repeated hints or threats of resignation. The Socialists had allowed this to happen because they feared the breakdown of three-party government, and because they believed that no one but De Gaulle could hold such a government together. But they were resolved not to let De Gaulle implant this kind of executive permanently in France, and they were obviously determined to retreat no further for fear of prejudicing the future. Philip declared a few days later in a speech at Lyon that in spite of the Socialist party's respect for De Gaulle, "it would not hesitate to break with the General if he were to maintain an intransigent attitude toward the Assembly. . . . We want him to stay in office, but we also want him to acquire the habits of democracy."

The controversy revealed a fundamental difference between the president and the Left over the true nature of parliamentary government. Neither view could be called antidemocratic in itself; either one could be defended with perfect validity. The De Gaulle thesis, still somewhat hazy in the mind of its author, seemed to resemble British cabinet government in general concept, except that the multi-party structure of France would naturally leave far greater authority in the hands of the chief executive.

It was marked with the presidential spirit even though it was rooted in the parliamentary principle. The Socialist position, on the other hand, veered toward the Communist thesis of government by assembly without quite arriving there completely. The Socialists hoped to weight the balance of executive-legislative relations in the direction of the legislature, whereas De Gaulle's plan was designed to tip the scales in favor of the executive.

A contributing factor in the growing discord between De Gaulle and the Socialists was the long-standing Leftist suspicion of some of the men around the General. From the earliest London days, the sentiment had existed that De Gaulle was more democratic than his entourage. One of the principal magnets for such doubts was Gaston Palewski, a twentieth-century version of the *éminence grise*. Born in 1901 of Polish-French stock, Palewski was educated in law at Oxford and became a Parisian journalist for a time. He quickly showed a genius for attaching himself to great men; he served as personal assistant to Lyautey in Morocco, then to Paul Reynaud in Paris. He joined De Gaulle in June 1940, and by 1942 had worked up to the post of the General's *directeur de cabinet*. After liberation, Palewski became De Gaulle's shadow and even in a sense his *alter ego*. Whenever De Gaulle attended a legislative session, Palewski would be seen a few feet away, always lounging against the same pillar, his thoughts masked by a smile that seemed to combine Machiavelli and Mona Lisa. As guardian to the door of De Gaulle's office, it was Palewski who decided whom the General should or should not see. He was probably one of the few men who exercised some direct influence over his chief. Although regarded as a political opportunist, Palewski was at bottom a Right-wing republican who believed in strong government with a clerical tinge. His enemies regarded him as the General's evil genius—a charge which Palewski himself rather savored.

If the Leftists were vaguely suspicious of Palewski, they felt certain that another Gaullist adviser was no real republican. "Colonel Passy" (the wartime pseudonym of Colonel Armand Dewavrin) had headed De Gaulle's secret service and intelligence bureau since 1940. His past was somewhat obscure; he was known to have risen to a colonelcy in the army engineers, but it was also bruited about that he had been associated with leaders of the fascist cagoulard movement. Passy was definitely a member of De Gaulle's inner circle, and five years of steady criticism from Leftist politicians had failed to shake his position. In the eyes of the Left, his very presence was a disturbing factor; as for the agency which he headed, they hinted darkly that it smelled of the Gestapo. A fraction of their distrust seemed to be confirmed after De Gaulle (and Passy) left office in 1946. It was shortly discovered that Passy, without De Gaulle's knowledge, had salted away a large chunk of his agency's secret funds, with a view to resuming his work quickly when the General's inevitable return to power should occur.

There were other men in the entourage who were much less vulnerable to attack: René Pleven, conservative but certainly not fascist; René Capitant, more a theorist than a man of action; young Jacques Soustelle, a professor of anthropology whose specialty was pre-Columbian cultures; André Malraux, whose life and work had always shown his leftist sympathies; Jacques Baumel, a prominent figure in the anti-German underground; Louis Vallon, an economic expert who had broken off his long association with Marcel Déat after Munich. But even such men, the Left feared, had developed a Messiah complex with respect to De Gaulle, and might follow him blindly into any adventure which more dangerous advisers might prepare. De Gaulle in turn was known to exact unswerving loyalty from the men around him, and to single out as a special elite those adherents who had joined him in June 1940. A top-ranking general who had not rallied to the cause until after the North African landings received from De Gaulle, after repeated requests, a photograph inscribed "To General ———, who chose the path of glory when it became readily accessible to him." One of the principal figures in the underground, who had served in the first post-liberation cabinet, later remarked to a friend: "De Gaulle has no use for me—I wasn't with him at London." This peculiar relationship between De Gaulle and his entourage thickened the cloud of suspicion which, by the end of

1945, had obscured the rainbow of co-operation between the Socialists and the President.

The New Year's Day skirmish, although settled by a token reduction of the military credits and a promise of early military reform, proved to be a kind of delayed-action bomb. Three weeks later, on January 20, De Gaulle suddenly called his cabinet into a special Sunday-morning session. The ministers' mystification turned to consternation when De Gaulle strode in, lectured them for ten minutes on their inclination to play party politics rather than to give him their full co-operation, announced his decision to resign, and strode out again. For the first time in modern French history, a man who had once possessed unlimited authority in the state abdicated completely and retired to his tent.

De Gaulle's brusque departure, like every other important act of the General's career, will always retain a controversial aspect. His letter of resignation baffled the average Frenchman even more than the act of departure itself, for it informed the nation that France's critical period was over and that De Gaulle could therefore take a well-earned rest. Many citizens concluded in bewilderment that the General must be either blind or emotionally unstable, for the country had rarely had so large a stock of unsolved problems on hand. Certainly De Gaulle's popularity in the country virtually collapsed during the weeks that followed. Some Frenchmen knew that De Gaulle had meant to use the radio that night to tell the country the real reasons for his break with the politicians, and that certain Socialist leaders, notably Vincent Auriol and Léon Blum, had dissuaded him on the ground that the nation's unity might be endangered. De Gaulle recognized that danger, and he also saw that a public appeal would turn him into the leader of an opposition faction rather than a symbol of national unity. His radio address, if delivered, might indeed have altered the course of French history.

At the root of De Gaulle's decision to step down was his realization that the Socialists would not help to build his kind of Fourth Republic, or anything remotely like it. His series of controversies with the Left, culminating in the New Year's Day incident, convinced him that the Socialists were "undependable." The final blow was the Socialist decision on January 16 to work more closely with the Communists in constitution-making. Instead of a Socialist-M.R.P. bloc, it appeared that a Left-wing majority was coalescing and that De Gaulle would become its prisoner. That he himself shared the responsibility for the Socialists' course was an idea which the General would never have understood.

De Gaulle further realized that his personal prestige had dropped sharply during the preceding months, and that to continue in office would probably increase his unpopularity. Finally, a few of the General's confidants already knew that he was convinced of the inevitability of a first-class international crisis, perhaps of a Russo-American war, within a year or two. Some members of the entourage freely predicted that De Gaulle would be back in power in six months, stronger than ever. To retire dramatically at a difficult moment, to let his reputation be mended by a spell of obscurity, to show the nation that no other man could fill his place, to be called back by popular acclaim when the new crisis arrived—such, apparently, was De Gaulle's intuitive strategy.

It was no ordinary cabinet crisis which France now faced. Deprived of the only prominent chief whom the nation had produced since liberation, the parties might proceed to ride off in all directions at once. The Communists pulled themselves together most rapidly. Assuming their "obligation" as France's first party, they proposed Maurice Thorez for the Gaullist succession, and called for a new Popular Front majority to rally around him. The Socialists wavered, but a caucus of their deputies finally voted sixty to thirty-eight not to enter a cabinet unless the M.R.P. as well as the Communists were included.

The M.R.P. was thrown into extreme confusion by De Gaulle's departure. It had ridden to electoral success partly because it was reputed to have the General's unofficial blessing. Fervent Gaullists were especially numerous in its ranks. An M.R.P. caucus found three-fourths of their deputies in favor of following De Gaulle into the opposition and refusing to enter a cabinet headed by anyone else. Most of the M.R.P. leaders disagreed, however, and finally brought the back-benchers around. They argued that democracy's fate in France was possibly in the balance—that if the M.R.P. were to leave the Communists in control of the cabinet, the latter party might move through gradual, superficially legal means toward a one-party dictatorship. The M.R.P. leaders felt too that blind support of De Gaulle would split France into Right and Left blocs, with the M.R.P. forced to abandon its Leftist ties and doctrines and its ambition to become the great Center party of the Fourth Republic. A few influential figures, such as Georges Bidault, were also moved by personal animosity against a chief who, as one underground leader put it, had behaved as "the disdainful master of our grateful hearts." As Foreign Minister, Bidault had hardly dared call either his policy or his soul his own, and more than once he had been on the verge of resignation in order to get out from under the General's haughty and domineering control. In the end, the M.R.P. leaders' victory over the back-benchers was so complete that only one deputy deserted the party in protest. That was twenty-seven-year-old Jean-Pierre Giraudoux, son of the famous novelist, whom the Communists cruelly described as "the master's most mediocre work."

The M.R.P.'s decision to stay with the team contained only one reservation: they would not accept a Communist as president. It was the Socialist party, therefore, which had to furnish a leader. Out of the pack emerged Félix Gouin, a tubby, owlish, hand-shaking politician who had been serving as president of the Constituent Assembly and therefore seemed to rank as a national rather than merely a party figure. Gouin, a southern lawyer with the Marseille charm, verve, and accent, had served in parliament for almost twenty years before the war. After voting against Pétain in 1940, he had been one of Léon Blum's lawyers in Vichy's 1942 Riom trials, and had later escaped to London to join De Gaulle. As president of the Consultative Assembly and then of the Constituent Assembly, he had won wide respect for his impartiality and his good humor. Gouin quickly put together a three-party cabinet, dropping out the Gaullist "technicians" who had been kept on in November. Thus the crisis passed almost before the country had time to recover from the initial shock.

De Gaulle's retirement meant a fundamental change in the political atmosphere, and in the effect which the interim regime might have on the new constitution. "De Gaulle has no friends," went the popular saying, "but Gouin has no enemies." Before the eyes of the constitution-makers there would no longer be a living example of a strong executive. Government by compromise, by negotiation, by balance of political forces, would again become the rule, much as it had been before the war. The reaction of many politicians was a thankful "Alone at last!" They would henceforth be freed from the constant threat of presidential pressure and independent action which De Gaulle represented. With Gouin in the presidency, the doctrine of a stronger executive no longer seemed quite so dangerous to the Left or quite so important to the Right. The idea of strong government was not dead, but it no longer hung imminent in Paris. It had withdrawn to the shadows of Marly forest, which De Gaulle had chosen as his retreat.

VI. THE RENOVATED RIGHTS
OF MAN

January marked a turning point in the constitutional debate. When the Committee reconvened after the resignation of De Gaulle, it had been decapitated by the promotion of André Philip to a post in Gouin's cabinet. Even more important, the Socialists' swing to the Left implied that the Committee would eventually backtrack on some of its earlier decisions.

Philip's successor as chairman, Guy Mollet, was an almost automatic choice. Mollet owed his elevation not so much to his personal qualities as to the fact that he ranked next to Philip in the Socialist delegation. A rather cadaverous figure with thinning sandy hair, horn-rimmed glasses, and the deep voice and solemn intonation of an undertaker, Mollet was one of the new men raised to prominence in the party by his underground work. He had been a highschool English teacher in Arras, and liked to point out that he was Robespierre's lineal successor as deputy for his native town. Mollet was also proud of his proletarian origin. He belonged to the so-called Left wing of the Socialist party, which meant in his case that he was a rigidly doctrinaire Marxian who disliked the bourgeois M.R.P. more than he loved the Communists. A sincere, straightforward, and rather humorless man, he was to prove a competent but not a distinguished substitute for Philip.

Two topics of vast proportions remained on the Committee's agenda for general discussion before the actual task of drafting could be begun. One was the Declaration of Rights; the other, the future status of the empire. Both topics were time-consuming, but it was the Declaration of Rights which produced the longer and more impassioned debate. In fact, the Committee devoted almost one-fourth of its total working time to that essentially theoretical bit of political philosophy.

The Committee refused to admit that this was a waste of effort. Almost every Frenchman was proudly convinced that one of France's greatest gifts to the world had been the revolutionary Declaration of the Rights of Man of 1789. The Committee believed, as René Capitant put it, that "on the morrow of a terrible crisis in which the ideology of totalitarianism had been preached," a new Declaration would be especially appropriate. It would, said Capitant, "determine the orientation of the new regime and would impress opinion both in France and abroad."

But the Committee was not prepared to give the Declaration the kind of binding force possessed by the American Bill of Rights. Without some sort of enforcement agency like the Supreme Court, the Declaration would obviously be little more than a set of pious commandments. The Right wing proposed such a supreme court, for which part of the M.R.P. showed sympathy; but the cause was hopeless because of the Left's solid opposition. Both Communists and Socialists feared that if citizens could appeal any law to the courts on the ground of possible conflict with a set of broad principles, the result would be permanent obstructionism.

Citing the horrible example of the Court which had slowed up Roosevelt's New Deal, the Left accused its rivals of aiming to set up a barrier against economic reform. The M.R.P. rather reluctantly joined the Left to bury the idea of judicial review from the start. Even Paul Coste-Floret described as "monstrous" the power of American judges to declare laws unconstitutional.

No committee member was heretic enough to suggest that the 1946 Assembly could improve on the classic purity of form of the 1789 Declaration. At the same time, a majority did feel that the old Declaration had long since been bypassed as to content. In 1789, the sole issue had been the political liberties of individual citizens with respect to an autocratic state. By 1946, the problem had broadened to include the social and economic rights of man in a more or less collectivist society. The Committee's task was to harmonize 1789 with 1946, either by adding a wing to the old structure or by rebuilding it entirely.

Three different concepts of the contents and spirit of the new Declaration gradually crystallized. The first thesis was that of the old-school liberals (mainly the Right and the Radicals), who sought to hold back the powerful current toward collectivism. They wanted to retain the 1789 Declaration with its guarantee of property as a sacred and inalienable right of man, and to give it a place of honor at the head of the new constitution. They proposed merely to add several new articles with mild guarantees of social and economic rights. But the liberals could not hope to resist the combined strength of the three major parties, all of whom insisted on a complete job of rewriting. The aim of the big three was to lay the groundwork for a collectivist society, and to eliminate the 1789 doctrine of "divine-right" property. They wished to place heavy emphasis on social and economic rights, and to demote political liberties from an absolute to a relative plane, subject to limitation by the state for the good of society as a whole.

Within the ranks of the collectivists, however, the M.R.P.'s philosophy of government diverged from that of the Socialists and Communists. The M.R.P. described its doctrine as "pluralism." Its spokesmen argued that the time had come to break with the severe individualism of 1789, which held that the individual citizen is the only natural component unit of society. The M.R.P. contended that other natural and organic units exist intermediate between the state and the individual. It held that these basic groups or "collectivities" (notably the family, the local community, and the professional organization) possess a separate organic existence, and therefore have natural rights which ought to be guaranteed and protected just as much as those of the individual.

The M.R.P. obviously drew this doctrine from the writings of Left-wing Catholics and from the social encyclicals of recent Popes. It bore at least a superficial resemblance to the corporative ideas preached by Mussolini, Salazar, and Pétain—a fact which the Left was not slow to point out. Leftists observed that when Pétain wished to replace Liberty, Equality, Fraternity with a new trilogy, he had set up *Famille* alongside *Travail* and *Patrie*.

The M.R.P. was keenly sensitive to these charges of corporatism, which it vigorously rejected. "Corporatism," declared its philosophic specialist Henri Teitgen, "consists essentially of integrating individuals by force in cadres which the state creates." He insisted that the groups which the M.R.P. wished to aid and protect were, on the contrary, living and existing collectivities rather than artificial creations, and that membership in them was not dictated by the state. Teitgen maintained that the M.R.P.'s doctrine, far from being related to fascism, was in fact democracy's best hope of survival. "Pluralism," he told the Committee, "is the true form of future democracy," and the sole alternative to totalitarianism. A collection of individuals left alone in face of the modern state would be unable to protect their rights. Only by guaranteeing the rights of organic groups against the state can democratic liberties be safeguarded. Those organic groups are "bastions of liberty" in a totalitarian age.

The organic group which concerned the M.R.P. most deeply was the family. Their interest here was not purely theoretical, but was tied up with the very practical population problem, an issue which seriously disturbed most Frenchmen. France's low birth rate seemed to doom the nation to steady decline; as Daniel Boisdon of the M.R.P. put it, "There are only two countries in the world where death prevails over life: Belgium and France." The population loss suffered between 1940 and 1945 was a further blow. That loss was officially estimated at more than 600,000 dead or missing (of whom over 150,000 were deportees who had died in Germany, and 30,000 were resisters who had been shot by the Germans). The M.R.P. contended, however, that the real cost of the war to France would be closer to a million and a half. Already the results had begun to show up in the form of a severe labor shortage, for which the only immediate remedy seemed to be a policy of heavy selective immigration.

The M.R.P.'s basic philosophy found little favor among the Socialists, and none at all among the Communists. The Marxian parties clung to the traditional Leftist thesis that the individual is the only natural unit of society. Certainly, asserted André Philip just before he left the Committee, individuals should be guaranteed the right to form groups of various kinds; but these groups cannot be regarded as collective beings, distinct from the individuals composing them, and possessing a separate organic personality. The M.R.P.'s doctrine, added Philip, might freeze the social structure into rigid categories, thus limiting the individual's freedom. As for the proposal of the M.R.P.'s blond Mme. Peyroles to "recognize the family founded on marriage as a natural institution, guardian of human liberties and foundation of all social life," the Left suspected that it aimed at the abolition of divorce, at the grant of a double vote to heads of families, and at "bourgeois and reactionary" discrimination against illegitimate children. After a long fight, the M.R.P. had to settle for a limp provision that the state would guarantee "the conditions necessary to the free development of the family."

A longer and more acrid dispute between the M.R.P. and the Left concerned freedom of instruction—which meant, in practice, a guarantee of the right to operate church schools. Few issues in French politics were so old or went so deep. Professor Ernest Lavisse used to tell his students at the Sorbonne: "If you want to understand the history of France since the sixteenth century, get it into your heads that there has never been but a single question —the religious question." All through the nineteenth century the anticlerical Leftists had fought to hold down church influence in temporal affairs, most particularly in education. They had finally triumphed during the Third Republic, and had made the public school system completely secular.

Some anticlericals had wished to go even further by giving the state a monopoly of education, but in practice church schools had been permitted to exist without a break throughout the Third Republic. One-fourth of all students in primary schools and half of all students in secondary schools regularly got their education from the Catholic brotherhoods. After 1900 the clerical issue gradually lost its intensity until, by 1940, it seemed that the old barrier between clericals and anticlericals was in the final stages of erosion. Traditional hostility survived, especially in rural districts where the *culs blancs* and the *culs rouges* had faced each other for so long. But politically, the problem seemed to be a relic of the nineteenth century.

It was Pétain who revived the issue in 1941 by granting a substantial state subsidy to church schools. After liberation the Catholics naturally asked that these grants be maintained, and thus reawakened the dormant anticlerical suspicions of the Left. De Gaulle found it advisable to let the subsidies quietly lapse in 1945, but the Church did not abandon hope. With a vigorous new confessional party on the scene, state aid might again become possible.

The M.R.P. leaders sympathized with this ambition, but tried to keep the question in the background; they were convinced that it would be fatal to revive the old clerical dispute at once. They were prepared to forget subsidies for the time being, but they were determined that the Declaration of Rights should guarantee liberty of instruction. Without that guarantee, they feared that the Left might some day try to close down church schools entirely.

Backed by the Right wing and the U.D.S.R., the M.R.P. spokesmen put up a vigorous battle before going under. They attempted to fit their case into the framework of pluralism, arguing that a state monopoly of education would smack of totalitarianism, and that only several school systems, like a variety of political parties or a diversity of philosophical attitudes, could ensure freedom. They also pled their case on the basis of family rights, one aspect of which would be the father's right to choose his child's education.

The phalanx of Left-wing schoolmasters on the Committee—Philip for a time, Mollet, Fajon, Hervé, Cot—leaped into the argument with fervor. They contended that the father possessed no absolute right to impose his will, but only a duty to give his child the kind of schooling which would prepare him, upon reaching maturity, to choose his own way of life. They argued that state schools alone could offer an unprejudiced approach to education, since church schools were "mental incubators" designed to inculcate a total view of the world. No child, Philip declared, should be exposed to Pascal without Voltaire or to Voltaire without Pascal. Absolute freedom of instruction they described as in fact a false liberty, since the child's mind is malleable and can therefore be shaped toward narrow prejudices. After all, asked Fajon, why should the Catholics insist on their own special schools? "We Marxists feel no need for our children to attend a Marxist school."

The outcome of the discussion was foreordained. Communists and Socialists, backed by the traditionally anticlerical Radicals, rejected an outright guarantee of freedom of instruction, and voted to describe education as a public service available to every child "in an atmosphere of liberty." Beaten in Committee, the M.R.P. vowed to renew its fight later on the floor of the Assembly.

When the Committee turned to the social-economic section of the Declaration, the gap between the Left and the M.R.P. narrowed considerably. It was in this sphere that the M.R.P.'s Leftist proclivities were most pronounced. The Communists made three-party agreement easier by announcing that they did not intend to press for revolutionary principles. "For the moment," declared Fajon, "there can be no question of establishing a socialist or a communist constitution"; in the present state of society, and "until the conditions of socialism are attained," the Communists were ready to affirm their respect for private property so long as it was not abused.

The hardest nut to crack was the new definition to be given to property rights. In 1789, property had been listed as one of the sacred and inviolable rights of man, on a level with liberty and personal security. The Radicals and Rightists were ready to stand on that 1789 text; but the Left and the M.R.P. rebelled. Property, declared Jacques Fonlupt-Esperaber for the M.R.P., "must no longer be an end in itself, but a means to serve the common good." Monopolies or the private control of key industries should be regarded as abuses of the right to hold property, and such abuses should be outlawed. As early as 1793, observed the Communists, Robespierre had proposed to make property rights subordinate to the law.

The text finally worked out by the Committee was strongly reminiscent of that Robespierrist doctrine. "Property," it read, "is the inviolable and sacred right to use, to enjoy and to dispose of objects guaranteed to each person by the law." The state would not be allowed to deprive any citizen of his property except for reasons of public utility, and on condition that a just indemnity be paid; but all monopolies and public services, the text concluded, should become the property of the nation. Theoretically at least, the Committee's new definition would open the way to the expropriation of any and all property. It posed a fundamental question: can society protect itself against unscrupulous individuals without ultimately putting all individuals under the heel of the state? If the individual's rights are made contingent rather than absolute, do those rights become meaningless? The same question was to arise again in connection with freedom of the press, which the Left wing wished to make subordinate to the law. The major parties believed that the Fourth Republic would have to face this dilemma rather than sidestep it, and that without a solution the Republic would be doomed to failure.

Except for these controversies, the Committee found itself in general agreement on the rights of contemporary man. The usual civil liberties were accompanied by a considerable number of new rights. Full equality before the law was guaranteed to women and to colonial natives; the principle of habeas corpus was introduced into France for the first time; the right of access to the courts for rich and poor alike was promised; discrimination based on such factors as color, religion, or opinions was forbidden. Every citizen was guaranteed the right to work in decent conditions and at a just wage, to join a union and to strike, and to receive state aid if incapable of working. In the first draft, resistance and insurrection against an oppressive government were described as "the most sacred of rights and the most imperious of duties." But the word "insurrection" grated on Communist ears, and was cut out at their insistence. The Communists also objected to an article promising that France would abandon part of its national sovereignty whenever other nations would do the same. The moment was inopportune for such an idealistic gesture, declared Fajon. On the contrary, what France needed was a vigorous reaffirmation of its sovereignty.

The Committee's draft thus shaped up as a document of a broad and generous nature, built to twentieth-century specifications, with nine-tenths of its articles accepted by all parties. It was the remaining one-tenth, however, which set the tone of the Declaration, and which gave promise of serious differences in the Assembly and the country as a whole.

VII. 100,000,000 FRENCHMEN

One of the most formidable tasks facing the Assembly was the constitutional reorganization of the empire. To the average deputy, the problem resembled a trek into the African bush without map or compass. Most educated Frenchmen possessed some academic knowledge of the size and complexity of the empire, and were deeply imbued with the conviction that the colonial peoples at heart loved and respected France. They were dimly aware that signs of native discontent existed, and they believed that unless France moved quickly to check that discontent, rival nations might profit by French weakness to chip away parts of the empire. But not more than a few dozen members of the Assembly were equipped to study imperial reorganization with any real understanding of the problems involved, or of the potentialities and desires of the overseas populations.

Prior to 1940, the issue of imperial reform had not arisen in any pressing sense. There had long existed a sporadic controversy between two broad schools of thought—assimilation versus association—but neither concept had involved revolutionizing the relationships between France and its possessions. The assimilationists had aimed to convert the colonial peoples into Frenchmen, by replacing the native cultures with French culture and absorbing the colonies into the highly centralized French political structure. The associationists, who gradually got the upper hand, had preferred to transform only a native elite into full French citizens, and to entrust this elite with a share in the administration. Both groups intended to keep the empire's center of gravity in Paris. Only the Communists, obedient to the teachings of Lenin, showed much sympathy for native separatist movements overseas.

Bewildering variety rather than logical symmetry characterized the empire as it stood in 1945. There were first of all the "old colonies" of Martinique, Guadeloupe, Guiana, and Réunion, all products of a century of assimilation. Their populations possessed French citizenship, and in 1946 the Constituent Assembly was to complete the assimilation process by promoting all four colonies to the status of French departments. French India and Senegal possessed a special status approaching that of the "old colonies," and the islands of Saint-Pierre and Miquelon were unique because their tiny population was made up entirely of French colonists.

On the surface, Algeria too seemed to be assimilated, since it was organized into three French departments. In fact, however, its status was colonial. French settlers were outnumbered eight to one by Arab and Berber noncitizens. In 1944 De Gaulle had taken a short step toward assimilation by granting citizenship to about 60,000 Arabs without requiring them to abandon Moslem law as a prerequisite. To assimilate the remaining eight million, however, would be a long process; and there was reason to believe that the Arabs themselves did not desire it.

Algeria's neighbors Morocco and Tunisia, along with Annam-Tongking and Cambodia in Indo-China, were still protectorates with native puppet rulers controlled by the French. In consequence, their populations were not French citizens but subjects of the native rulers, who still possessed theoretical sovereignty. The rest of the empire was administered directly by French colonial officials, with local self-government virtually nonexistent. This was the status of the federations of French West Africa and French Equatorial Africa; of Madagascar and the Comores Islands; of Somaliland, Cochin-China, New Caledonia, and Oceania. Most of these colonies contained only a handful of French settlers; in the Ivory Coast, for example, there were four thousand Frenchmen scattered among four million natives. Two mandated areas, Togoland and Cameroon, had been administered like colonies under League of Nations supervision. Their future, like that of the protectorates, could not be unilaterally settled by the Constituent Assembly.

The idea of converting the empire into some form of commonwealth or federation did not originate with the French underground. Instead, it was imported from Algiers by De Gaulle and the Free French returning from exile. The proposal had a number of roots. Gratitude was one: De Gaulle owed some recompense to the colonies for their aid to his Free French movement after 1940. For two years, more than half the troops in the Free French forces had been African natives. National prestige was another: France's only hope of winning back the status of a first-rank power seemed to depend on knitting the empire together. The phrase "a hundred million Frenchmen" rang with satisfaction in the ears of French patriots. Necessity was a third root: the loss of Syria and the Lebanon, the revolt in Indo-China, the growing sentiment of nationalism in Asia and Africa vaguely worried the French and moved them to seek a barrier against the breakup of their empire. Idealism was a fourth: the Left wing in France had traditionally favored improving both the political and the social status of the natives. In consequence, it was generally agreed in the summer of 1945 that the overseas peoples ought to help draft the constitution, and no hostile voice was raised when De Gaulle authorized every territory to elect deputies to the Constituent Assembly.

Although it was De Gaulle who had brought the idea of imperial reform from Algiers, he and his advisers had developed no positive plans. Their negative aims were a bit clearer, at least to those persons who recalled the Brazzaville Conference of French colonial officials in January 1944. At the head of the recommendations adopted at Brazzaville was this warning: "The effect of the civilizing work accomplished by France in the colonies dispels any idea of autonomy, any possibility of evolution outside the French imperial bloc. Even the distant establishment of 'self-government' [sic] in our colonies is to be set aside." Progress toward dominion status was therefore ruled out by the Gaullists, at least for the African continent.

The Brazzaville Conference did lay plans for improving the social and economic lot of the native peoples, and after De Gaulle's return to France his government took some positive steps in that direction. A native labor code was promulgated, and an eventual end to forced labor was foreseen. In the field of colonial self-rule, however, De Gaulle was extremely cautious. His cabinet confined itself to setting up several colonial assemblies with restricted membership and limited powers. Not even De Gaulle's Colonial Ministers Paul Giaccobi and Jacques Soustelle had yet caught the vision of what Soustelle later called a "Copernican revolution" in the imperial realm. Giaccobi's major contribution was the phrase "French Union," which he first used in March 1945 to describe the future federation.

The Constitutional Committee was plainly at a loss in attacking the problem. Colonial deputies were so few in the Committee's ranks that it seemed logical and proper to call on the Committee on Overseas France for aid. The latter body, made up in majority of overseas representatives, was presumably better equipped to propose a specific plan.

It was a curious blend of federalism and centralization which finally emerged from the Overseas Committee's deliberations. Marius Moutet, its Socialist chairman (and shortly to become the perennial Minister for Overseas France), introduced the plan as "a leap into the unknown," but nevertheless defended it as a necessary gamble if France were to hold its colonies. The project adopted Giaccobi's term "French Union" as the name of the new structure, and declared that membership in this Union would be based on "free consent." The status of "subject" would be wiped out; every French national, from Parisian to neolithic Congo tribesman, would become a citizen and would enjoy full equality of rights. Each overseas area would be authorized to elect a territorial assembly, with the power to shape local policies and to control the local administration. Up to this point, the plan was federal in spirit. The federal capstone, however, was left off. The draft contained no provision for either a federal assembly or a federal executive at the top. Instead, the overseas areas would continue to send deputies to the French legislature in Paris, just as they had done to the Constituent Assembly. All natives would be given the suffrage, and both natives and white colonists in each area would be lumped together for voting purposes.

This plan, although less completely federal than some native deputies desired, had far-reaching implications. If membership in the Union were really to be based on free consent, a territory might conceivably refuse to enter the Union or might later secede. If the territorial assemblies were to receive broad local autonomy, they might strike out on the road leading to separatism. If the overseas populations were to receive fully equal rights, they might dominate parliament, for sixty million people lived overseas as compared to only forty million in continental France. Finally, if natives and colonists in each territory were to be lumped into joint electoral colleges, the small colonist element would be snowed under and would lose all representation both in the Paris legislature and in the territorial assemblies.

The Overseas Committee's plan offered something specific as a point of departure, but it certainly did not dissipate the fog enshrouding the French Union question. The long debate which followed was the most confused and contradictory of all the Constitutional Committee's labors. Unfortunately, the empire was far too complex an organization to be made over on the basis of pure logic; and when forty-two Frenchmen pit their Cartesian training and prejudices against an empirical problem, the outcome is likely to be cloudy.

As a general rule, the discussion set the Socialists and Communists against the M.R.P. and the minor parties. The Left was inclined to accept the Overseas Committee's plan for the time being, and to look beyond it toward complete federalism as the proper goal. Both Socialists and Communists dimly foresaw a future federation of peoples, each with its own culture, its own responsible government, and its own citizenship, crowned by some sort of federal parliament. They knew, however, that many of the colonies were still too primitive to function as states in a federation. Most of them agreed with the bureaucrat who, when told that Algeria wanted immediate statehood, snorted, "Nonsense! where would they get the stenographers?" Therefore they advocated that federalism be achieved on the installment plan.

Their aim was to begin at the bottom with territorial assemblies, and to expand the powers of these bodies as the natives' capacity for self-government increased. For the time being, matters of common interest to the whole Union would continue to be decided by the Paris legislature, in which the overseas territories would be represented on a minority basis. Once the territories reached maturity, this representation would be suppressed. The Paris legislature would become merely the national assembly for continental France, on a level with the assemblies of Madagascar, West Africa, and the rest. The common interests of the Union would then be taken over by a truly federal assembly. In preparation for that historic day, André Philip proposed to set up at once an advisory Council of the French Union. Out of this nucleus would eventually develop the dominant federal assembly.

The Left indignantly denied Rightist charges that its program might lead to the breakup of the empire. "Federalism in no way implies separatism or secession," cried the Socialist Gilbert Zaksas; and Pierre Hervé added: "Does federalism lead to dismemberment? That is false. It would be more accurate to expect such a result from a policy of all-out assimilation." Yet the Leftists at times showed their embarrassment and their uncertainty. Hervé himself once let slip the remark that "we wish to lead the peoples under our protection toward autonomy or even independence"; and both Etienne Fajon and Guy Mollet admitted that "federalism might lead to a recognition of the right of secession." Nevertheless, the Left argued, the only proper solution was to let the overseas peoples evolve freely in whatever direction they might choose. To strait-jacket them would be the surest way to bring on trouble.

In contrast to this approach, the M.R.P. and Right were more cautious, more suspicious of federalism, more determined to maintain the tensile strength of imperial ties. Their hazy goal was not to develop a series of separate nations loosely joined in a federal union, but to make the overseas possessions into French provinces or, as Pierre Cot put it, "annexes to the mother country." The M.R.P.-led bloc was ready to abandon assimilation in the cultural sense, but intended to preserve it politically.

The principal author of this policy was the M.R.P. deputy Paul Viard, Dean of the Algiers Law School. Viard urged that separatist movements be headed off by converting all native subjects into French citizens at once. He realized, however, that the sixty million newly created French citizens might soon demand sixty per cent of the legislative seats in Paris, and that such a demand would be hard to refute. He therefore suggested that French citizenship be subdivided into two categories: "citizens of French statute" (i.e., those subject to French law) and "citizens of local statute" (those who would choose to retain their own law and customs, such as the Moslems and the peoples of Black Africa). By implication, citizens in the latter category would have no claim to full political equality. Besides, they would vote in a separate electoral college, which would prevent them from submerging the white colonist element. Viard suggested that if the natives' self-esteem were offended by this plan, it could be soothed by giving them heavy representation in a purely advisory Council of the French Union. Even in such a Council, however, Viard argued that continental France ought to be given two-thirds of the seats. The overseas delegates, he insisted, must be "bathed in a French atmosphere."

The Left reacted vigorously against Viard's proposals to make the natives "second-class citizens" and to require them to vote in a separate electoral college. "The most profound aspiration of the native populations," asserted Marius Moutet, "is to feel that they are treated on a basis of equality." Maintenance of the double electoral college, he warned, would be regarded as a symbol of racism and might stimulate separatism. Mohand Achour, an Algerian Arab sitting as a substitute Socialist committeeman, protested at the idea of two types of citizenship. "Is there such a difference between Moslems and occidentals?" he asked ironically. "The former keep all their wives under one roof, while the latter have a woman in every quarter. [Laughter; protests from the M.R.P.]" The Left also questioned the wisdom of forcing either first- or second-class French citizenship on native peoples who might prefer to become citizens of Madagascar, Viet Nam, or some other federated state within the French Union.

The product of this long and fuzzy debate was a series of a half-dozen articles scattered through the constitutional draft, so loose and vague that no party voted against them. At bottom, these articles embodied most of the Left-wing demands; they left the future almost completely open. Even the M.R.P. and Right agreed to base membership in the Union on "free consent." They knew that in practice the phrase would be little more than a pious wish, or even a "pharisaism," as Paul Coste-Floret bluntly put it. The draft forbade discrimination based on color or beliefs, and specifically outlawed forced labor. It endowed the native populations with "all the rights attached to the status of citizen," but it purposely avoided a choice among "French citizenship," "citizenship of the French Union," or citizenship of a local territory such as Madagascar. No guarantee of the double electoral college was included, and the Left-wing majority promptly abolished it in the new electoral law. By general consent, all the overseas territories were granted elective assemblies, plus the right to send deputies to the legislature in Paris. The Left proceeded to vest the new territorial assemblies with relatively broad powers to control the administration. Besides, the colonial administration was revolutionized; the post of governor was abolished, and it was decided that in his place there would be a political figure subject to direct control by the Paris assembly.

The Committee's longest controversy occurred over the nature of the new Council of the French Union. Once the principle of its creation was accepted by all parties, the M.R.P. and Right swung their weight behind the idea of making it an upper house of parliament. They urged that it participate in electing the president of the republic and that it have the right to examine all bills adopted by the National Assembly. Both Communists and Socialists absolutely refused to let bicameralism be brought in thus through the back door; they set up the Council as a narrowly limited body with purely advisory powers on questions affecting the whole Union. Some Leftists viewed the Council as a body which might eventually develop into the real unicameral assembly of the French Union; but all Leftists were determined not to let it grow into a new Senate.

The French Union structure which finally emerged from Committee was a pretty nebulous affair, marred by gaps even more than by inconsistencies. Some skeptical Frenchmen preferred to describe it as "an insufficiently licked bear." But at least it did not try to force the polyglot empire into a rigid, logical framework. With its hybrid character of federalism and centralization, it was capable of future development in almost any direction. In a time of uncertainty, that was perhaps a virtue.

VIII. VARIATIONS ON A THEME
BY AURIOL

The leaders of the Socialist party, like tight-rope artists, were keenly aware of the hazards involved in leaning too far either to the right or to the left. They had corrected their balance in January by a brusque shift toward the Communists. By the middle of February, they were beginning to wonder whether they had not traded one risk for another. M.R.P. leaders were protesting vehemently against the kind of constitution which now seemed to be in sight, and were threatening that they might call on the voters to reject it. For the first time, the thought came home to many French politicians that their work might actually be thrown out by the people.

The two months from mid-February to mid-April were completely taken up in the search for a three-party compromise. It was the Socialists who came forward as chief bearers of the olive branch. Caught in the middle politically, they stood to suffer most if the country were to split into two blocs over the constitution. If they should be forced to go along with the Communists alone, they would face the risk of domination or even absorption by the "brother party." They had already tried the experiment of collaboration in the labor movement, and there the Communists were in the process of "plucking the Socialist chicken." On the other hand, a swing back toward the M.R.P. might drive the Communists into the opposition, from which vantage point they could loose their lightning upon the Socialists as traitors who had sold out to the bourgeoisie. Neutral observers recalled the sad story of Buridan's ass, and wondered whether the Socialists too would starve to death while hesitating between "the bucket of M.R.P. holy water and the peck of revolutionary oats."

The role of great compromiser was assumed by the Socialists' ablest diplomat, Vincent Auriol, newly elected president of the Assembly. On February 21 Auriol called the leaders of the major parties into his office and warned them that unless the constitution was ratified by a healthy majority, democracy would be gravely endangered in France. From that day forward, Auriol's office became the real constitutional laboratory. His informal "committee on compromises" superseded the Constitutional Committee on fundamental issues, and turned the latter into little more than a drafting organ.

No one could doubt the genuineness of the Socialist desire for compromise, for party interest and national interest happened to coincide in their case. But in the case of the other two parties, this fusion was less clear. Both the Communists and the M.R.P. expressed cautious satisfaction at the new trend toward conciliation, and promised to do their part. But both groups had to weigh a complex set of factors, some of which indicated that a breakdown of three-party unity or even the defeat of the constitution might offer political advantages.

The Communists hesitated to risk a break with the M.R.P. if that would endanger the ratification of the constitution. They attached great importance to having their type of draft accepted by the country, since they regarded such a constitution as a useful framework within which they could expand their strength in France. They realized that the defeat of a draft sponsored by them might seriously weaken the party at the polls, for it would check the forward wave on which the Communists had ridden since liberation. It would also strengthen the prospect of De Gaulle's return to power with a program of strong government. On the other hand, there would be clear advantages in driving a deep wedge between the M.R.P. and the Socialists, and forcing the latter to fight shoulder to shoulder with the Communists in the referendum campaign. Such a strategy would further the Communist aim of "workers' unity" and absorption of part of the Socialists' troops.

The M.R.P. also feared the potential results of a defeat of the constitution. They knew that if the first elected assembly since liberation were to fail in its major task, a severe blow would be dealt to representative government, for the Constituent Assembly was in a sense a test of the effectiveness of such a regime in France. Another seven-month period of quibbling over esoteric constitutional principles would further delay recovery and would deepen public discontent. On the other hand, M.R.P. leaders sincerely felt that democracy could not work in France without a relatively strong executive, and without effective counterweights to the assembly's power. During the winter of 1945-46, an M.R.P. study committee had been meeting long and frequently in an effort to reconcile some of dictatorship's advantages with a democratic system. One of its members declared bluntly that unless such a reconciliation could be achieved, "la démocratie est foutue." Furthermore, M.R.P. leaders could already see that it would be profitable to lead a fight against an unpopular draft constitution. If the prospect of political gain should coincide closely with their doctrinal convictions, the M.R.P. might find it advisable not to make too many concessions.

While the fundamental problems at issue were transferred to Auriol's office, the Constitutional Committee proceeded to jettison much of what one cynical observer called "the Picasso aspect" of its draft project. In other words, it pruned away many of the secondary clauses which the Committee had earlier voted to insert in the constitution. Each of these points had drawn the fire of at least one party, and so might endanger a three-party accord. The Socialist-sponsored policy of mutual concessions therefore required their elimination.

Operating on this theory, the Committee cut out the "party statute" and the recall of unfaithful deputies by the party machine; it abandoned both the obligatory vote and the plural vote for heads of families; it dropped proportional representation out of the constitution, reserving it for the more easily amendable electoral law; and it gave up the idea of a semijudicial body to validate the election of deputies.

This result was achieved at the cost of steadily rising friction. The M.R.P. quickly saw that mutual concessions on these secondary points amounted largely to a one-way street. Most of the clauses in question had been adopted when the Socialist-M.R.P. bloc dominated the Committee, so that to abandon them meant a series of concessions to the Communists. M.R.P. leaders were ready to admit that it is more blessed to give than to receive, but they were not sure how far the principle should be carried in politics. From conciliation the Committee turned to haggling and weighing one sacrifice against another. The spirit of compromise turned into a boomerang, for each concession by the M.R.P. increased tension within the party and put the M.R.P. leaders under heavier pressure from their followers.

While the temperature steadily rose in the Committee, some progress was being painfully accomplished in Vincent Auriol's office. Auriol's aim was to find a lowest common denominator among the three big parties on the major issues of bicameralism and presidential powers. After ten days of effort a solution seemed not only possible but probable. The representatives of all parties tentatively agreed that instead of an upper house of parliament there should be two purely consultative bodies: an Economic Council, to examine certain bills prior to their discussion in the National Assembly, and the Council of the French Union, whose right to render advisory opinions would be extended to cover all bills adopted by the Assembly. This "tricameral" scheme, after so much talk of the evils of bicameralism, occasioned a good many sarcastic remarks. A cartoon in a satirical weekly pictured Auriol seated on the tablets of the law and shouting into the telephone, "Thirty-seven chambers and six presidents, that's my final offer!"

As for executive powers, the Auriol compromise provided that the president of the republic would be elected by a two-thirds rather than a simple majority of the Assembly, and that he might submit a list of several potential premiers to the Assembly, which would then make the final choice. The power of dissolution would not be granted to the executive, but the Communists agreed to accept the system of automatic dissolution provided that it be used only during the last half of an assembly's five-year term.

Auriol's apparent victory proved to be premature. The M.R.P. delegates had tentatively endorsed the proposals, but an M.R.P. caucus the next day rejected the plan as inadequate. The party insisted that the Council of the French Union must share in electing the president of the republic, in order to free the president from dependence on the assembly and to make him "something more than a national zero." It also urged that the two proposed consultative councils be fused into one body, which would thereby possess greater authority and could serve as a real second chamber of parliament.

The indefatigable Auriol returned to the task at once. By March 6 he felt close enough to success to make a public appeal to the heads of all parties. In an open letter, he listed the points of agreement and suggested a give-and-take on the two unsettled issues. To please the Communists, the two consultative councils would be kept separate; to please the M.R.P., the Council of the French Union would be allowed to help elect the president.

This time it was the M.R.P.'s turn to give grudging approval while the Communists held up their hands in horror. Concealed in Auriol's scheme the Communists thought they detected the shadow of the old Senate. They pointed out that the Senate had managed to broaden its powers after 1875, and warned that the Council of the French Union would try to do the same if it were given even one prerogative of a political nature. The Communist party, Jacques Duclos announced, would never permit the revival of "un quelconque Sénat."

Faced by this stalemate, the M.R.P. for a moment seemed inclined to give way, and to accept a new face-saving compromise produced by Auriol's fertile brain. By this compromise, the president would be elected by the Assembly plus representatives of the departmental councils. But before the plan matured, a new and minor issue suddenly intruded to bring on the long-delayed crisis. Three months earlier, the old Socialist-M.R.P. majority had agreed to insert a procedure for testing the constitutionality of laws by referendum. Since that date the point had never been raised again. But on March 29, when it reached the Committee's agenda for final action, the new Socialist-Communist majority reversed the earlier decision and agreed to junk the whole procedure for testing laws. M.R.P. leaders looked on this reversal as the last straw. In the past, they had lost no sleep over the constitutionality mechanism, but the procedure assumed a new importance now that their other proposed counterweights to the assembly had been rejected. They therefore announced that unless the Left would reconsider, the M.R.P. could no longer accept the constitutional draft.

The issue which the M.R.P. thus chose for a showdown was of second-rate importance, but it had first-rate results. Time was running out; little more horse-trading was possible if the Assembly was to finish its work before the seven-month deadline. On April 3, François de Menthon formally requested the Left to reconsider its decision on the constitutionality procedure, and again the Socialist-Communist committeemen stood firm against it. De Menthon then announced that his group had instructed him to resign as Reporter-General, and to inform the Committee that the M.R.P. could no longer sponsor the draft as it stood. The breach in tripartism was open at last.

No one could yet be sure, however, that the breach was irreparable. "Rupture or poker game?" asked *Combat*; and indeed, there was a widespread sentiment that the M.R.P.'s decision was only a brusque maneuver in a continuing war of nerves. M.R.P. leaders made it plain that their policy henceforth would be one of "wait and see," and that if adequate concessions were made to their wishes during the public debate to come, they would still accept the constitution *in extremis*. It seemed almost unbelievable that tripartite unity should break down after Auriol had brought the big three to within one step of successful compromise. French politicians therefore faced the future with equanimity. They knew that time was short, but they felt that hope of broad agreement was still far from dead.

IX. "CIVIC SERMONIZING"

While the constitutional *pièce de résistance* was still simmering in Auriol's office, the Assembly diverted its attention for a week to an *hors d'oeuvre*, the Declaration of Rights.

The Constitutional Committee, haunted by its seven-month dead-line, had sought to speed things up by completing its work on the Declaration early in March and sending it to the Assembly for advance approval. In this way, the ground would be cleared for the body of the constitution to come up for public debate early in April.

The Committee's choice as special *rapporteur* to shepherd the Declaration through the Assembly was Gilbert Zaksas, Socialist. Zaksas was one of the more unusual figures brought to the surface by the resistance movement. As a young lawyer in Toulouse, he had headed a tiny underground group called *Libérer et Fédérer*, which had a slightly Proudhonesque flavor of federalism. Born in Lithuania in 1910, he was one of the rare immigrants who have reached even temporary prominence in modern French politics. His foreign birth was an initial black mark against him, but still more serious were his unorthodox French syntax and his Baltic accent. These idiosyncrasies, along with his headlong eagerness to hold forth in Committee, soon exposed him to the mild ridicule of his colleagues.

The first draft of Zaksas' official report on the Declaration was torn to shreds in Committee, and a second version was handled almost as roughly. Some tragicomic scenes occurred in the Com-mittee room, with Zaksas at one point being baited by René Capitant until he wept with rage. For a while it seemed that the Committee might have to mark time for a few days in order to permit someone else to write a substitute report, but a subcom-mittee finally helped Zaksas turn out a satisfactory revision, and thus assured him of his brief moment in the spotlight. When the Assembly eventually adjourned, the Socialists found Zaksas a dis-tant if not congenial civil service post in central Africa. One un-kind spirit thereupon wrote his political epitaph by defining Zaksas as "an eastern European dialect now spoken only on the banks of the Congo."

Few deputies had any illusions as to the practical importance of the Declaration, even though its moral influence might be great. Pascal Copeau's phrase "civic sermonizing," used in connection with a Right-wing proposal to add a Declaration of Duties, might have been applied to the Declaration of Rights as well, since there would be no sanctions to enforce it. But the Declaration did provide the opposition parties with useful propaganda weapons, for it had already aroused the hostility of some sections of public opinion. The church hierarchy was up in arms because there was no guarantee of liberty of instruction; some farmers were nervous over the definition of property rights; and the Committee's refusal to add a flat guarantee of freedom of the press was suddenly being inflated into a major threat to democracy.

A flood of more than eighty amendments met the project on the floor, most of them proposed by the small Center and Right groups, a few by the M.R.P. Both the Socialists and the Communists stood foursquare behind the Committee's draft: the former because it best reflected their doctrines, the latter for reasons of "political opportunity," as Jacques Duclos explained with his usual jovial irony. Duclos made it plain that the Communists did not take the contents of the Declaration very seriously. In contrast to 1789, he observed, the France of 1946 "has no new social order to offer as an example to the world. . . . I do not hesitate to confess that we can complete the Declaration of 1789 not so much by texts as by acts." But the Communists were determined not to let the debate degenerate into a long dog-fight over amendments which might thus delay and perhaps endanger the adoption of the entire constitution. "Let us be wise enough," cried Duclos, "to subordinate the secondary to the essential; let us hasten to give a new constitutional base to the French Republic."

The Radicals, U.D.S.R., and Right wing found themselves in an excellent tactical position, since they could come forward as the only true defenders of civil liberties and of the immortal Declaration of 1789. They charged that the Left wing had actually repudiated the principles of 1789 instead of expanding and "prolonging" them, as Guy Mollet and Zaksas insisted was the case. They ridiculed the Left-wing thesis that the Declaration of 1789 was merely a "charter of the triumphant bourgeoisie," which should now be modernized into a "Declaration of the Rights of

Man and of the Worker." They balked at the Socialist-Communist tendency to see human rights and liberties as relative things which may change as society and its structure evolve. Instead, they proclaimed, certain rights are absolute and eternal, sound in all times and places, as valid in 1946 as they were in 1789.

The M.R.P.'s position was more embarrassed. It was determined to put up one more fight for its doctrine of pluralistic democracy, but it was not sure how far to push the fight. In the end, the M.R.P. straddled. It joined the Radicals and Right to back a considerable number of unsuccessful amendments. On the other hand, the M.R.P. decided to make a showdown issue of only one article —that dealing with education. On this issue the Catholic hierarchy had been beating the drums so loudly that the M.R.P. had to listen. The General Assembly of Cardinals and Archbishops of France on March 13 had announced that no Catholic could accept a constitution without a flat guarantee of church schools. It took real courage for the M.R.P. leaders to resist such pressure, yet they did resist and ended by accepting a compromise. Since they could not persuade the Left to guarantee liberty of instruction outright, they assented to a Left-wing offer to drop out a phrase describing education as a public service. That phrase might have made education subject to a complete state monopoly, like any other public utility. Omitting it meant by implication that church schools would not be closed, and that the current modus vivendi (operation of church schools, but without subsidies) would be maintained.

For a time it looked as though the M.R.P.'s retreat on the school issue might cost it church support. The Right-wing P.R.L., which hoped that the hierarchy's blessing might be transferred to its own brow, loudly denounced the M.R.P. as a band of traitors who had accepted the "Godless" school. The campaign worried the M.R.P., but in the end the hierarchy refused to break with a party of the future in favor of a party of the past.

The issue of freedom of the press offered the Radicals and Right an excellent opportunity to brand the Declaration as antidemocratic. The Committee's draft provided that "any man is free to speak, write, print, publish; he may, either through the press or in any other manner, express, circulate, and defend any opinion to the extent that he does not abuse this right, notably with a view to violating the liberties guaranteed by this Declaration or injuring the reputation of any individual." This guarantee seemed sweeping enough, but Edouard Herriot as spokesman for the opposition demanded that there be added one simple phrase, "Freedom of the press is guaranteed." From this springboard Herriot launched into an attack on the government's press policy since liberation. He repeated the old charges that the Center and Right-wing press was muzzled, and that the Radicals had been forced to fight the October election campaign "with wooden swords against machine-gun nests." He alleged that so long as official permits were required to start a new paper, the strongest parties would possess totalitarian power.

The dispute in this case concerned practical politics rather than principles, yet there was a principle behind the Left's refusal to accept an outright guarantee of freedom of the press. Socialists and Communists argued that such a guarantee would actually restore the false liberty and the license of the prewar press. It would prevent the repression of libelous sheets like *Gringoire*, and would throw the press back into the pockets of moneyed or foreign interests. The charge of muzzling since liberation they described as a red herring. Current restrictions on publishing, they argued, were necessary and temporary evils because of the severe paper shortage. Here again, the Assembly split over a fundamental question: are liberties safe once they are made contingent rather than absolute? It was the same question which underlay the long dispute over the nature of property rights. The Left accepted Lacordaire's dictum that "between the weak and the strong, it is liberty which oppresses and it is the law which offers freedom." They rejected Herriot's proposition, but in doing so handed the enemies of the constitution an excellent battle cry for use in the referendum.

After seven days of oratory during which, as Pierre Hervé put it, "the saliva of 1946 ran as red as the blood of 1789," all thirty-nine articles of the Declaration were at last approved. The Socialists and Communists had beaten off every important amendment, but the margin had usually been narrow because the M.R.P. so often joined the opposition. In consequence, it would be easy to convince the voters that the Declaration was a purely Marxist and revolutionary document—which was far from being the case. The Center and Right were prepared to show the voters that freedom of the press and of education had been thrown out the window, and that no citizen's property would henceforth be safe. They also heaped ridicule upon the Declaration for its awkward style, its compromising and equivocal nature on some points, and its tendency to be a catch-all. One critic sarcastically remarked that only a single right of man had not been mentioned: "Imbecility being unfathomable, its expression is solemnly guaranteed by the present document."

In fact, the Declaration was far less dangerous than its enemies tried to paint it. It indicated a state of mind—a belief in collectivism and a directed economy—with which some might not sympathize, but it certainly was not built on a totalitarian philosophy. *Combat* accurately described it as a temporary nonaggression pact among the three major parties. Interpreted by democratic leaders, it offered the possibility of greater social justice than did the historic Declaration of 1789. An antidemocratic party might of course use it to destroy all personal liberties; but such a party would hardly be deterred by any collection of thirty-nine commandments. As a set of principles, the Declaration offered hope of a better future for the common man. Viewed from the angle of practical politics, however, it unquestionably helped to defeat the constitution in the May referendum.

X. PIERRE COT, CONSTITUTIONAL OBSTETRICIAN

"On the seventh day of the creation, having contemplated the work of tripartism, the M.R.P. took alarm. It recoiled before the prospect of government by Convention." So wrote a prominent commentator immediately after the rupture of April 3. Figuratively speaking, it was indeed the seventh day when the breach came. Less than a week remained before François de Menthon was scheduled to present the text of the constitution for debate on the floor of the Assembly. The M.R.P.'s *coup de théâtre* left politicians wondering whether all hope of a three-party agreement had been destroyed, and whether the Left could find an adequate last-minute substitute for De Menthon in the key post of reporter-general.

Despite the shock caused by De Menthon's resignation, it was generally believed that a solution would be found. The gap between the M.R.P. and the Communists did not seem too wide to be bridged, especially in view of the possible results of a failure to bridge it. The Left therefore maintained all the concessions which it had previously made, in the hope that the M.R.P. might still be tempted to change its mind. The tempo of interparty negotiations was stepped up rapidly during the two remaining weeks, both in Auriol's office and in the Constitutional Committee; and beginning on April 9, floods of eloquence were let loose on the floor of the Assembly itself.

Viewed in retrospect, these two final weeks leave an impression of shadowboxing and total futility. The net result was zero, for neither the M.R.P. nor the Communists gave way on any important point. If anything, both rivals became more intransigent once the initial plunge had been taken, and each one blamed its enemy for blocking a viable compromise. A prominent M.R.P. official privately expressed the conviction that the Communists had deliberately decided to block a compromise in order to drive a further wedge between the Socialists and the M.R.P. The M.R.P.'s genuine suspicion of Communist motives was buttressed by partisan interest. M.R.P. leaders realized that if they were to give in to Left-wing demands, many of their voters would "jump ship." An M.R.P. caucus examined this potential loss and estimated that the party's strength might be cut by one-third. These lost voters would be attracted to the minority parties of Center and

Right which would capitalize on the M.R.P.'s "treachery" and "weakness."

As for the Communists, they seemed to enjoy a heads-I-win, tails-you-lose position. If the M.R.P. should eventually capitulate, the Communists would get the kind of constitution they wanted and would wreck the M.R.P. If the M.R.P. should hold out, it would bear the overt responsibility for the breakdown in three-party unity, and would permit the Left-wing parties to back the constitution alone as proletarian brothers-in-arms against the "forces of reaction." The Communists reflected that France had never in its history answered "no" in a plebiscite or referendum, and that the French were thirsty for an end to the provisional period. The gamble therefore seemed safe enough, and Jacques Duclos publicly announced that his party was indifferent to the M.R.P.'s final choice.

Of all the questions raised by the rupture of April 3, the most pressing was that of a successor to De Menthon as Reporter-General. De Menthon had been preparing for the task for four months; his successor would have little more than four days. The Left-wing parties looked over the field and found only one man equipped to perform such a feat—Pierre Cot. Unfortunately, Cot had lately resigned both from the Committee and from the Radical Socialist party after a series of squabbles with his group. He had shifted over to the M.U.R.F., a tiny faction of Communist affiliates. By a complex bit of sleight of hand, Cot was given a seat on the Committee as the M.U.R.F.'s representative, and was immediately named Reporter-General by the Socialist-Communist majority while the other committeemen looked on in sour silence.

The adopted father of the completed constitutional draft was probably better fitted for his arduous task than any other man in the Assembly. A brilliant orator, persuasive, fluent, and subtle, widely read and thoroughly versed in constitutional law, Cot scorned the idea of jamming the project through the Assembly with Socialist and Communist support alone. His goal was to convince the M.R.P. and the other opposition parties that the Committee's draft was by no means so bad as they believed it to be.

The draft, according to Cot, contained a system which would lie midway between classical parliamentary government on the one hand and government by assembly on the other. The system, he explained, was based on the concept of checks and balances rather than separation of powers. He described the separation of powers principle as an antiquated one, like the flywheel of a primitive steam engine, while the Committee's blueprint would resemble the complex set of highly integrated parts which make up a modern airplane motor. This up-to-the-minute mechanism, Cot promised, would give France a government "more powerful, stronger and more democratic than before the war." To support his check-and-balance thesis, Cot pointed to the existence of various limitations on the sovereign assembly: a president of the republic who could not be overthrown; a body of judges supervised by a new High Council of the Judiciary; two advisory councils to help guide the assembly's work; and local councils throughout France and the French Union to balance the central power.

If Cot's sophistry did not convince the opposition parties, his virtuosity won their admiration. From April 9 to 19, his figure dominated the public debate. Pacing from end to end of the tribune, tossing off Latin phrases and *bons mots* with the greatest of ease, he orated, reasoned, pleaded with the stubborn recalcitrants to come into the fold. No one could doubt that Cot thoroughly enjoyed the limelight, and that he was not insensible to the idea that history might record the admiration which his hearers felt. It was no mean opportunity to be the potential Hérault de Séchelles of the twentieth century—provided, of course, that one did not have to end like Hérault at the guillotine. And indeed, Cot came as near to evangelizing the Assembly as any man could have done. No irritation or bitterness ever showed in his attitude, even when the opposition baited him. With full good humor and an apparently sincere desire to meet the critics halfway, he toiled till the very last moment in the cause of unity.

Cot's task was an exceptionally difficult one. What he hoped to do was to convince the opposition groups that they had misunderstood the Committee's draft, and had taken the appearance for the reality. His position would have been far stronger if he could have presented an unadulterated draft of the Communist type, frankly establishing a system of government by assembly. In committee, Cot had pleaded for such a system and had called it by name. As Reporter-General, his case for the Committee's draft had to be based on a grudging admission that government by assembly was not adapted to France's current needs, and that it might actually be a dangerous type of regime. He therefore had to spend most of his time trying to prove that several feeble checks on the Assembly would add up to something really effective.

The M.R.P.'s position, as stated from the tribune by De Menthon, was that even though the draft did not expressly create a system of government by assembly, it did not contain enough guarantees against such a system. De Menthon pointed out that his party had renounced its concept of pluralism in order to reach a compromise, but it would not renounce its demand for real counterweights to the assembly's power. The M.R.P.'s remaining wants were few: it asked only that the president be elected by two houses of parliament instead of one, and that the Council of the Republic be recognized as an upper house of parliament with strictly limited powers. The M.R.P. was ready to submerge all its other grievances if it could attain those two goals.

A more sweeping type of opposition came from the U.D.S.R. and the Right wing. René Capitant, their most effective spokesman, rejected the Committee's "system of false beards" which disguised what he called "the absolute monarchy of the assembly." He demanded that instead of a "confusion of powers" the proper goal should be an equilibrium between the executive and legislative branches. Neither Capitant nor any other orator advocated the American presidential system; but he insisted on a bicameral legislature and on the grant of full dissolution power to the executive. He and Edouard Herriot charged that the project made the president merely "a clerk and postman," and added that the judiciary would come under political control because half the members of the new High Council of the Judiciary would be named by the Assembly. The Committee's draft, Capitant concluded, "may be the constitution of the Germanic Holy Roman Empire, but it is not the constitution of the French Republic."

In a desperate effort to break the log jam, Vincent Auriol resumed his daily sessions with the leaders of the big three, but neither side would budge. The Communists and Socialists were so suspicious of a new Senate that they refused even to let the debates of the Council of the French Union be published in the *Journal Officiel* along with those of the Assembly. Auriol finally got the Left to agree that the Council's proceedings might be published in a semiofficial Special Bulletin, but the M.R.P. scornfully rejected the proposal as a farcical bit of window dressing. The dispute was carried to the ridiculous point of discussing whether or not the word *Officiel* added to the title *Bulletin Special* might satisfy the bicameralists without frightening the unicameralists. A group of medieval scholastics could not have done much better.

By April 16, the Assembly had adopted all except a few controversial articles which were still under Auriol's microscope. The showdown could be put off no longer, for the Assembly's final vote was scheduled for April 19. Paul Coste-Floret on behalf of the M.R.P. put the first of a series of critical amendments, proposing to describe the Council of the French Union as a second chamber of parliament. Prior to the balloting, Coste-Floret compared his proposal to the historic Wallon amendment of 1875, whose adoption by a margin of one vote had permitted the republicans to accept the constitution of the Third Republic. The Left, ignoring the threat, rejected the proposal by 288 to 260.

From that moment—barring a political miracle—compromise became almost hopeless. On April 18, President Gouin himself walked unannounced into the Assembly and made a desperate appeal that men of good will submerge their differences. He warned that a further extension of provisional government would endanger democracy and would "build the foundations of French policy on sand." Gouin characterized his intervention as "a cry of alarm which, in spite of everything, can still be a cry of hope and union." The Assembly rose to a man and lustily sang the *Marseillaise*, but the effect of Gouin's appeal was nevertheless worse than dubious. The M.R.P. bitterly resented it as an unfair attempt to use presidential pressure, and a Right-wing deputy called out mockingly that De Gaulle never would have used such tactics.

That evening the lights in Auriol's office burned till midnight, while he made one final effort to bring the party leaders together. Never before had the great compromiser seemed so close to success, even though he could now offer nothing more than face-saving solutions. Auriol proposed that the debates of the Council of the French Union be published in the *Journal Officiel*, and that the president of the republic be elected by the Assembly plus two hundred special electors. Both Maurice Schumann for the M.R.P. and Pierre Hervé for the Communists took a conciliatory attitude, but as usual they could not bind their parties and therefore had to refer the plan to their respective caucuses. On the morning of April 19, while the Socialist and M.R.P. groups were still deep in debate, the Communists voted to reject the Auriol compromises, and anounced their decision in a communiqué to the press. This communiqué they sent directly to the M.R.P.'s caucus room, where it naturally broke up the meeting and relieved the M.R.P. from making a choice. The Communists made their gesture even more brusque by by-passing the Socialist caucus— perhaps in order to avert a desperate Socialist effort to hold things together. Thus the lines were drawn beyond any possibility of change when the Assembly met for the final vote.

The session of April 19, even though its outcome was foreordained, had the atmosphere of one of the great days of French parliamentary history. Packed galleries and crowded benches heard each party's star performer recapitulate his group's past and present stand. It was a solemn and impressive oratorical display, but it had no more effect than writing on water. When the ballots were cast that night, the Communists, M.U.R.F., and Socialists were joined by only nine bolters from the Center groups (eight of them from the colonies). The constitution, instead of being a bond of unity, had produced a clear split between Left and Right. Pierre Cot's evangelism had brought meager results; but the draft had gotten past its first test, and by a sufficiently impressive margin (309 to 249) to make its fate seem safe in the referendum. There seemed no reason for Cot to be disturbed at a Right-wing deputy's parting shot: "I hope that you may enjoy a long life, *monsieur le rapporteur-général*, but as for your constitution, it is about to die!"

XI. REVOLUTION IN A SPARE MOMENT

During the dark days of the German occupation, resistance leaders had dreamed of a purer and stronger France whose democratic spirit would be revealed in the economic and social as well as the political sphere. Utopia was still far off when the first Constituent Assembly convened; but when the Assembly adjourned on April 26, it could point with pride to a list of reforms which for bulk (if not for quality) broke all French legislative records.

Many of those reforms were jammed through during the final week of the session, after the Assembly had completed its major task of constitution-making. The Center and Right-wing parties urged adjournment as soon as the constitution was adopted. Their aim was to get back to their districts for the referendum campaign; their argument was that "structural reforms" could wait until after the people had judged the new constitution. The Left-wing parties, however, insisted that there must be no delay. They feared that the next legislature might not contain a clear Left-wing majority committed to economic reform. Besides, they felt that it might be unhealthy to go before their voters without a record of promises fulfilled. Therefore they voted to continue the session for one more week, and fell to the task of legislation with buzz-saw speed. The climax came during the final twenty-four hours, which saw the remarkable total of thirty-five new laws placed on the books.

When the Assembly adjourned, France found itself endowed with a mixed economy, partly socialized and partly capitalist, with broad state control over most aspects of economic life. State ownership and operation were extended to the Bank of France and the four largest deposit banks, the insurance business, and the gas, electricity, and coal industries. In addition, the Assembly broadened the system of old-age pensions to cover most citizens; it reinforced the social security laws, notably with respect to miners; it extended the powers of the new plant production committees set up by De Gaulle; and it improved the status of tenant farmers and share-croppers (who cultivate approximately half the arable land in France) by the adoption of an omnibus bill protecting them against such injustices as arbitrary eviction and encouraging them to become landowners. It pointed the way toward a new colonial policy by promoting the natives to full citizenship, by abolishing all forms of forced labor in the empire, and by establishing an "overseas development fund" to finance projects of economic and social betterment.

The Assembly's record in the field of nationalizations will doubtless serve as its most lasting monument. Ever since Popular Front days, and even more since liberation, the idea of expropriating "the trusts" had possessed a powerful appeal both as a plan of reform and as a slogan. Few Frenchmen had any clear idea of the economic factors involved in such a program of nationalizations, but many of them felt that it would broaden the distribution of wealth and would break the political influence of big financial and industrial interests. They had not forgotten the peculiarly narrow and short-sighted attitude of most French capitalists toward essential social reforms before 1940. After 1944 the idea took on a kind of mystic quality; it seemed to symbolize progress toward a new era and to offer a cure for most social and economic ills. This intense popular reaction against the economic oligarchies was another face of the revulsion against the political system of the Third Republic. Good patriots felt that the old regime's economic structure as well as its political machinery had helped bring on the disaster of 1940. The pro-Vichy record of many of the so-called two hundred families and of the upper bourgeoisie in general added fuel to the antitrust sentiment. In March 1944, even the

Right-wing members of the National Resistance Council signed a program calling for "the eviction of the great economic and financial feudalities from control of the French economy"; and De Gaulle added his approval in cloudy but unmistakable terms.

After liberation, however, it became clear that there were varying concepts of how, when, and what to nationalize. The Rightists, once they had begun to regain some self-confidence, showed that they had not departed from classical liberalism except under pressure, and that they did not intend to be pushed very far from home base. André Philip ironically characterized their utopia as "a free fox in a free hen coop." The M.R.P. accepted the principle of a directed and semi-collectivized economy, but wished to move in that direction slowly and cautiously. Only the Socialists and Communists remained intransigent; they demanded that a long list of industries be expropriated with little or no compensation, and that these enterprises be run by boards of state, labor, and consumer representatives.

During De Gaulle's year in power, only halting steps were taken to reform the economic structure. Before the Assembly met, he had nationalized or seminationalized only the coal mines of the northeast, the Renault automobile plant, the Gnome-et-Rhône aircraft motor works, and the commercial air line Air-France. De Gaulle argued that the French economy should contain the widest possible "free sector," with state ownership applied only to a few monopolies. The state's role, in his eyes, was not to operate the economic system but to guide and plan. "We insist," he declared, "that the state should keep the levers of control in its own hands. . . . It is the role of the state . . . to prevent groupings of private interests from running counter to the general interest." But, he added, hasty and ill-advised measures would be likely to defeat their purpose. No enterprise should be taken over until plans had been thoroughly worked out in advance.

The Left's victory in the October 1945 elections forced De Gaulle to move ahead more rapidly. He therefore sponsored the bank nationalization bill, which was his first and only fundamental "reform of structure." By this measure the state took over the Bank of France (which enjoys a monopoly of note issue), as well as four deposit banks which together held fifty-five per cent of the country's total bank deposits. Control of each bank was entrusted to a board of directors appointed in part by the Minister of Finance and in part by the bank employees' trade unions. In addition, loan policy was vested in a new national credit council representing labor, agriculture, commerce, and in general all branches of activity in France. By this reform, the famous *mur d'argent* which in prewar days had blocked a number of Left-wing cabinets was at least partially razed. The Left complained, however, that De Gaulle had been too timid. It held that more banks should have been nationalized; that the general public should have been given representation on the boards of directors; and that the former owners should not have been compensated so generously (with negotiable government securities bearing 3 per cent interest).

De Gaulle's resignation in January freed the Left-wing majority from its major restraint. His successor, Félix Gouin, announced a long list of enterprises which the new government intended to nationalize. Time was short, however; only three months of the session remained, and each nationalization bill was so complex that it required long study in committee. Only three bills could be reported out by April, and they emerged from committee only after the most strenuous efforts.

A measure providing for state ownership and operation of the gas and electricity industries ran into especially rough weather. The economic liberals of the Center and Right flatly opposed it, the M.R.P. insisted that the expropriated owners ought to be compensated with securities bearing 3½ per cent interest, and the Communists and Socialists split over the issue of centralized versus decentralized organization. The Left-wing parties finally worked out a painful compromise, agreeing to set up two national public corporations for gas and for electricity, but permitting regional and intermunicipal operation within these corporations.

The insurance and coal industries offered fewer headaches.

Only the largest insurance companies were taken over; all together, they handled sixty-five per cent of the business in France. Each one was permitted to keep its individuality, and was placed under a tripartite board of directors, representing the government, the public, and the insurance workers. A national insurance council was created to furnish over-all guidance. The coal industry was concentrated in a single public corporation, the *Charbonnages de France*, with regional subsidiary organizations in the various coal basins. In each case, the Left wing's cherished formula of tripartite boards of directors was adopted; and in each case, the ex-owners were compensated with government securities.

The coal nationalization bill, jammed through on the eve of adjournment after a ludicrous debate of an hour and a half on the floor, brought to a temporary end the Fourth Republic's march toward collectivism. Six weeks later, a general election wiped out the Left's clear majority, and convinced the Socialists and Communists that their strategy of haste in preference to careful planning had been a wise one. They had placed on the books a first installment of structural reforms before it was too late; time and experience, they felt, would bring efficiency into the newly nationalized enterprises.

It was perhaps inevitable that most of the state-run industries should fall into a condition of near-chaos during the months that followed, and that almost every one should go heavily into the red. In addition, political wirepulling sometimes took precedence over the public interest in setting up the new boards of directors. For example, the board of directors for the coal industry, appointed by the Communist Minister of Industrial Production, turned out to be almost solidly Communist in membership; and the nomination of directors for the nationalized banks produced violent disputes between the Left (who wanted to appoint trade union officials) and the M.R.P. (who wanted "technicians"). But these weaknesses, the Left believed, were temporary ones. A great many Frenchmen looked with sympathy on the experiment of a mixed economy, half-collectivist and half-liberal. They hoped that it might serve as a workable compromise between divergent economic doctrines, and that it might prove to be the best potential barrier against totalitarianism.

The economic sphere was not the only one in which the Assembly carried out revolutionary changes. Some Frenchmen viewed as even more drastic the law which closed all licensed brothels in France. This shift from an historic policy of licensed regulation to one of outright abolition was essentially the work of the M.R.P., whose program of protection to the family and stimulation of the birth rate logically required a more rigid repression of organized vice.

Prior to adoption, the bill stirred up a lengthy debate in the country, with the experts on social hygiene dividing almost evenly. Its sponsors produced statistics to show that venereal disease in Paris had increased tenfold between 1939 and 1945, while its opponents argued that a prewar abolition experiment in Strasbourg had backfired and had actually raised the disease rate. The controversy became so warm that even political arguments were dragged in. Abolitionists charged that the Gestapo had found the *maisons de tolérance* a fertile field for their investigations after 1940; partisans of licensed regulation retorted that the prewar abolitionist leaders in Alsace (where the movement had then centered) had turned out to be pro-Nazi. A Communist paper solemnly reported that the brothel-keepers were pouring heavy subsidies into the coffers of the P.R.L. The measure was finally adopted by a special no-debate procedure, which spared all parties the necessity of taking a public stand or casting a recorded vote.

Another knotty problem tackled by the Assembly concerned the status of the new post-liberation press. In 1944, the publishers of clandestine newspapers had seized all plants and offices which had operated during the Vichy period. De Gaulle had approved these seizures, but as the months passed it became obvious that a policy of "squatters' rights" could not continue forever. No problem was involved where the plants of outright collaborationist sheets were involved, for such property was subject to confiscation as soon as the courts returned a guilty verdict. In many cases, however, legal action had not yet been taken against the owners, and grave doubt often existed as to whether there was valid proof of collaboration with the Germans. Acquittal would entitle the owners to demand the immediate return of their plants, which in turn would force one or more resistance newspapers out of business.

The Assembly was faced by a choice not between pure justice and rank injustice, but between old and new vested rights. Its decision, more political than juridical, was in favor of the squatters. It transferred to the state the property of all publishing and advertising agencies which had continued to function during the German occupation. Even those owners who might eventually be acquitted of collaboration charges were denied the right to recover their property, but they were to be granted compensation. All such property was turned over to a government agency, which was empowered to administer it and to arrange for its sale or lease to organs of the post-liberation press. Cries of anguish went up from the Center and Right-wing parties, which would have gained new support in the newspaper field if the property had been restored to its original owners. Their appeals to abstract justice might have been more convincing if the owners in question could have pointed to prewar records of honesty and integrity in the journalistic field and to active participation in the anti-German resistance.

When the Assembly at last adjourned, it could look back upon an impressive list of achievements, but it could not expect to receive much applause from the country at large. The first six months of revived democratic government had struck a sour note. It was rare to find a private citizen who had a good word to say for the expiring Assembly. Even members of the majority parties took up a defensive attitude; Edouard Depreux, head of the Socialist parliamentary group, found it necessary to lecture readers of the party organ *Populaire* on their general tendency to disparage the Assembly. Hostile critics of the more violent sort branded it as "a circus" or a collection of total incompetents.

"Soon," declaimed a Radical leader, "nothing but ashes and dust will remain of this rotten Constituent." When De Gaulle left office, a Rightist editor blazoned the headline, "Triumph of the Eunuchs"; and *Combat* once called on the deputies to give up and go home.

Much of this criticism was undeserved, and some of it was dangerous. The Assembly's faults as well as its virtues were derived from its democratic nature; many of those who condemned it were consciously or unconsciously condemning representative government in France. If first-rate talent and unselfish statesmanship were rare, that was because the Assembly contained a fairly faithful cross section of the French people as a whole. The deputies may have lacked experience, but their per capita content of idealism and good intentions was probably above normal. Most of them sincerely wished to use their office to help rebuild and rejuvenate France; they chafed at their seven-month deadline and at the stifling discipline of the new party system.

Some critics justly felt that the deputies suffered from a kind of political astigmatism. They never quite managed to put postwar problems in their proper perspective, to focus sharply on the task of getting France back on its feet. As a result, wrote the penetrating commentator André Stibio, "the Assembly's work will always give the impression of having been written on the margin of the nation's existence, of its misery, its confusion, the vital problems which it must face." This failure to get at the root of France's ills was, however, not peculiar to the politicians. It was shared by General de Gaulle and by a heavy proportion of the French people as well.

Some of the most biting criticism was aimed at the rigidity of the party system, which, it was alleged, falsified democracy by acting as a screen between the French people and their government. Much was made of the "three orchestras" which constituted the Assembly, of the "laic and obligatory Holy Trinity" which perpetuated itself through the new electoral system. The attacks had their ironic aspect, for one generally accepted flaw of the Third Republic had been the indiscipline and multiplicity of parties. The critics failed to explain how representative government could work except through the medium of organized parties. Perhaps the party system did stiffen the barriers between various segments of political opinion, and make the task of compromise more difficult. But at bottom, the parties simply mirrored the deeply divided opinions of the French people as a whole. Until most Frenchmen could agree on a common minimum of aims and methods in government, democracy was likely to function in a halting and ineffective manner. That discouraging lesson at least should have been implicit in the record of the first Constituent Assembly.

XII. STILLBIRTH OF
A CONSTITUTION

André Le Troquer, the one-armed Socialist Minister of Interior, was noted for what the French call un caractère difficile. Shortly before the Assembly adjourned, an M.R.P. deputy asked him if a "no" majority in the referendum would wipe out the new electoral law as well as the constitution. "The conclusion is correct," remarked Le Troquer acidly, "but the hypothesis is absurd."

Le Troquer's comment may have been effective sarcasm, but it was bad prophecy. It nevertheless reflected the state of mind of the Socialists and Communists, who saw no need to fear the country's verdict. In the October 1945 elections, the two parties together had polled 49.8 per cent of the total vote, and they felt sure that enough Center and Right voters would join them to raise the figure by five or ten per cent. They reminded themselves again that France had never answered "no" to any past referendum or plebiscite, and they reflected that the phrase "Il faut sortir du provisoire" ought to be worth several hundred thousand votes.

The campaign for and against ratification, billed at first as a battle of ideas, quickly turned into a battle of slogans. The contents of the constitution lay almost forgotten while the Communists cried, "Bar the way to reaction!" and the M.R.P. warned, "Block the threat of one-party dictatorship!" The Communist-controlled C.G.T. found even more curious virtues hidden in the constitution: "Vote 'yes,'" it proclaimed, "in order to give the French people more food, more clothing, shoes, and household utensils at reasonable prices." The Right triumphantly announced that the daughters of Clemenceau and Foch were voting "no," while the Left replied that the National Federation of Tuberculous Persons had officially gone on record for "yes." Only a minority of citizens got around to reading the constitutional draft and basing their decisions on what they found there.

Most politicians regarded the referendum as a warm-up bout before the main event, which would be the general elections soon to follow. That was notably true of the Radicals and the P.R.L., both of whom were brimming with confidence. "The wind is swelling our sails!" Edouard Herriot had cried at the recent Radical Congress; and P.R.L. leaders privately predicted that they would win from 100 to 150 seats in the next legislature. They therefore toured the country with the warning that civil liberties were in danger and that an eventual Communist dictatorship lurked behind the innocent-looking constitutional façade. What right-thinking citizen, they asked, could accept this "monster born of tripartite fornications"?

It was the M.R.P. which carried the real burden of the fight against the constitution, and which was eventually to reap most of the electoral profit. Maurice Schumann sounded the M.R.P.'s keynote, warning that it would be safer to "remain provisionally upon the republican path rather than to enter definitively upon the road to dictatorship." Georges Bidault assured the voters that another seven months of provisional government would have no ill effects on French diplomacy, and implied that a "no" majority would reassure the Anglo-Saxon powers. The Catholic hierarchy gave almost solid support to the anticonstitutional forces, although public statements by the bishops were carefully ambiguous. The Church's choice was easy to make when the M.R.P. and Right

were on the same side of the fence. M.R.P. leaders also hoped until the last moment that Charles de Gaulle might break his self-
imposed silence and come to their support. But De Gaulle sat
tight-lipped in his forest retreat, gambling on the M.R.P.'s ability
to win the fight without him. By this strategy he could continue to
pose as a national symbol above party disputes.

The campaign of the proconstitution forces was a lukewarm and
halfhearted affair, especially on the part of the Socialists. They
rejected a Communist offer to go before the country arm in arm,
as in Popular Front days. Such tactics, they felt, would encourage
the idea that the draft was purely Socialist and Communist in
inspiration. Therefore they convoked their followers to separate
meetings, and took the negative approach that any constitution
would be better than no constitution at all. Above all, urged André
Philip, France must avoid the appearance of living permanently in
a provisional status.

While the Socialists adopted the role of more or less brilliant
second, the Communists stumped the country with their customary vigor. In their enthusiasm, they made a strategic error
which may have cost them victory. They suggested that it was time
for France to try a government headed by a Communist; and the
old battle-cry began to go up in Communist mass meetings,
"Thorez au pouvoir!" The effect was electric. It gave the enemies
of the constitution a bogey to wave in front of hesitant voters, and
it both frightened and infuriated many Socialists. The latter felt
aggrieved that the Communists should want to replace Félix
Gouin with Thorez. In addition, many Socialists were still smarting from the outcome of the C.G.T.'s national congress in April,
when the Communists had ridden roughshod over the reformists
to take control of the trade-union movement. Communist leaders
quickly realized their error and tried to repair the damage, but it
was too late. To many potential "yes" voters, it seemed that the
Communists had admitted a connection between the new constitution and Communist hopes to take power in France.

In spite of this slip, the Left could still feel optimistic on the
eve of May 5. A French public-opinion poll showed a last-minute

"yes" majority of fifty-four per cent. Virtually every party leader and government official privately predicted that the constitution would carry by a narrow but safe margin. Even the heads of the M.R.P. were prepared to accept what seemed to be the inevitable, and to pin their hopes on the elections to follow.

Early on the morning after the referendum, the M.R.P. Minister of Justice reportedly telephoned to Minister of Interior Le Troquer and asked in perfect innocence by what margin the constitution had been ratified. A peppery exchange followed before Le Troquer realized that Teitgen had not been trying to rub in the Left's defeat. The "absurd hypothesis" had become a reality; fifty-three per cent of the electorate had rejected the constitution.

When the embarrassed false prophets examined the statistics, they could see clearly enough what had gone wrong. The Communists had held the support of their voters wherever they were strong, but the Socialists had suffered several hundred thousand desertions. The referendum, in the minds of many citizens, had turned into a plebiscite for or against the Communist party. Frenchmen ranging from Right-wing Socialists to the P.R.L. had decided that a "yes" majority might open the way to eventual totalitarian control by a single party. The fact that a heavy majority of them had not read the constitution was no deterrent to this belief. They had been told that the constitution was, or might be, dangerous; better, then, to vote it down and take no chances. Mixed in with this vague and inchoate reaction was a widespread tendency to vote "no" in general protest against the state of things in France—especially the continuing shortage of food and consumers' goods.

From the empire came returns which deserved more attention than they got. Without exception, wherever white colonist voters were in the majority the constitution was rejected; wherever native voters dominated it was approved. The key to these results was the fact that citizens alone were allowed to vote. Throughout North Africa, Black Africa, and Madagascar, citizenship was restricted almost entirely to the white colonists. They balked at the prospect of new political and social guarantees for the natives, at the threat that the white minority would be swamped by a flood of new citizens, and at the idea of relaxing the bonds of empire. Only in territories where the natives had long since been promoted from subject to citizen (Senegal, French India, and the four "old colonies") was the constitution approved by huge and triumphant majorities. These results suggested that the French Union problem had merely been skirted by the first Constituent Assembly, and that the new Assembly would find itself faced with a far more complex dispute. Upon its successful solution might depend the fate of the empire.

Some observers read into the referendum results a positive as well as a negative significance, and thought they detected a fundamental change in French political optics. Traditionally, any test of strength between Left and Right would find all Leftists rallying solidly against the clericals and the "forces of reaction." On May 5, instead, many moderate Leftists had joined the Right against a threat from the Communists. Some Frenchmen felt that if this trend were to continue, it would be "the most notable phenomenon in French political life since the Dreyfus affair." It might mean that part of the Left wing, rallying around the principle of human liberty, would modify Gambetta's phrase to read, "Le communisme, voilà l'ennemi!" The prospect brought a rebirth of hope in the minds of those who looked toward a powerful Left-Center bloc, linking together all the proponents of social justice through democratic methods. Time alone could confirm or refute this hope; much would depend on whether a threat from the Right might arise to outweigh the Communist danger.

All this, however, was speculation in May 1946. One thing was certain: six months of effort had gone for nothing, and at a time when France could ill afford such waste. Responsibility for the fiasco was shared by the Communists and the M.R.P., either of whom could have maintained three-party unity by retreating a single step during the last days of the constitutional debate. If the gap between them had been wide, deep, fundamental, then it would have been easy to understand their failure to get together. The fact that the gap was so narrow suggests that political calculations outweighed all other factors. As a result, division in the country was deepened, yet the issues were scarcely clearer than before. French democracy had revealed both its strength and its weaknesses in the months since its revival. No one could yet say which aspect would dominate; but at least democracy was still alive, and would have time for a second test of its resiliency.

CHAPTER SIX

Repeat Performance: The Second Constituent Assembly

I. THE WILL OF THE PEOPLE

No one could doubt that the people had spoken on May 5. The only question was, what had they said? The referendum had offered the voters a single choice: take the constitution or leave it. Their reply—and that by a narrow majority—had therefore been essentially negative. It was the task of the party leaders to read into the results such positive indications as might be discovered by a process of combined common sense and intuition.

Not only the answer given by the voters, but also the motivation for that answer, had been primarily negative. The majority had concluded that the so-called "Pierre Cot constitution" might serve the Communist party as a mechanism for arriving in power by legal methods. They felt that the heavy concentration of power in the unicameral assembly would leave no real constitutional barrier against the will of a single party which might sweep a general election. Few of them stopped to reflect that if the Communists should ever win a clear majority in the country, constitutional checks and balances would be mere tissue-paper barriers. Emotion rather than reason told them that somehow Communist strength ought to be channeled: that the Communists must be given a share of governmental power, but not so large a share as to endanger the republic.

Just how could a constitution assure such channeling? The answer was not very clear in the voters' minds. They felt vaguely that safety might lie in distributing power among several organs of government, even at the cost of speed and efficiency. If they favored granting a little more independence to the executive, their purpose was not to make the government more vigorous but rather to set up a barrier against the spread of Communism. By a curious irony, a majority of Frenchmen had already reached the point where they were more concerned with governmental brakes than with accelerators. The constitutional problem had come to be dominated by a double negative: the fear of a strong man, the fear of a strong party, either of whom might be suspected of wishing to destroy democracy. So long as such a man and such a party existed in France, it was perhaps inevitable that the idea of making democracy work with vigor and efficiency should take a back seat.

The politicians had little time to reflect on the referendum results; they were swept at once into a new electoral campaign. For the parties which had won the referendum victory, it was an opportunity to follow up their advantage and to ride the wave of success. For the Left wing, an electoral victory would mean revenge, while a second defeat would be taken as proof that the post-liberation leftist tide had passed its crest and was beginning to recede.

In consequence, every party dodged the arid constitutional issue with conspicuous success. Most of the party newspapers, in *Combat's* ironic phrase, "maintained a studied silence, heavy with reciprocal suspicion and afterthoughts." Vague and resounding affirmations took the place of explicit proposals. The M.R.P. proclaimed that it had saved France from a system of government by assembly, and that it would now see to the creation of "a parliamentary regime whose powers will be in equilibrium, and a government which will be stable but controlled." These fine words were more than matched by the Communists, who promised that they would defend to the death those "humane and generous principles" in the defeated constitution, such as equal rights for women and freedom of conscience in a lay state, which the reactionaries were out to destroy.

Only the Socialists had something a little more tangible to offer; they disinterred Vincent Auriol's compromises which had almost brought the big three together in April. President Gouin publicly announced that the Socialists were ready to accept a two-house parliament, with the upper house empowered to help elect the president of the republic and to exercise a suspensive veto over legislation. He specified only that the upper house must not be a "younger brother" of the old Senate: that it must have no share in choosing, maintaining, or overthrowing the cabinet. Gouin's remarks suggested that the Socialists were ready to meet the M.R.P. at least halfway.

Some Socialists were ready to go even further. The lesson of the referendum, they felt, was that collaboration with the Communists could bring the Socialists nothing but disaster. A clean break at once, they argued, might still save the party in the June elections; it might win back the thousands of voters who had bolted in the referendum. Since the party's leadership was divided, Minister of Interior André Le Troquer decided to point the way himself. In a campaign speech, he brutally dragged into the open the Communists' record during the "phony war" period, and labeled Maurice Thorez a common deserter. Ever since Thorez' return from Moscow, anonymous posters had from time to time described him as "Maurice Thorez—*premier parti de France*," and slogans chalked on the walls had added, "*Pétain au pouvoir, Thorez au front!*" An attack by a cabinet minister, however, was something new. Other Socialist leaders, who had no desire to see the party split in two in the midst of the campaign, hastily repaired the breach. As Edouard Depreux put it, "We will never permit the reactionaries to arbitrate the difference which separates us from Bolshevism, for it is a conflict within the working class." Thus the Socialists continued to straddle, even though their internal division was obviously on the increase.

The tone of the electoral campaign was much more bitter and

THE SECOND CONSTITUENT ASSEMBLY

vindictive than had been the case in October. Not only were the
Socialists and Communists sniping at each other, but the M.R.P.
and P.R.L. were engaged in a thinly disguised civil war for the
official blessing of the clergy. The P.R.L. charged that the M.R.P.
had sold church schools down the river in the recent Assembly,
and hinted that the M.R.P.'s economic doctrines were probably
too extreme to please Rome. M.R.P. leaders were annoyed at this
campaign, yet at the same time they praised God for the existence
of a neighbor like the P.R.L., which could serve as lightning rod
for the charge of "reactionary." They predicted privately that the
P.R.L.'s attacks would not cost them more than ten per cent of
their support in the country. That limited loss, they added, would
be a blessing in disguise, since it would purge the party of Right-
wing hitch-hikers who opposed the M.R.P.'s social-economic doctrines.

The only sign of political harmony was to be found in the
Center, where the Radical Socialists and the U.D.S.R. announced
the formation of an electoral coalition with the formidable title
Rassemblement des gauches républicaines. This coalition was the
meager outcome of long and involved negotiations among the
leaders of a half-dozen splinter groups. The goal was to attract into
a new Center party the great mass of floating independent voters
whose temperament in prewar days had been Radical Socialist.
This mass of drifters, estimated to total from one to three million,
naturally fascinated a great many politicians who were fertile in
ideas but short of troops.

The principal obstacle to the success of the scheme was Edouard
Herriot, whose massive figure towered above the other Center
politicians. Herriot was too influential to be either absorbed or
by-passed; no plan could succeed without his approval. And it soon
became clear that Herriot's consent would depend on whether the
rattling Radical Socialist machine—and M. Herriot himself—were
to be made dominant in the proposed new party. The mountain's
labors therefore produced only the *Rassemblement* mouse, in
which the Radicals preserved their name and clear pre-eminence.
Limited though it was, the *Rassemblement* nevertheless turned

out to be more than a temporary electoral coalition. Its federal bonds became tighter in the months that followed, and it seemed destined to survive indefinitely unless a revival of Gaullism should produce a schism.

Election day on June 2 brought out the largest number of voters on record. Exactly as in the referendum, 47 per cent of those voters backed Socialist or Communist candidates while 53 per cent chose the parties which had fought the constitution. The Left-wing bloc thus lost the clear majority which it had enjoyed in the First Constituent. That result was expected; but more surprising was the distribution of strength within the Right and Left blocs. On the Left, the Socialists ran true to form by losing a third of a million votes; but the Communists, who in private had been more than pessimistic, actually marked up a slight increase in total popular vote. On the Right, the M.R.P. not only failed to decline as expected, but was hoisted overnight into the position of France's first party. No single party in any modern French election had attained the M.R.P. total of 28.2 per cent of the popular vote. The leading French public opinion poll, which had predicted 22 per cent for the M.R.P. on the eve of the election, retired in confusion to re-examine its methods. Meanwhile the *Rassemblement des Gauches* and the P.R.L., which had been tasting triumph for several weeks past, were bitterly disillusioned to find that neither one had made appreciable gains.

What kind of party had the M.R.P. become? As expected, it had lost some conservative votes to various Right-wing groups, but the loss had been more than offset by the M.R.P.'s absorption of a large share of the floating Center vote. To that extent, the party had shifted its center of gravity slightly away from the Right. However, many ultraconservative citizens had been forced to stick with the M.R.P. for lack of an alternative. Just prior to election day the P.R.L. had committed partial hara-kiri by withdrawing from the race in thirty districts and leaving the M.R.P. with no competition on its right. The P.R.L. had decided that its candidates in these districts had no chance of success, and would only divide the anti-Communist forces. Grudgingly, therefore, they left the field open to their chief rival in order to assure the defeat of their worst enemy. In so doing, they partially counterbalanced the M.R.P.'s shift away from the Right.

The M.R.P. victory further proved that most of the church hierarchy had refused to listen to the P.R.L.'s siren song. The clerics had perhaps concluded that the M.R.P.'s social program harmonized best with Catholic ideals as applied to conditions in France. Even more clearly, however, they could see that the M.R.P. offered the most promising barrier to the spread of Communism.

The Communists undeniably were the co-victors on June 2. Their ability to hold their five million voters immediately after the referendum fiasco was a tribute to their tenacity, their tight organization, their propaganda methods, and their effective leadership. Their prestige was bound to suffer slightly because they were no longer France's first party, and their tactical position was weakened by the disappearance of the Left-wing majority. But they viewed the results as good, far better than they had expected; and their leaders were privately jubilant.

It was the Socialist camp which wore the deepest mourning. Their setback, contrasting with their bright hopes in 1945, was not only a disappointment; it suddenly raised the specter of accelerating decline and eventual extinction. The fate of the British Liberals, ground under by two vigorous neighbors, was too recent and too near at hand to be overlooked. Off the record, many Socialists used harsh words toward their own leadership, and bewailed the internal division which had caused the party to zigzag between the M.R.P. and the Communists. One young deputy complained that his party's failure to choose a line and follow it consistently had alienated first one and then another group of voters. Furthermore, he added, the Socialists had aided both their rivals in the process. By working in alliance with the Communists, they had stamped the latter with the seal of democratic purity; by collaborating at other times with the M.R.P., they had strengthened the M.R.P.'s claim to be a true movement of the Left.

As Frenchmen studied the significance of the double victory scored by the M.R.P. and the Communists, they realized that their traditional multi-party system might be in the process of dissolution. For the first time in decades, there arose the prospect of a two-party system, in which minor groups might continue to exist, but only as satellites of the two giants of politics. Paradoxically, most Frenchmen were appalled at the idea. Even those who had long considered the multi-party structure a major source of instability hesitated to see power pass into the hands of two powerful political machines. But the real danger, they felt, was the division of France into Communist and anti-Communist blocs. They feared that such a split, far from simplifying and stabilizing the operation of the government along British or American lines, would be likely to lead toward eventual civil war, for the two parties would differ not on secondary issues but on the very fundamentals of political and social philosophy. Power could not alternate between two such blocs in the Anglo-Saxon manner. The republic could be either soviet or anti-soviet, but it could not conceivably be now one and now the other.

The Communists alone could foresee the development of two blocs with equanimity. Even the M.R.P., apparently marked by destiny to be the other survivor in the struggle for existence, rejected the idea of a two-party system. During the months that followed, M.R.P. leaders kept repeating that one of their major goals was to prevent such a development, notably by locking the gates between their party and the Right wing, and by consolidating the M.R.P. as a movement of the Center. They nevertheless clung to their highly centralized organization and their propaganda methods, and insisted that a monolithic party like the Communist could not be successfully opposed except by another monolith. Many Frenchmen wondered whether the M.R.P. could possibly stop the evolution which by now seemed well under way.

When party leaders shifted their field of vision to the overseas election results, they were suddenly struck by the possibility that the sixty-four "colonials," so obscure in the First Constituent Assembly, might actually hold the balance of power in the Second

Constituent. The elections confirmed the rough cleavage between French colonist and native voters which had already appeared in the referendum. Most of the colonists were by now obsessed by the Black Peril, and chose conservative deputies (usually U.D.S.R. or M.R.P.) committed to defend the rights of the white minority. Native political leaders, on the other hand, had definitely decided to throw in their lot with the Socialists or the Communists, who would fight to preserve the rights won in the defunct Assembly. As a result, the Left parties picked up additional strength in Black Africa, Madagascar, and the Antilles—not enough to offset the M.R.P. victory in continental France, yet sufficient to close the gap considerably.

Most striking of all were the Algerian results. In place of Dr. Bendjelloul's colorless group of "tame" Arabs who had sat in the First Assembly, a vigorous Arab party called "Friends of the Manifesto" swept eleven of the thirteen native seats. All of the Manifesto deputies, including their leader Ferhat Abbas, had just emerged from prison, where they had been held since the bloody Algerian riots of May 1945. Their program was little known in France, but it was presumed to be extreme. Abbas himself, a handsome, hawk-nosed pharmacist from Sétif, had once been a follower of Dr. Bendjelloul and an exponent of the complete assimilation of Algeria by France. He himself was a product of assimilation: educated in French Algerian schools, he was the son of an Arab official who had reached the dignity of Commander of the Legion of Honor. After serving as a volunteer on the Western front in 1939-40, Abbas had brusquely reversed his position, and in his Manifesto issued in 1943, had demanded "a free Algeria joined to a free France." Shortly after his election, he was credited with remarking that "the Algerians are tired of being the bastard sons of France." His declared goal was autonomy rather than complete independence, but there were some rumors of an alliance between Abbas and Messali Hajd, exiled leader of an extremist faction which demanded that all ties with France be broken. He was also known to be in contact with the Moslem reformist groups called the Oulemas, whose program was pan-Islamic. Time was to show, however, that Abbas was far more loyal to France than his chief rival Messali.

The effect which a noisy group of Algerian autonomists might have on the constitutional discussions was obvious. But in addition, party leaders quickly calculated that if Abbas should throw his strength to the Communists and Socialists, he would raise the Left wing's total to 293 votes, or exactly half the membership of the Assembly. The potential importance of the eleven-man Manifesto group was therefore far out of proportion to its size. In subsequent months, Abbas was to take full advantage of his key position, and to assume a role of peculiar importance in the new Assembly.

11. *"On prend les mêmes et on recommence"*

The "Re-Constituent" Assembly which convened on June 11 was a slightly altered carbon copy of its predecessor. Three-fourths of its members, including almost all the prominent ones, were repeaters, and its president was once again Vincent Auriol. The Socialist delegation had shrunk a little, and the M.R.P. had spilled over into the U.D.S.R. benches; but there was no sign of any sweeping change in French political forces. The voters had rejected the handiwork of the First Constituent, but they had returned most of the same men to have another try. That somewhat ironic situation was in part the result of proportional representation, which softened the effect of a shift in the popular vote, and which virtually guaranteed against defeat the top-ranking candidates of the major parties.

Only a few newcomers drew the attention of the galleries. Most of them were resurrected leaders of the Third Republic, who took seats either with the Radicals or the Right wing. There was dapper little Paul Reynaud, premier at the time of the 1940 collapse, who had spent the years between in Vichy jails. Reynaud's efforts to rebuild an important political following had failed, but he had finally decided to re-enter politics as an independent. Although it was unlikely that Reynaud could ever regain his prewar prestige, he did stand out as a skillful politician and first-rate speaker in the dreary wastes of the far Right. Edouard Daladier, the man of Munich, was back too: a gray and shadowy figure drifting almost unnoticed in and out of the legislative hall. Daladier had gone down to defeat in October under a hail of invective and overripe tomatoes; but in June, after what *Populaire* called a "semi-confidential" campaign in his old district, he had managed to squeeze back into office. Alongside Daladier on the Radical benches were two other former cabinet ministers, Paul Bastid, former member of the National Resistance Council, and Vincent de Moro-Giafferi, the eminent criminal lawyer.

Far over on the Right appeared General Henri Giraud, De Gaulle's pathetic rival for leadership at Algiers. Like a modern Cincinnatus in reverse, Giraud emerged from his military obscurity to win election on a joint Peasant-P.L.R. ticket. His second intrusion into politics was to prove as brief and unimpressive as his first at Algiers. Gray, distinguished, ramrod-straight, Giraud sat impassively on the independent benches, rising at rare intervals to warn his colleagues that the empire was in danger of disintegration. When the Assembly at last adjourned, Giraud retired from politics and was seen no more.

On the Left, in a small enclave between the Communists and the Socialists, sat Ferhat Abbas and his ten followers. The Assembly's secretariat had assigned them seats on the extreme Right, but Abbas had announced that if necessary he and his group would "sit standing" next to the Communists. The secretariat hastily capitulated and let the Algerians have their way.

The composition of the Constitutional Committee, like that of the Assembly, showed continuity rather than change. Twenty-five of the forty-two members were repeaters, and André Philip was returned by acclamation to the post of chairman. A few influential figures were missing: René Capitant (who had been beaten for re-election), François de Menthon and P. E. Viard of the M.R.P., and Congo-bound Gilbert Zaksas. But Pierre Cot was back in his old place, along with the M.R.P. spokesmen Coste-Floret and Teitgen, the Communists Fajon and Hervé, the Socialist Guy Mollet, and the synthetic Peasant Jacques Bardoux. As in the previous Committee, an M.R.P. deputy was made Reporter-General: Paul Coste-Floret stepped into the shoes of François de Menthon, who was in line for a cabinet post.

Bolstering the Committee as new arrivals were Paul Bastid, talented constitutional lawyer who was destined to replace Capitant as chief minority spokesman; Paul Ramadier, bearded Socialist lawyer and wheelhorse politician; and Count Lionel de Tinguy du Pouet, youthful M.R.P. deputy from the Vendée. A year of obscurity had allowed Ramadier to live down his record as Minister of Food Supply just after liberation, when he had been hanged in effigy on various street corners. Behind his kindly and unimpressive manner (his pseudonym in the resistance had been "Violette"), Ramadier possessed a remarkable knack for working out compromises among discordant factions. De Tinguy, a high-ranking civil servant who had spent the war years as a prisoner in Germany, was the son of a conservative deputy from France's most conservative department. He represented the extreme Right-wing faction within the M.R.P. The last important newcomer was Ferhat Abbas in person. Technically, Abbas had no right to a seat, since his group was not quite large enough to receive committee representation. The major parties, however, hesitated to keep Abbas out on a technicality. To the Communists, his presence was of great potential importance. If he could be counted on to line up with the Left, his ballot would give the Communists and Socialists twenty-one of the forty-two votes, and would allow the Left to block any M.R.P. or Right-wing proposal in Committee. The only difficulty was that the Communists could not be sure of Left-wing solidarity this time. In fact, most of the signs were pointing toward a renewal of Socialist-M.R.P. cooperation.

Although the Assembly's personnel had changed little, its spirit had definitely altered. There remained none of the enthusiasm which had marked the opening session of the First Constituent. A grim and rather uneasy tension had taken its place. All parties agreed that the time for stalling was past. The spadework on the constitution had been done; it was generally felt that three months would be enough to smooth out the major difficulties. This time the constitutional problem was given a number-one priority over all other legislation. Structural reforms in the economic sphere would have to wait.

The call for speed was endorsed by Félix Gouin's presidential successor, Georges Bidault, who announced that his new cabinet was embarking for "the shortest possible cruise—the Château d'If." Bidault's election on June 19 by a near-unanimous vote was regarded as a logical choice, now that the M.R.P. had become France's first party. The Communists had tried to head it off by proposing that the Gouin cabinet continue; but the Socialists, smarting from their electoral defeat, declared that they intended to trade their heavy burden of governmental responsibility for a mere "jump seat" in the cabinet.

The rise to power of the diminutive former professor of history seemed a fitting reward for his courageous role in the underground movement. Bidault's anti-fascist record dated well back into pre-war days, when as columnist for *L'Aube* he had opposed Franco and denounced the Munich settlement. Likewise, the sincerity of his belief in a Leftist social-economic policy was above dispute. Whether Bidault could offer the caliber of leadership which France desperately needed was more uncertain. His enemies hinted that he was not sufficiently free of church influence (whence the label "choir boy" which the Communists liked to use); and they also cast doubt on his strength of character. As Foreign Minister, some of his speeches before the Assembly had been incredibly bad, and critics had been heard to describe him as "Demosthenes before the pebbles." Bidault therefore faced a serious test when he assumed the republic's highest office. Events were to show that he would meet that test with relative if not absolute success.

Bidault's cabinet, like that of Gouin, was a three-party affair, with a larger proportion of M.R.P. ministers and fewer Socialists. The Radicals were invited to make it a foursome, but they preferred to continue their opposition role. Recognized by everyone as a stopgap, the unwieldy coalition ministry turned at once to a collection of inherited headaches, the worst of which were to be the wage issue and the Indo-Chinese question. Meanwhile, the new Assembly tackled the problem of how to interpret the constitutional referendum.

III. VOICE FROM THE WILDERNESS

Three days prior to Bidault's election as provisional president, and before the Constitutional Committee could set to work, the political world was jolted by Charles de Gaulle's brusque re-entry into the constitutional debate.

A patriotic ceremony at Bayeux on June 16 was the occasion which De Gaulle chose to emerge from his monastic silence. Ever since January, he had remained in strict seclusion in a government-owned hunting lodge in Marly forest. No word had come from him during the referendum campaign; but once the voters had done their duty and a new Assembly was ready to begin its work, De Gaulle concluded that it was high time to offer guidance. The "Bayeux program" was the first formal statement which he had ever made on the constitutional issue. As usual, he confined himself to principles, leaving to others the task of filling in details. But those principles were precise enough to mark a new stage in De Gaulle's evolving and still misty viewpoint.

Three points stood out in the General's manifesto. First, he declared, France must have a stronger and more independent executive than the one provided in the Pierre Cot constitution. Second, parliament must be made up of two houses, the upper house to represent territorial areas and professional and family groups. Third, the French Union must be completely rebuilt on federal principles, with the initial federal organs to be set up at once by the constitution.

Two of these principles—bicameralism and federalism—were new to the General's political vocabulary. The third—a strong executive—had always taken topmost importance in his mind. The chief novelty in De Gaulle's new program was the role attributed to the president of the republic. In the past De Gaulle had overlooked the possibilities of that somnolent official. His concern had been to strengthen the real executive, the premier, within the framework of the parliamentary system. As recently as January 1, during his dispute with the Socialists, he had accepted the parliamentary principle that the executive should be responsible to the legislature at all times. He reaffirmed that principle at Bayeux, but at the same time he suddenly adopted the phrase "separation of powers," and demanded that the executive, legislative, and judicial branches be "clearly separated and strongly balanced." "It goes without saying," he continued, "that the executive branch cannot emanate from the parliament without producing that confusion of powers in which the government [i.e., the cabinet] would soon become nothing more than a collection of delegates."

Here, side by side, De Gaulle placed two contradictory ideas. He proposed that the executive should be responsible to parliament, but should not emanate from it. One concept was parliamentary, the other presidential. In an effort to reconcile the two systems, De Gaulle turned to the nonresponsible president of the republic as a kind of *deus ex machina*. The president would hover above party conflicts, above the legislature, above everything except that vague entity called "the general interest." Chosen by a broadened electoral college (but not by the people directly), the president would select the premier and the ministers, and would when necessary dissolve the assembly in order to let the voters arbitrate disputes between the assembly and the cabinet. The president would be free of control by the legislature, and the real functioning executive (the premier) would emanate from him. His prestige would be further enhanced by making him president of the French Union as well as of the republic.

The foggiest aspect of De Gaulle's plan was the relationship between president and premier. By implication, it seemed that the former might overshadow the latter. De Gaulle's intense desire to give the executive branch more authority and independence led him to graft certain aspects of the presidential system onto the main parliamentary trunk. Gradually he had come to believe that the premier could not be made free and strong without either abandoning the parliamentary system or setting up a strong president behind the premier. In the latter case, the nonresponsible president would become the real source of executive authority. The idea resembled the doctrines of Right-wing republicans before 1914, except that De Gaulle's vagueness left room for a presidency with even more personal prestige and independence of action.

The Bayeux speech struck Paris and the Constituent Assembly with loud reverberations. No political leader could judge its potential effect in the country at large, for there was no way to measure De Gaulle's popular influence. After his resignation his prestige had sunk almost to the vanishing point, but even his enemies admitted that it had begun to revive by early summer. The referendum fiasco, the sputtering progress of economic recovery, the dearth of new leadership of national stature, and De Gaulle's own strategy of silent and splendid isolation, all helped to restore luster to the tarnished halo. On the other hand, visitors to Bayeux on June 16 reported that De Gaulle's self-resurrection had stirred up only mild enthusiasm. Several hundred of his most ardent backers who had come from Paris for the ceremony tried several times to start the chant, "De Gaulle au pouvoir!" but the demonstration fell completely flat. Bayeux gave further proof that some elements in De Gaulle's entourage were more impatient and less republican than the General himself. It also left unanswered the question of De Gaulle's hold upon French hearts.

The quickest reaction to the Bayeux program came from the Communists. They accused De Gaulle of proposing a presidential semi-dictatorship, and of attempting with "Machiavellian naïveté" to prepare his return to power. "The program of Louis Napoleon!" cried Pierre Hervé. The Socialists less passionately but no less firmly rejected the Bayeux program as reactionary and authoritarian. Léon Blum anxiously expressed the fear that De Gaulle's speech might hamstring efforts at a constitutional compromise. Of all the parties, the M.R.P. was most deeply embarrassed by the new turn of events. Behind the scenes, M.R.P. leaders had to admit that the Bayeux program had much in common with their own doctrines, but they regarded the speech as brusque and ill-timed. They felt that it might endanger an agreement between the M.R.P. and the Socialists, and push the latter back into the arms of Maurice Thorez. The M.R.P. press therefore dodged the central issues raised by De Gaulle, and played up the General's warning that a weak state would invite dictatorship.

The greatest enthusiasm naturally came from the Right wing, most of whose leaders hailed De Gaulle as a convert to their cause. More surprising was the favorable reaction of the Radical Socialists, whose personal regard for the General had never been more than lukewarm, and whose nostalgia for the Third Republic had nothing in common with the thesis of a stronger executive. But the Radicals saw a chance to make political capital of De Gaulle's acceptance of bicameralism, and of his new tendency to set himself up in opposition to the three big parties.

Within the little band of ultra-Gaullists, the Bayeux speech came like manna to the children of Israel. At last they had something positive upon which to work, instead of being forced to guess where their leader stood. The man who was moved most deeply was René Capitant, who had failed of re-election to the Assembly and was available for some kind of active service. With his accustomed fervent and headstrong enthusiasm, Capitant announced the formation of a society called the Gaullist Union for the Fourth Republic, whose aim it would be to rally men of all parties who accepted the Bayeux program as the basis for the new France.

Capitant also plunged into a re-examination of the constitutional question as illuminated by the Bayeux revelations, and shortly emerged with a fresh analysis which he published under the title *Toward a Federal Constitution*. Although the brochure never drew De Gaulle's public blessing, it amounted to a semi-official commentary on the Bayeux speech, and the fullest statement to date of Gaullist constitutional ideas.

What Capitant tried to do was to integrate the idea of a strong executive with De Gaulle's new thesis of imperial federalism. The blueprint which he drew up was strange and wonderful to behold. It maintained the parliamentary system for continental France, but combined it with a presidential system for the French Union as a whole. The president of the republic (and of the French Union) would appoint premiers in France and in certain other advanced parts of the Union. These premiers would be responsible to their respective legislatures, in true parliamentary fashion. In more backward areas, however, the president would name a kind of viceroy and a ministry responsible only to the president himself. In addition, a federal cabinet for the entire French Union would be set up in Paris to administer foreign affairs, national defense, and finance, and this cabinet would be directly responsible to the president.

Capitant was frank to admit that his scheme would make the French president one of the most powerful men on earth. Such authority, he contended, is necessary in the modern world: every great power today possesses a strong executive. He also accepted as obvious the fact that De Gaulle was the only living Frenchman capable of filling such a post. He believed that De Gaulle would be able to establish the system so solidly that it could continue to function even if weaker men were to succeed him as president.

The flurry created by the Bayeux speech quickly died as it became clear that De Gaulle did not intend to follow it up. Instead, he returned to his hermit-like existence, this time at Colombey-les-Deux-Eglises in Lorraine. In Paris, Capitant busied himself with getting his brochure published, and with trying to figure out how to convert his Gaullist Union from a name into a functioning organism. The Constituent Assembly, freed of the threat of continuing pressure from De Gaulle, heaved a sigh of relief, even though the M.R.P. was still vaguely disturbed by the idea that the Bayeux manifesto might some day be repeated. Capitant soon concluded that the Assembly was hopeless, and that no amount of pressure could bring it to adopt the Bayeux program. By the end of July, he had set his sights on the referendum and on a Third Constituent Assembly as the only hope. The French people, he believed, would again reject a compromise constitution if De

Gaulle should advise them to do so. The Gaullist Union would then come forward bearing the Bayeux program, and would be swept triumphantly into power to save the country from anarchy and civil war. A moment was to come in September when it almost seemed that Capitant had read the future aright.

IV. THE LABORS OF PENELOPE

While the Gaullists schemed and read their crystal ball, the new Constitutional Committee moved rapidly into action. The Committee's initial choice was this: should it start over from scratch, as De Gaulle, the Radicals, and the Right demanded; or should it merely revise the so-called Pierre Cot constitution, salvaging as much as possible of the latter? The M.R.P. was in a position to swing the balance either way. Its decision was unhesitating: it voted with the Left wing to revise rather than replace the Pierre Cot draft.

The effect of the M.R.P.'s choice was twofold. It meant greater speed, and it meant that the Bayeux program was virtually buried as a model for the new draft. M.R.P. leaders hoped to borrow some ideas from De Gaulle, but their central aim was to work out a middle-of-the-road constitution which might satisfy all parties except perhaps the extreme Left and Right. Such a document, they believed, would check the division of Frenchmen into Left and Right factions, and would encourage the growth of a Center bloc built around the M.R.P. and the Socialists. A Bayeux-style *constitution de combat* might be more in harmony with the M.R.P.'s own constitutional theories, but in this case theory seemed less important than practical political results.

Wisely, the Committee wasted little time re-exploring the jungle of the Declaration of Rights. By common consent (except for mild Communist opposition), it junked the long academic Declaration which had been so painfully drafted in March, and replaced it with a more general preamble labeled Declaration of

Principles. By this device, the party leaders sidetracked further debate on such thorny issues as property rights, liberty of the press, and freedom of instruction. The new preamble led off by reaffirming the contents of the 1789 Declaration of Rights, and added all the newer social and economic principles which had been generally accepted. The only dispute came when the M.R.P. tried to have the 1848 Declaration of Rights blanketed in as well. The anticlerical Left and the Radicals quickly headed off this maneuver, which they recognized as a scheme to introduce a guarantee of freedom of instruction through the back door.

Turning at once to the body of the constitution, the Committee unanimously accepted two changes which seemed to be dictated by the recent referendum. First, the bicameral principle was approved, with the reservation that the upper house should be expressly denied the right to overthrow cabinets. Second, the president of the republic was given back his traditional right to name the premier. But the Committee took away with one hand what it gave with the other. The Left insisted that the premier would have to be approved by the Assembly before he could form a cabinet. This requirement, the Left argued, would make for greater cabinet stability. As Pierre Cot put it, "A marriage has more chance of lasting when one chooses one's wife."

Both of these changes were swallowed by the Communists, but from that point onward they began to balk. They refused to admit that the country had voted for any further strengthening of the president or the upper house, nor would they accept additional limitations of any kind on the power of the assembly. History therefore began to repeat itself: a loose coalition of the Socialists and the M.R.P. overrode Communist objections on one issue after another.

Four principal changes were made in the Pierre Cot draft by this Socialist-M.R.P. entente. The powers of the president were slightly broadened, and his election by both houses of parliament assured; the upper house (labeled Council of the Republic) was given a different electoral base from that of the lower house; the High Council of the Judiciary was freed of any suspicion of control by the Assembly; and a committee of experts was set up to refer unconstitutional laws to the people. Not one of the changes was far-reaching; taken all together, they represented no more than the bare minimum necessary to satisfy the M.R.P. In fact, they closely resembled the so-called Auriol compromises which had almost brought the parties together in April. The most notable concession by either party came when the M.R.P. once more abandoned its thesis of full dissolution powers for the executive, and accepted the Socialists' view that dissolution must be a mere safety valve rather than a weapon. That concession cleared away the biggest constitutional stumbling block between the two parties.

The old Socialist-Communist lineup did not disappear completely, but it showed signs of life only at rare intervals. One instance was when the Left bloc voted that the president of the republic should be elected by open rather than secret ballot. The Left argued that the secret ballot had covered all sorts of shady maneuvers during the Third Republic, and had contributed to the surprise defeat of Clemenceau in 1919 and Briand in 1931. Their real motive, however, was a more practical one. They were afraid that under cover of the secret ballot, Charles de Gaulle might be chosen first president of the Fourth Republic. They knew that such was the M.R.P.'s silent hope in urging continuance of the secret ballot. Protected by anonymity, some Left-wing deputies might disobey party orders and thus give the General a majority.

A far more significant remnant of Socialist-Communist co-operation had to do with the French Union. During the life of the Second Constituent Assembly, that issue finally emerged from the fog into the spotlight, and threatened to dominate the entire constitutional debate.

Before the Assembly convened, it had seemed likely that the French Union clauses of the Pierre Cot draft would survive intact. That aspect of the constitution had drawn virtually no criticism in continental France during the referendum campaign. Immediately after the referendum, the Gouin cabinet had met and had announced to the overseas natives that none of their newly promised rights would be withdrawn. M. de Laurentie, Director of Political Affairs in the Ministry for Overseas France, had added publicly: "It can be affirmed without hesitation that the French Union system as defined by the First Constituent Assembly remains above dispute."

It did not take long for this rosy haze of unanimity to evaporate. Colonial deputies representing colleges of white voters had found the latter on the warpath against the First Constituent's French Union plan. These voters demanded a complete revision, and sent their deputies back to Paris filled with the fear of God and the elector. A second factor which shook many French politicians was the election of Ferhat Abbas and his fire-eating lieutenants in Algeria. The sentiment arose that if this was the fruit of the new policy of generosity, perhaps it would be wise to take another look at the tree which had borne it. They were disturbed too at reports of the rising nationalist movement in North Africa, and of an anti-French slogan allegedly in use among the Arabs: "Traveling bags or coffins!" Finally, De Gaulle's Bayeux speech, which placed the question of empire at the very heart of the constitutional problem, struck the M.R.P. in particular with a severe jolt.

Shortly after the new Assembly met, the M.R.P. suddenly announced its conversion to "progressive federalism" as the basis for the French Union. The term implied a sharp reversal of the M.R.P.'s earlier position. In the First Constituent it had followed the lead of Paul Viard, consistently rejecting the Left wing's federal doctrine in favor of a centralized French Union. The M.R.P.'s decision not to reappoint Viard to the Constitutional Committee was an early sign that its ideas were in a state of flux.

Curiously enough, the right-about-face of the M.R.P. did not mean that it had suddenly joined hands with the Left. On the contrary, it intensified the differences between them. Lengthy debate was necessary before party positions became relatively clear, and varying concepts of the term "federal" could be defined. When clarity finally emerged, the differences boiled down to these: (a) Should the framework of a federal commonwealth be set up at once from the top, by an Assembly dominated by continental

Frenchmen; or should it be built from the bottom over a period of years? (b) Should the constitution guarantee a share in government to the white colonist minority; or should the colonists be left to shift for themselves, a tiny minority in a huge native electorate?

To the Socialists and Communists, it seemed logical to build a federal French Union from below, and to delay its completion until the colonial populations could send their fair share of constitutional architects. The existing Assembly, they felt, was unrepresentative of the overseas natives, for only ten per cent of the deputies were colonials. They wished to begin with local assemblies in every overseas area, elected by a suffrage that would make no distinction between natives and French colonists. Each assembly, they argued, should work out its local statute of government in collaboration with the Paris parliament. At the end of several years, a truly federal constituent assembly should be convoked to place the capstone on the new structure. Only then, declared André Philip, would there be something to federate; and only then would the populations be prepared to make a free choice of their destiny. In the meantime, the overseas areas would continue to send deputies to the Paris parliament. The Left felt that its program could be achieved by re-enacting, with slight changes, the loose and nebulous French Union clauses of the Pierre Cot draft. Its version of federalism was strongly backed by the overseas native deputies, whose votes were so important to the Socialists and Communists. Political advantage thus fused with idealistic motives in crystallizing the Left's viewpoint.

The M.R.P.'s variety of progressive federalism, on the other hand, sprang from ideas similar to those of De Gaulle. Both the M.R.P. and De Gaulle feared that unless positive imperial bonds were created at once, the empire might fall apart before the Union could be consummated. The M.R.P. felt, therefore, that the Assembly must immediately set up federal organs in Paris. The president of the republic must be given the additional title of president of the French Union; and an Assembly of the French Union must be created, distinct from the two-house French parliament, to deal with matters affecting the whole Union. When pinned down, the M.R.P. spokesman Paul Coste-Floret admitted that this assembly would be given little power at first; but he argued that its authority would grow gradually. The M.R.P. also insisted that the structure of government in the various overseas territories should be determined in Paris, in order to keep the degree of local autonomy within bounds. Finally, it demanded that some seats in all elected bodies be reserved for the white colonist minority. This M.R.P. program won strong support from the *Rassemblement des Gauches* and the Right, some of whose deputies proposed to go even further. They again suggested a "second-class" citizenship for the natives, and they proposed that all the native deputies be shifted out of the Paris parliament into the powerless Assembly of the French Union.

As the two sides squared off for a showdown fight, the colored and Arab deputies decided that in union there might be strength. They therefore seceded from the old Intergroup of Overseas Deputies (which included colonists as well as natives) and set up a narrower but tighter-knit Intergroup of Native Deputies. The dominant figure in this new body was Ferhat Abbas, who, with his ten Algerian followers, served as a pole of attraction which had been lacking in the earlier Assembly. Visible proof of his influence was furnished on the floor of the Assembly, where colored deputies from other colonies gradually began to migrate to the benches adjoining the Manifesto party. First came the two Madagascar autonomists, then two colored members of the U.D.S.R., and finally a scattering of representatives from Black Africa. Their arrival shifted the Right-Left balance just enough to give the Left a clear majority once more.

The Native Intergroup's ideas on the French Union were incorporated in a draft plan put together by Abbas himself. On July 31 that plan, with some modifications, was accepted by the Constitutional Committee by a twenty-one to twenty margin. The victory was a major one, and the possibilities of the plan were formidable. It was built around the Socialist-Communist interpretation of progressive federalism, with the Union to be built from the bottom over a period of years. Each overseas territory would be free to enter the French Union as either (a) a free state linked to France by international treaty, (b) an autonomous unit, or (c) an integral part of France proper. By a loophole consciously placed in the draft, any territory might also choose to remain outside the French Union. Full French citizenship would be granted to all residents of the Union except those already possessing another citizenship (e.g., the Moroccans). Every remnant of inequality between native resident and white settler would be wiped out. On the French Union issue, the Left wing's triumph was total; but it was also temporary. During the weeks that followed, that issue was destined to bring the threat of a cabinet crisis, and to produce the intervention of President Bidault himself.

The French Union problem was the final topic on the Committee's agenda. Six weeks had sufficed to unravel the rejected constitution and to reweave its pattern in slightly different form. On August 2 came the climactic vote on the revised draft as a whole; and just as in April, one major party refused to go along with its rivals. This time it was the Communists who declared that "the project exceeds the limits of reasonable compromise," and who threatened to carry their opposition into the referendum unless changes were made on the floor of the Assembly. The prospect of three-party unity seemed further off than ever, especially since the M.R.P. had no special desire to win over the Communists. Paul Coste-Floret, the M.R.P.'s Reporter-General, had little of Pierre Cot's zeal to evangelize the heathen; he would be satisfied to hold together the Center bloc. Yet, strangely enough, he was to succeed in achieving Cot's goal of tripartite unity, and the unwitting author of his success was to be Charles de Gaulle.

V. DUET OR TRIO?

There was a strangely familiar air about the draft constitution which emerged from Committee in August

1946. Except for its French Union clauses, it resembled its unlucky April predecessor like a half sister. André Philip declared (and Paul Coste-Floret agreed) that the Committee had modified the old draft in detail but not in spirit. The total effect of the changes was to shift the proposed system one short step further away from government by assembly. The new text was a kind of halfway house between the Pierre Cot constitution and the abhorred system of the Third Republic. It did not approach either British cabinet government or the program of General de Gaulle.

Some critics (mainly in Gaullist and P.R.L. circles) felt that the M.R.P. had sold its referendum victory for a mess of pottage, and had actually retreated further than it was ready to do in April. Irritated at this "weakness," a Rightist deputy remarked that the letters M.R.P. must stand for *Mouvement de Rotation Perpetuelle;* and *Combat* added that the M.R.P., like Paul Claudel's God, "moves straight ahead by way of devious paths." There was a little truth in the charge. M.R.P. leaders, reassured by their June electoral victory, now felt strong enough to risk alienating some of their voters in order to build a coalition with the Socialists. At bottom, however, the M.R.P.'s position was more consistent than the critics would admit. During the April crisis, the party had advanced a final set of four demands which would have permitted it to accept the Pierre Cot constitution. Those demands coincided on all but one point with the changes which appeared in the August draft. It was the Socialists more than the M.R.P. who had shifted ground since April.

If the new draft had set up a strong upper house or a powerful executive, a violent campaign of abuse might have been expected from the Communists. The draft did neither, but the abuse followed anyway. With straight faces and apparent sincerity, men of the caliber of Duclos and Fajon alleged that the draft had been tailored to measure after the Bayeux pattern; that it restored the Senate in disguised form; and that it was a dangerous and reactionary document which opened the way to "a Prince-President."

The representatives of other parties were not quite sure what to make of these fantastic statements. They were convinced of one thing, however: Communist strategy would continue to aim at preventing the consolidation of a Left-Center bloc. In the long run, that consideration would be likely to outweigh their constitutional doctrines. It seemed logical to suppose that the Communists had once again turned to a policy of bluff designed to frighten the Socialists and to break up the Socialist-M.R.P. entente. If the bluff should fail, the Communists would have to fall back on a lone referendum campaign against all the "forces of reaction," in the process of which they might chip away more of the Socialists' strength.

There was reason to believe that the Communists this time expected the failure of their bluff, and that they were preparing for a solitary fight against the constitution. All through July and August, they had shown a new spirit of intransigence rather than compromise, a willingness to isolate themselves from all other parties and to break lances for lost causes. As a reward for isolation, they could pose as the only Frenchmen who had never ceased to fight Munich and Vichy, and who remained the scourge of doubtful patriots. One example was their fight to unseat Edouard Daladier, Paul Reynaud, and Frédéric-Dupont; another was their attempt, after the acquittal of the Vichy premier P.-E. Flandin, to reorganize the High Court of Justice as a frankly political rather than a judicial body. The Communists' effort to turn justice into a political process, together with their thesis that a parliamentary majority should be able to unseat regularly elected deputies at will, threw a curious light on their concept of democracy. To risk such exposure in the midst of the constitutional debate was a serious business. That risk was worth taking, however, if the Communists intended to fight alone in the referendum. The effect would be to divide all Frenchmen into two simple categories—patriotic, anti-Munich, anti-Vichy republicans on the one hand and reactionary friends of Pétain on the other. That, at any rate, would be the picture which the Communists could present to the voters.

The opening of public debate in the Assembly on August 20 seemed to confirm the assumption that the Communists would fight the constitution. Etienne Fajon announced bluntly, "We are in complete disagreement with the system embodied in the most important articles of the project." He was backed by the subtler arguments of Pierre Cot, who suddenly moved down from his assigned place with the M.U.R.F. to the front row of Communist benches, on Jacques Duclos' right hand. One journalist speculated that if Cot's leftward migration were to continue in the next legislature, it might be necessary to install a jump seat for him outside the regular semicircle.

The Communists soon had reason to be even more discontented. On August 27 the Assembly voted to lift the French Union chapter out of the constitution and to send it back to the Committee for revision. The character of this chapter, sponsored by the Communist-Socialist-native bloc, had terrified good French conservatives and nationalists, who labeled it "secessionist anarchy." Edouard Herriot expressed the fear that it might work to make France "the colony of her former colonies." President Georges Bidault concluded that the time had come to swing a big stick. Bidault, along with the entire M.R.P., was convinced that the French Union clauses as they stood might lead to the breakup of the empire, and he felt that the head of the government could not keep hands off in such circumstances. He therefore threatened that unless the Left wing would agree to a revision, he would resign the presidency. The Left, faced by the prospect of a cabinet crisis, capitulated, much to the disgust of some of the native deputies.

This was the moment chosen by Charles de Gaulle to throw his second constitutional grenade. The effect of his Bayeux speech had been quickly dissipated, but his new attack, delivered in the form of a statement to the press on August 27, came near wrecking the Assembly's efforts of the preceding two months. In the end, by a strange irony, it was to accomplish the miracle of rallying all the major parties in support of the constitutional draft.

De Gaulle's rejection of the new project was blunt and total. A whole series of detailed criticisms streamed from his pen, but the principal emphasis was upon the inadequate powers of the president, the dangerous slackness of the French Union chapter, and the failure to assure the cabinet of enough cohesion and enough independence. De Gaulle demanded also that the legislature be stripped of the right to initiate expenditures, that the prerogatives of the upper house be broadened, and that the electoral law be referred to popular referendum. It was plain that the General's ideas had been slowly taking shape during the summer months. His concept of the president's role had moved beyond the Bayeux stage, even though he still failed to make it clear how a nonresponsible president could be vested with first-class powers within a parliamentary system. Between the lines it appeared that De Gaulle, like René Capitant, had decided to link the question of presidential authority with that of a federal union, and that the General had thereby taken a notable step in the direction of the presidential form of government.

De Gaulle's blast rocked the M.R.P. from top to bottom. In the corridors of the Assembly, Maurice Schumann was heard fervently damning Capitant as the guilty party who had persuaded De Gaulle to intervene at such a moment. The M.R.P. still claimed to be "the party of fidelity," with De Gaulle as its symbol and inspiration. Its leaders—even those like Bidault who had long wished to throw off the "De Gaulle mortgage"—knew that an open break with the General might cost the party millions of votes. Besides, many prominent members of the M.R.P. felt that De Gaulle's views on government were basically sound. On the other hand, the M.R.P. had chosen to sponsor a compromise draft before the Assembly. To repudiate the work of their Reporter-General Paul Coste-Floret at this stage would be highly embarrassing, and even dangerous. It would destroy the nascent Center bloc, and it might produce another negative majority in the referendum. The fruit of such a policy might even be the breakdown of democratic government.

The M.R.P.'s alternatives, therefore, were to stand fast against De Gaulle and thereby split the party, or to follow De Gaulle and thereby split the country. M.R.P. leaders knew that the P.R.L. and other rivals would seize the chance to promote the party's disintegration. To make matters worse, they were suddenly beset by doubts about their Socialist partners. Were the Socialists preparing to tack to the Left once more? At the Socialists' national congress late in August, the provincial rank and file of the party rose up in more or less righteous wrath to throw out Daniel Mayer as Secretary-General and replace him by Guy Mollet, the candidate of the so-called left wing of the party. Almost simultaneously, the Socialists in the Assembly decided to shift over to the Communist position on one constitutional issue—the election of the upper house by direct rather than indirect vote. The M.R.P. feared that this reversal might be only the first in a series, and that their fragile compromise with the Socialists might again collapse. Their nervousness in this connection was to prove unjustified, but it contributed to the M.R.P.'s internal crisis.

While De Gaulle's attack sowed dissension in M.R.P. ranks, it cut the ground from under the Communists. They could no longer describe the draft as a Bayeux-model constitution designed to please the General and to serve as a vehicle for his return to power. Their threats to vote against the project abruptly ceased, and their silence showed that they were giving new thought to their strategy. De Gaulle's statement had at least made it easy for them to reverse their position. In their eyes, De Gaulle's hostility to the draft could be offered as proof that it was safely republican.

The Socialist reaction to De Gaulle's statement was one of indignant resentment, mixed in some cases with surprise and disillusionment. Léon Blum, for example, recalled that six months earlier he had expressed confidence in De Gaulle's sound republicanism; now he openly confessed his doubts and fears. Blum still believed that the General's intentions were pure, but he charged that De Gaulle had unwittingly turned the corner which would lead him ever further toward a presidential, and eventual an authoritarian, regime. The left-wing Socialist daily *Franc-Tireur* was more brutal. "The Republic married De Gaulle by correspondence," it announced; "*elle a été . . . trompée.*"

The only political figure who greeted De Gaulle's statement with unrestrained joy was René Capitant. For the first time, life was breathed into his embyro Gaullist Union. Recruits began to flock in; offices were hastily opened in Paris and other cities; the idea spread that the Union might become De Gaulle's personal vehicle in the next referendum, and perhaps even his official party in a Third Constituent Assembly. Within three weeks, the Union was claiming half a million members, and Capitant was publicly predicting that France would lapse into civil war if the Assembly's constitution were to be adopted.

The Gaullist Union's leaders concentrated their fire on the M.R.P. (which they called "the party of lip-service fidelity") in an effort to split that group wide open. They were indifferent to the fact that the success of such tactics would leave the Communists far and away the largest party in France. Capitant was convinced that the emergence of two great blocs was not an evil but a necessity, and he believed that De Gaulle was the only Frenchman capable of leading the anti-Communist bloc.

Enthusiasm led the Gaullist Union to open its doors to all comers, and among the converts there were a good many Frenchmen who could scarcely have been called Gaullists during the Vichy period. At the close of a large rally in Paris, for example, part of the crowd marched off singing monarchist songs. Capitant's failure to screen the membership displeased De Gaulle, and kept most of the General's most prominent followers outside its ranks. It also left the Union wide open to the charge that it was the spiritual heir of the prewar semi-fascist leagues. Second-rate leadership and doubtful republicanism hampered the Union's effectiveness, and eventually destroyed it entirely.

The month that followed De Gaulle's attack of August 27 was the most confused and complex period in the entire constitutional debate. The party leaders wandered steadily deeper into a thicket of compromises and sub-compromises, of crises and pseudo-crises, which ended by becoming almost inpenetrable. Vincent Auriol's office again became the scene of top-level negotiations. M.R.P. agents made almost daily pilgrimages to the retreat of "the hermit of Colombey." Georges Bidault, aided by Minister of State Alexandre Varenne, busied himself with plans for a substitute French Union. On the floor of the Assembly a mountain of more than three hundred amendments had to be leveled, and some of them found the Socialists and M.R.P. in opposite camps. Rising tension brought the most fantastic crop of rumors—that a Gaullist maquis was gathering in the mountains, that Thorez had gone to Moscow for instructions, that American agents had met the Count of Paris in Lisbon with a view to a royalist *coup d'état*. Three times at least during that critical month, it seemed that all hope of three-party unity had been destroyed.

A special source of hard feeling was the fact that the Algerian and Malagasy autonomists controlled the fate of several important amendments. Whenever the Assembly split into Right and Left blocs, the handful of deputies around Ferhat Abbas (eleven Algerians plus four natives from Madagascar, the Comores Islands, and French India) were enough to give the Left victory. For example, they enabled the Left to beat off a final M.R.P.–Right-wing attempt to salvage freedom of instruction; the margin was 274 to 272. M.R.P. and Rightist leaders were exasperated at this "alien interference" in the affairs of continental France. They asked bitterly if the voters would be presented this time with "a Communist-Socialist-Islamic constitution" as a substitute for the Pierre Cot draft. In vain Abbas pointed out that he and his followers were not in Paris by choice, and that they would much prefer to sit in a new Algerian parliament. The ill feeling persisted nevertheless.

In spite of all these ill omens, the Socialist-M.R.P. entente survived intact and ended by winning Communist adherence as well. This achievement—without which a Third Constituent Assembly would have been almost inevitable—must be marked up to the credit of both the M.R.P. and the Communist leaders. The M.R.P. resisted the temptation to assure its own short-run future by attaching itself to De Gaulle's coattails; the Communists chose to compromise with the M.R.P. rather than run the risk of bringing De Gaulle back to power through a Third Constituent Assembly. Each side gave up as little as possible to the enemy, and was heavily motivated by partisan considerations and by fear. But the fact remains that April was not repeated, and that a basis for agreement was achieved.

Those final constitutional skirmishes centered around one major issue—the character of the French Union—and two relatively minor ones—the method of electing the upper house, and the question of secret or open ballot in choosing the president. In the upper house dispute, it was the M.R.P. which retreated far enough to prevent a Right-Left split; in the other two cases, the Socialists and Communists gave ground.

The upper house issue was the first to be settled. Late in August the Socialists had shifted over to the Communist position, favoring popular election by proportional representation rather than indirect election by the local councils. The inevitable result would be to weaken the upper house still further by making it a political mirror of the lower house. For two weeks the M.R.P. stubbornly refused all the offers of compromise suggested by the tireless Vincent Auriol. Its unyielding attitude reflected the intra-party stress caused by De Gaulle's intervention; many M.R.P. back-benchers had decided that a rupture with the Socialists would be better than a break with De Gaulle. All the prestige and influence of Georges Bidault were needed to tip the scales. Bidault, appearing before an M.R.P. caucus on September 11, pleaded with his colleagues to shake off their hypnotic fear of De Gaulle and to accept the Socialists' compromise offer. His appeal won the caucus over, but only by a bare six-vote majority. The compromise was accepted, and a Right-Left split narrowly averted. The solution provided that the first Council of the Republic would be chosen by indirect popular election (as the Left wished), but that the permanent system for electing the Council would be postponed for decision by the future Assembly.

The French Union showdown was longer and more complex. Bidault, who had gotten the original chapter withdrawn for revision, presented the Constitutional Committee with a substitute plan built around the M.R.P.'s concept of "progressive federalism." It plugged up the loophole of secession, assured the white colonist minority of special representation, converted the native peoples into "citizens of the French Union" rather than full-fledged French citizens, guaranteed that the Paris parliament would measure out the autonomy to be granted to each overseas area, and provided for the immediate creation of three federal organs in Paris—the president, an Assembly of the French Union, and a High Council of States.

The Left-wing–native bloc in the Committee set out at once to water down Bidault's proposal. It was so successful that Bidault once more had to use personal pressure; he appeared before the Committee on September 19 and made it plain that he would resign as president if his plan were not restored in its original purity. The Left wing, faced a second time with the threat of a cabinet crisis, again capitulated. On September 20 the Committee accepted the Bidault-sponsored plan with only minor changes.

That decision immediately produced a counter crisis. Ferhat Abbas and several other native deputies sitting in the Committee as alternates or observers walked out, and the entire Intergroup of Native Deputies decided to resign from the Assembly en masse unless Bidault would compromise. That afternoon, when the Assembly began its general debate on the French Union chapter, every native deputy quietly arose and left the hall. Even wizened little Prince Douala Manga Bell of Cameroon, the sole colored deputy on the M.R.P. benches, filed meekly out when tapped on the shoulder by a fellow African. It looked as though the much-advertised new imperial federation would be set up by fiat of the mother country alone.

At this critical moment Auriol and Marius Moutet, Socialist Minister for Overseas France, stepped in as conciliators. They brought Bidault and the native deputies together for a lengthy talk, out of which came an agreement in extremis. The natives agreed to accept the Bidault plan with its rigid organization and its guarantees of French sovereignty, while Bidault agreed to alter two provisions which smacked of racial inequality. As a result, the double electoral college was transferred from the constitution to the less sacrosanct electoral law, and the native peoples were assured of "first-class" citizenship. All Frenchmen and natives in the

Union (except citizens of the associated states like Morocco) were given a dual status as "French citizen" and "citizen of the French Union." The latter phrase retained only one purpose: it applied to citizens of the associated states as well, and thus brought the Moroccans, Tunisians, and Viet-Namese into the fold.

Abbas and the native deputies were back in their regular places the next day, but a residue of bitterness remained. When Bidault praised the Assembly for adopting his plan and described the French Union as "an institution whose like cannot be found anywhere else in the world," the natives pointedly refused to join the applause and exchanged sour looks. Further evidence of resentment came a few days later, when Abbas dropped his usual conciliatory tone and brought on the most violent parliamentary incident since prewar days. As Abbas mounted to the tribune for the last time, a Right-wing deputy shouted, "What's that salaud doing here anyhow?" Provoked by this greeting and by further interruptions, Abbas broke up the meeting when he charged that France had not been able to defend its empire in 1940, and that French colonial policy had been one of the worst blots on the record of the Third Republic. Half of the deputies immediately walked out, and one group of firebrands headed by Maurice Schumann laid siege to the tribune in an effort to drag Abbas down by force. The Communists naturally rallied to his defense, and a free-for-all was narrowly averted. The incident, occurring in the final hours of the constitutional debate, was in sharp contrast to the First Constituent Assembly's love feast over French Union matters. Perhaps it was also a portent of the storms which were to shake the Union during the months to come.

The issue of open versus secret ballot in electing the president of the republic was the last to be settled, and it came nearest to destroying the whole complex structure of compromise. A decision was seemingly reached on September 12, when the Left-wing bloc rejected the secret ballot by a margin of 275 to 273. The M.R.P., however, refused to abandon the struggle. M.R.P. leaders hoped that the secret ballot might be the key to a reconciliation with De Gaulle. Their scheme was to assure De Gaulle that they would back him for the presidency if he in return would stop criticizing the constitution. The success of this strategy hinged on the use of the secret ballot, without which the General would have little chance of being elected.

On September 24, only five days before the Assembly was scheduled to accept or reject the constitution, the M.R.P. asked the Constitutional Committee to reconsider the secret ballot issue. Its proposal went down to defeat by a 21 to 21 tie vote. All of the M.R.P. and Right-wing delegates immediately walked out of the Committee room, and Paul Coste-Floret announced that he intended to resign as Reporter-General. History seemed about to repeat itself. Once more the weary Socialists rushed forward with the olive branch, but this time they were not rebuffed. Vincent Auriol called together his famous "committee on compromises" on the twenty-fifth and proposed that the secret ballot dispute, together with several other irritating lesser points, be settled by the simple process of postponement. These controversial points would be omitted from the constitution, and would be left for the future legislature to decide in the form of organic laws. Meanwhile a gentlemen's agreement, unwritten but binding on the major parties, would guarantee that the first president of the Fourth Republic would be chosen "in accordance with republican tradition"—that is, by secret ballot. Suddenly the skies cleared. On the twenty-sixth, it was announced that everything was settled, and that the three principal parties would all back the compromise draft. Ratification was at last assured.

It was something of an anticlimax when the Assembly, at 4:00 A.M. on September 29, voted its approval by the overwhelming margin of 440 to 106. In a burst of rather forced enthusiasm, the deputies rose once more and sang the *Marseillaise*. Vincent Auriol hoarsely congratulated the Assembly and quoted from Benjamin Franklin, and the deputies scattered just as the sun rose. Only a few superstitious politicians noted that it was the eighth anniversary of the Munich pact. The task of constitution-making was definitely over, and success in the referendum seemed assured. Only one small point of doubt remained: could Charles de Gaulle, if he chose, challenge and defeat France's three major parties?

VI. THE WOES OF "DECADENT TRIPARTISM"

When the Second Constituent Assembly adjourned on October 5, the traditional cry "Vive la république!" went up from the Left-wing deputies. "And may God protect France!" retorted a voice from the back benches of the M.R.P. On that rather dubious note the Assembly's labors came to an end. The ultra-Gaullist *Etoile du Soir* wrote contemptuously, "We have known other assemblies in which there flourished a like degree of bad faith, nonsense, shamelessness, incoherence, and other elements necessary to great legislative efforts, but we have never known one so cold and dreary." The reaction of the general public, however, was not contempt but general indifference and lassitude. The voters had already gone to the polls four times in eighteen months; now they were faced by another referendum, to be followed by the election of a lower and then an upper house. They were tired of voting, bored with the long squabble over constitutional minutiae, disgusted with continuing shortages of food and consumers' goods. Their temper was far from revolutionary; it was a curious blend of irritation and apathy.

The Assembly's legislative record, compared to that of its predecessor, was a meager one. Not a single "structural reform" in the economic sphere had even come up for discussion. The trend of the June elections had weakened the impetus toward legal revolution. Besides, many politicians who accepted the need for a semisocialized economy (notably in the M.R.P.) felt that the First Constituent Assembly had produced near-chaos by its pell-mell nationalizations, and that it was time for a breathing spell during which some order could be restored.

Except for its constitutional draft, the Assembly could point to only two constructive measures of broad importance: a civil servants' statute and a law concerning the reconstruction of war-damaged property. The former was the culmination of ten years of effort by the civil servants' union. It standardized appointment, promotion, and salary policies throughout the sprawling French administration, and set up a central director with some degree of co-ordinating power. The long-overdue reconstruction bill obligated the government to finance the rebuilding of private homes, shops, and factories destroyed or damaged during the war. It was estimated that a million and a half buildings scattered through seventy-four of France's ninety departments would be affected, and that seven million citizens would benefit by the law. The Assembly was careful, however, not to open the doors of the treasury at once. The threat of further inflation, of a "financial hemorrhage," was too obvious, especially when building materials and home furnishings were still not available. The law therefore gave bombed-out persons nothing more than a mortgage on the state for future collection at the discretion of the Ministry of Reconstruction. The plight of the *sinistrés* was by no means relieved; but a major preliminary step had finally been taken.

Paralleling the Assembly's career, the Bidault cabinet by October had accomplished the major part of its "summer cruise." Public opinion had centered much more on its behavior and its problems than on the work of the Assembly. Government by coalition, by balance of political forces, received a prolonged test in the face of increasingly difficult conditions. The results of the test brought growing disillusionment. The Bidault period, remarked André Stibio, might properly be labeled the era of decadent tripartism.

The cabinet's toughest problem lay on its doorstep when it took office. That was the wage issue—and, behind it, the whole question of the continuing inflationary spiral. The Fourth Republic had inherited from Vichy a system of wage and price controls. Before liberation those controls had kept wages constantly behind prices. One of the first acts of the De Gaulle government had been to order blanket wage increases in an effort to restore the balance. But living costs had immediately started upward once again, leaving wage scales far behind. In spite of this injustice, there had been no serious strikes since liberation. The C.G.T.'s Communist leadership had exacted remarkable discipline from its followers, at the risk of losing strength to those "lewd vipers" the "Hitlero-Trotskyites." On the eve of the June elections, however, the line had changed. The C.G.T., perhaps for electoral reasons, suddenly plumped for an across-the-board wage increase of 25 per cent.

No party could deny that a readjustment was due and overdue. If prices did not come down and if distribution did not improve, wages would have to go up. The only question was, how could justice be done to the workingman without giving the inflationary spiral another whirl skyward? The Communists argued that because production had doubled since liberation, a flat 25-per-cent rise could be absorbed by industry without any resultant increase in prices. They cited figures to show that industrial profits were on the upgrade, whereas the wage-earners' share of the national income had dropped from 48 per cent in 1938 to 41 per cent in 1946. President Bidault replied that anything beyond a 15 per cent boost was out of the question, and that the wage issue would have to be fitted into the whole economic-financial picture.

There were a few Frenchmen who suggested guardedly that a bold stand against wage rises, coupled with aggressive steps to reduce prices, might be the turning point in the struggle against inflation. The situation, they argued, was right for it: note circulation had been slowing up for two or three months, and black market prices were beginning to drop. Vigorous measures would force prices downhill, would squeeze the black market, and would stabilize the financial situation. Hindsight a year later vindicated this opinion. The policy would have been both far-sighted and courageous, but in view of the C.G.T.'s attitude it might also have amounted to political suicide, with the Communists as chief beneficiaries. No political leader—not even M. Bidault—dared to run that risk.

Instead, after some jockeying, Bidault called together representatives of all industrial, agricultural, commercial, and labor interests to draw up a set of recommendations. This conference eventually thrashed out a sliding scale of increases averaging slightly more than 15 per cent, with higher grants to low-paid workers. The farmers' organization was persuaded to approve this recommendation in return for a C.G.T. promise to raise farm price ceilings. It was also agreed that some underpriced industrial products would have to be readjusted. During the late summer, therefore, the inflationary spiral began again. Wages were hoisted to the new level; but at the same time farm prices jumped, and Minister of National Economy De Menthon decreed adjustments in certain industrial prices. Labor's gains were rapidly nullified, and with millions of francs in new currency appearing each week, there was no end in prospect.

The Communists' role in the wage controversy led some Frenchmen to reflect anew on the party's strategic aims. Inflationary wage increases could bring neither economic recovery nor justice for the workingman; the Communists knew that well enough. Perhaps their motive was purely defensive, to head off rising discontent among their voters. But why was the party so lukewarm toward the only effective method of aiding the masses: a tough policy of wage, price, and profit control during the long period of penury? True, the Communists had steadily proclaimed their desire to get France back on its feet, and they deserved much of the credit for post-liberation recovery. But could they sincerely expect and desire recovery in a non-Marxian regime? Some Frenchmen began to wonder if the Communists' disguised purpose was not to help along the self-destruction of a doomed society, deferring the final crash until they themselves would be sure to inherit power.

Bidault's second major problem was also inherited; it concerned the fate of Indo-China, the most populous part of the French Empire. Ever since Japan's surrender in August 1945, the provinces of Annam and Tongking had been controlled by a native government headed by a president whose current pseudonym was Ho Chi Minh. Ho's political career had begun in 1920 when, as a photographer's assistant in the Paris slums, he had joined the new Communist party. A period of training in Russia followed, and then two decades as a party agent in China and Annam. His record during the Japanese occupation was obscure; apparently his Viet Minh league resisted both the Japanese and the French with equal fervor.

Ho's Viet Nam government, a coalition of Annamese nationalist and Communist groups, aspired to absorb the rich rice basin of Cochin-China as well as Annam and Tongking; but the French, aided by a temporary British occupation, succeeded in holding onto that province. Major hostilities seemed likely as French reinforcements moved slowly out to the Far East. They were averted, however, by an agreement signed with Ho Chi Minh in March 1946. This agreement provided that the Viet Nam republic would become a part of a new Indo-Chinese Federation and of the French Union. Plebiscites in Tongking, Annam, and Cochin-China would determine the wishes of the population in each province.

It soon became evident that the two governments were poles apart in interpreting the March accord. The French, for reasons of prestige, were determined not to lose their predominant influence in Indo-China. It contained two-fifths of the population of their whole empire, and its loss would knock the props out from under their French Union scheme at the very start. Their aim, therefore, was to construct a new Indo-Chinese Federation made up of five states, of which only Annam and Tongking would be Viet Nam controlled. The other three, it was hoped, could be kept friendly and docile, and could easily outvote the two Viet Nam states. To this end, treaties were signed with the rulers of Cambodia and Laos, and a French-sponsored native government was suddenly set up in Cochin-China. These steps infuriated the Viet Nam leaders. What they wanted was to reduce French influence to nothing more than a shadow. They aimed to absorb Cochin-China outright, to deny the Indo-Chinese Federation any real powers, and to dominate the whole region by sheer weight of numbers and superior dynamism.

Such divergent views could hardly have been reconciled, even if there had been a desire for understanding on both sides. Two lengthy conferences sought to implement the March agreement, but all progress was blocked by the question of who would control Cochin-China pending the plebiscite. The Viet Nam delegates finally walked out in disgust; but a last-minute *modus vivendi* between Ho and Bidault kept the lid on. It was obvious, however, that the Bidault cabinet had been unable to come within shouting distance of a real solution. The alternatives which Bidault faced were almost hopeless ones. His own party was the most determined to give no ground, even though it must have known that convalescent France could not hold Indo-China by sheer force. The only other choice, urged by the Communists, was to give the Viet Nam what it wanted in the hope of preserving some crumbs of French influence. But the wisdom of that choice hinged on the Viet Nam leaders' sympathies for France and on their good faith, both of which were more than doubtful. Here was a case where colonialism had borne strange and bitter fruit.

It was not the cabinet's handling (or mishandling) of the foregoing problem which irritated public opinion and produced the phrase "decadent tripartism." The real source of discontent was the progressive breakdown in cabinet solidarity. France had long known coalition cabinets, but it had never before seen such flagrant civil war within a government. Each of the three parties held certain ministries, and increasingly tended to regard those departments as private fiefs. Each one claimed credit for the cabinet's achievements and shifted the responsibility for errors onto "the other two bandits." Ministers began to snipe at one another by press communiqués. In September the Communists undertook a vicious press campaign against François de Menthon, "*ministre de l'hausse*," "agent of the trusts," for having authorized increases in certain industrial prices. The M.R.P. in return dragged Minister of Industrial Production Marcel Paul over the coals daily for alleged favoritism and incompetence. When a deficiency appropriations bill came before the Assembly for debate, each minister's requests were blasted by the other two parties in the cabinet. France was treated to an example of coalition government at its worst. The opposition, instead of attacking the cabinet from the outside, was within the cabinet itself. Collaboration gave way to cohabitation; instability was replaced by near-paralysis.

The result was a widespread reaction of disgust toward the organized parties, and a growing sentiment in favor of breaking their hold in some way—perhaps by a different electoral system, perhaps by setting up an executive with power to crack the whip. The parties, by their bickering, thus played directly into the hands of critics like Charles de Gaulle and those whom *Populaire* called the "Radicalo-reactionaries." Such critics could easily show that the new constitutional draft, buttressed by the system of proportional representation, would tend to prolong the type of government which France had known since De Gaulle stepped down. No other factor weighed so heavily in the constitutional referendum of October.

The 1946 laboratory experiment in government left an offensive odor in the nostrils of many truly democratic Frenchmen. At the same time, it made them realize that some elements were ready to profit by the imperfections of French democracy in order to destroy democracy itself. They concluded, therefore, that it might be dangerous to correct the evils of decadent tripartism by harsh and uncompromising methods. The fundamental fact was that France was deeply divided on political, economic, social, and religious issues. The parties helped to maintain that division, but they were its consequence much more than its cause. Men like De Gaulle believed that France could not long survive such division, and that a degree of unity could be enforced through a constitutional mechanism plus the influence of a strong leader. Men like Léon Blum believed that France's division could only be overcome by a gradual evolutionary process; that for the time being, the collaboration of the three major factions was indispensable even though almost impossible; that time and returning prosperity might erode some of the internal barriers, allowing a coherent and stable majority to emerge. Should the system and the spirit of tripartism be destroyed, as the Gaullists urged, or could it be outgrown, as Blum suggested? There was the issue which separated French republicans two years after liberation, and which would continue to separate them during the months to follow.

VII. ST. CHARLES AND THE
THREE-HEADED DRAGON

At one end of the lists, General de Gaulle; at the other, the three largest parties of France. That, essentially, was the character of the October referendum campaign. The contest seemed hopelessly unequal. The proconstitution forces had controlled more than three-fourths of the votes cast in previous elections. On De Gaulle's side there were only the Radicals, the U.D.S.R., the Right, and the Gaullist Union; and all except the Gaullist Union were thoroughly defeatist in spirit. The referendum therefore offered a clear test of the influence which De Gaulle could still exert in France.

The General wasted no time in stating his position. At Epinal only twelve hours after the Assembly adopted the constitution, he asked rhetorically whether it would meet France's needs, and answered, "Frankly, no!" Once again he summarized his own constitutional doctrines, still marred by the same obscurities as in the past, but hardening now into a fixed pattern: a president who would really be a chief of state, a cabinet which would be a solid and coherent team, a French Union with effective institutions at the center, an upper house which would balance the lower. In addition, he struck out with unprecedented harshness at the "omnipotence" and "division" of the parties, and at their readiness to abandon principles for tactical ends. For the first time De Gaulle adopted the royal "we" throughout his speech, but he expressed an "iron disdain" for the charge that he had dictatorial ambitions. His tone, complained Emmanuel d'Astier, was that of "an irritated Jupiter."

De Gaulle did not follow up the Epinal address with a country-wide personal campaign. He retired once more into silence, saving his ammunition for the proper moment just before referendum day. He was privately convinced that a one-man crusade could not defeat the constitution. His aim was therefore more modest: he would seek to raise the proportion of "no" votes to at least 35 per cent, in the hope that this figure plus the abstentionists would total more than half the registered electorate. He would then be in a position to argue that a clear majority of Frenchmen had refused to accept the constitution, and could thus justify a campaign for immediate revision.

The task of active proselyting fell by default into the hands of the Galluist Union, whose leaders toured the country with a tub-thumping appeal to all elements of discontent. They got the feeblest sort of aid from the Radicals and the Right, who in some areas did not even form campaign committees. The Radicals, as usual, sailed close to the wind and thought first of electoral results. They followed De Gaulle in opposing the constitution, even though their own constitutional ideals were closer to the Coste-Floret draft than to De Gaulle's strong-executive doctrine. Paul Bastid set the tone by describing the draft as "the result of intermittent and passionate amours between the Socialists and the M.R.P." Edouard Herriot confined himself to one major speech, in which he described the new constitution as a hypocritical reworking of the Pierre Cot project. What Herriot really opposed was the dominance of the three big parties, which was bound up with the electoral law rather than with the constitution. To break that dominance, he was ready to play with political fire, and to risk the consequences of a Gaullist victory.

The M.R.P., although it had survived thus far without any serious defections, was still keenly embarrassed by the General's attitude. The Epinal speech for the first time contained a scarcely veiled thrust at the M.R.P.; but the leaders continued to hope that De Gaulle would not excommunicate them outright, and that by temporizing they could hold the votes of Gaullists even while backing the constitution. Maurice Schumann in L'Aube performed some tortuous feats of mental gymnastics in an effort to prove that when De Gaulle said "Frankly, no!" he really meant "Yes."

.

In line with this strategy, the M.R.P. avoided any show of enthusiasm over the constitutional draft. It contained "*du bon et du médiocre*," they asserted, but at least it had been purged of the evils of the Pierre Cot project. The M.R.P.'s lukewarm attitude was matched by, and contributed to, the uncertainty and division of the Church hierarchy. In May the Church had formed a solid phalanx in favor of a "no" vote. In October, a few rare clerics came out on one side or the other, but the majority of churchmen could find no word of consolation and guidance for the sorely tried elector.

The Communists, remembering their costly error during the May referendum campaign, this time moved with all the caution of a man stepping among eggs. Unlike the M.R.P., they did not toss daily verbal bouquets at De Gaulle, but they did refrain from attacking him and concentrated their venom on the Gaullist Union. As the campaign proceeded, however, they became increasingly irritated at the M.R.P.'s attitude. M.R.P. speakers suggested that the thing to do was to adopt the constitution and then proceed to revise it. They implied that De Gaulle was in accord with such a procedure, and that the paths of the General and the M.R.P. had diverged only temporarily. Stung by this talk, the Communists began to urge the need for a "massive majority" of "yes" votes in order to block a revisionist campaign led by the reactionaries and a new General Boulanger.

If trouble was brewing between the M.R.P. and Communists, it was headed off by De Gaulle's final double-barreled blast in the press on October 10 and 11. The General left the M.R.P.'s sophists like Schumann with no ground to stand on. He declared that when he had said "Frankly, no!" at Epinal, he had not meant "vote yes"; and he contemptuously dismissed the idea of adopting a bad constitution with a view to revising it later. The referendum, he asserted, "is a question of life or death for the country. If this constitution is adopted, anarchy and disorder will reign in France." He charged bitterly that the Assembly had made the president a phantom "perhaps because of the fear that Charles de Gaulle might one day become president of the republic." With some justice; he reminded the voters that he had a long record of fruitless appeals to his unheeding countrymen, and that he had always turned out to be right in the end. For the first time he referred publicly to the threat of a new war, and implied that France would again fall under foreign domination unless a strong executive were set up to protect French sovereignty. His conscience was now clear, he concluded; when the crisis comes, "it will not be said that I failed in my duty to enlighten the country."

De Gaulle's final attack came just at the moment when a wave of pessimism and nervousness was striking the proconstitution forces. Until three or four days before the referendum they had expected to coast to victory, but they suddenly began to wonder if they had not been overconfident. Reports from the country indicated a swing toward De Gaulle. A few resounding resignations from the M.R.P. were announced—notably that of Deputy Jacques Vendroux, De Gaulle's brother-in-law. Most inopportunely, the lid suddenly popped off a whole series of "scandals" which the opposition seized upon avidly. The biggest of these graft exposures was alleged to implicate men as highly placed as Félix Gouin himself. Gaullist Union speakers called down the wrath of divine and human justice upon the crooked politicians who, they claimed, were swimming in "scandals of wine, of textile ration points, of dried beans, of wet beans, and so on ad nauseam." It seemed possible that De Gaulle's lofty pronouncements and the Gaullist Union's earthy ones might snowball all the country's discontent and disillusionment, and carry the new draft over the same precipice as the first. By the eve of October 13, however, the period of jitters seemed to have passed. Most final forecasts estimated that the "yes" majority would probably approach 60 per cent.

As the returns came in on referendum night, the pessimists had good reason to wonder if they had not won a Pyrrhic victory. Nine million citizens had voted for their constitution; but eight million had voted against, and eight million more had refused to turn out at all. Not since 1881 had there been so high a proportion of abstentionists. "All Gaul is still divided into three parts," remarked one observer; "those who say reluctantly yes, those who say unconditionally no, and those who simply don't give a damn."

De Gaulle's strategy had succeeded even beyond his own hopes, for he could now offer plausible evidence that 64 per cent of all Frenchmen were hostile to the new constitution. If he had chosen to remain silent as in April, the constitution might easily have carried by two to one. No one could now believe that he was a political has-been, a figure out of history who belonged in a Valhalla of not-quite-dead warriors. De Gaulle was an active political force, whose continuing hold over a large minority of the voters had been proved. What the M.R.P. leaders had feared was true; their troops were the most susceptible to De Gaulle's persuasion. Some M.R.P. voters had followed the General into the "no" camp; others, confused by the contradictory pleas of Bidault and De Gaulle and by the uncertainty of the bishops, ended by staying away from the polls entirely.

France had a constitution at last, but for how long? The way was open for a revisionist campaign at once; the referendum had given De Gaulle and Capitant an apparently solid launching platform. But revisionism would depend on De Gaulle's willingness to lead it personally. It would not arise spontaneously from below—that at least was certain. Most Frenchmen were tired of constant trips to the ballot box, and they felt that too much time had already been wasted in constitutional hair-splitting. No one but De Gaulle would be capable of stirring the people out of this torpor.

And what if De Gaulle should undertake such a crusade? There were a few thoughtful Frenchmen even among his admirers who feared that it might boomerang. A party or a movement bound together by nothing but revisionism would, they felt, inevitably become an antiparliamentary league built upon the use of the plebiscite. Such a threat would rally all sound republicans around the constitution as it stood, and would lead them to oppose even the revision of its worst defects. In much the same way, republicans had come to the defense of the 1875 constitution after 1930, at a time when they ought to have considered adapting it to modern needs. Thus the effect of a revisionist campaign might be to discredit revision entirely. Simultaneously, De Gaulle would almost inevitably fail to cure the evil of political disunity. Instead, his call for revision and for an end to party divisions would split France into two roughly equal factions, with the gulf between them deeper than ever. Such were the ominous perspectives of revisionism in October 1946.

There was another major question which emerged from the referendum results: where would the M.R.P. go from here? Would they climb onto a Right-wing bandwagon driven by De Gaulle, and thus abandon their attempt to build a Center bloc? The referendum greatly strengthened those in the party who favored such a policy, and dealt a severe blow to the anti-Gaullist Bidault group. Some prominent members (perhaps including national president Maurice Schumann) now felt that the "yes" campaign had been a serious mistake, and held that the party ought to take the quickest road to Canossa—or, in this case, Colombey. They bolstered their case by citing one observer's bearish opinion that 95 per cent of the M.R.P. voters had abandoned the party in the referendum. They declared that Bidault had "truckled" long enough to the Communists, and urged that the leadership take its cue from the voters.

Calmer reflection suggested, however, that the M.R.P. still was in a position to choose its course, and that the old course might be the wiser one. The referendum results suggested that the party would be able to survive a split with De Gaulle, even though its size would be cut. The October 13 statistics offered interesting evidence concerning the nature of the party's strength. In every area where the M.R.P.'s roots were deep and its leadership able, it had held the loyalty of its troops. Its bolters came from regions where M.R.P. inroads were recent, where its party organization was shaky and its leadership weak. These bolters were the latecomers, mostly ex-Rightists who had never fully accepted the M.R.P. program. Even without their support, the M.R.P. would still be a powerful force, and might even work more effectively toward a Center bloc. For that matter, the bolters might be forced to return to the M.R.P. for want of an alternative. The party still held its old electoral trump card: it had no dangerous rival for the mass of non-Marxist voters. Neither the P.R.L. nor the *Rassemblement* was vigorous enough to rally that huge bloc of citizens. Only a party actively led by De Gaulle would be able to threaten the M.R.P. on its right.

The echoes of De Gaulle's pre-referendum attack on the constitution reached overseas France, and probably influenced the voting there on October 13. The result was a repetition of April, even though the French Union clauses had been greatly modified since then. White colonist voters again refused to approve the constitution wherever they dominated the polls; but where native voters were in control, the majority was heavily "yes." The native attitude was realistic. They knew that they had lost ground since April, but the project nevertheless still contained some important new rights. Besides, their Socialist and Communist leaders recommended adoption. The white colonists, however, were not appeased by the improvements in the French Union chapter which Bidault had engineered. To them, the empire was still in danger, even if the worst mistakes of men like Pierre Cot had been corrected. In fact, they generally voted down the "improved" draft by even greater majorities than in April. The mental barrier overseas between colonizer and colonized was evidently getting more rigid rather than less so. In direct proportion, the need for able statesmanship in Paris increased. Clearly, creating the French Union would not be an easy process.

Whatever the October referendum proved or failed to prove, whatever the portents hidden in the statistics, the Fourth Republic did at last possess a constitution. Two more months of transition, and the provisional era would finally be over. France could begin to prepare for moving out of the constitutional tent which had served as emergency housing since liberation. But there were few Frenchmen who were confident that the permanent structure would be much of an improvement. They hoped for the best; but, borrowing Léon Blum's phrase, they wondered if the nation was not merely moving "from the provisional to the precarious."

CHAPTER SEVEN

From the Provisional
to the Precarious:
Launching the Fourth Republic

I. THE END OF THE BEGINNING

The constitution which one-third of the French people took to their hearts on October 13 (with something less than enthusiasm) was not the kind of document to satisfy any citizen's dreams or to hold out the promise of a golden age. Like most compromises, it was widely regarded as an unlovely child, of obscure parentage and doubtful legitimacy. Sheer lassitude, however, led them to accept it with passive satisfaction. They cared little about its detailed contents, and rarely even took the trouble to ask which party's ideas were best reflected in it. True, a few still pointed at the Communists and uttered the political equivalent of "Galilean, thou hast conquered"; but the question of measuring defeat and victory seemed unimportant. What the mass of Frenchmen wanted was to get on with the process of establishing the government for which they now possessed a framework, and to let that government—if it could—come to grips with the material problems facing France.

Two years had gone by since liberation. In a sense, it was unfortunate that the end of the provisional period should coincide so closely with that second anniversary. Reflective minds were led to take stock of the past and the present; and a survey of the reborn republic's achievements since 1944 was bound to bring a degree of disillusionment. "The liberation was rich with infinite possibilities," wrote André Stibio gloomily. "How many of these possibilities have been realized? The question is better left unanswered." Edouard Herriot, full of nostalgia for the old regime, remarked caustically that "two years have been sufficient for the Fourth Republic to sink into disrepute, to break all records for scandals." And *Combat*, irritated by the lack of a tough and consistent economic policy, sardonically titled an editorial "*Laurel et Hardy au pouvoir!*"

Recovery there had been during those two years; no one could deny that. A major triumph was the rise of coal production, until it surpassed the prewar level. The Communists could claim most of the credit for this achievement, for their leaders had goaded the miners into steadily greater efforts and had sat successfully on the strike lid. But the victory of coal was partly due to the use of more than 50,000 German prisoners of war in the pits, and those laborers could not be held much longer. Besides, the coking coal which heavy industry needed could not be dug out of French mines, but could only come from the Ruhr. Without coke from beyond the Rhine, steel production continued to lag behind at half the prewar level.

Along with coal, the restoration of the railways was a real achievement. The heavily damaged right-of-way, bridges, and equipment had been patched together with remarkable speed, until the tonnage carried in 1946 reached 102 per cent of the prewar figure. The output of electric power and of cement also reached and then surpassed the 1938 level, although it still fell far short of crisis needs. Agricultural production too had taken a sudden spurt. After the miserable harvests of 1944 and 1945, which scarcely reached 50 per cent of the prewar level, the 1946 crop neared bumper proportions. Livestock numbers steadily increased and were beginning to approach normalcy. As for overall industrial production, it had risen in 1946 to 85 per cent of the 1939 figure, although that general average concealed great variations.

These successes, important though they were, left most Frenchmen bitter and discontented. They knew that faulty distribution still made life a struggle for existence, except for those who could resort freely to the black market. They knew that the average Frenchman's buying power—even if he could find something to buy—had been cut in two since 1938. They knew that France was still in the nineteenth century so far as modern housing was concerned, and they saw no evidence that the Fourth Republic had any plan for catching up. Unofficial figures showed that more than three-fourths of the buildings in France had been constructed before 1914; that 23 per cent of the inhabitants of Paris lacked running water, almost half lacked private toilet facilities, and 85 per cent had no central heating. "Among the great states of western Europe," *Combat* grumbled, "our country has the largest number of slum dwellings: three times as many as England in 1939 and two and a half times as many as Germany."

Some Frenchmen knew, too, that little had yet been achieved to lay the foundations for a modern industrial structure in France. The nation faced the future with a decrepit industrial plant which had already been archaic in 1939. The complaint went up that the provisional governments had followed a "policy of facility," a kind of laissez faire with respect to long-range planning, concealed behind a maze of government regulations and controls inherited from Vichy. Not until December 1946 did the almost-legendary "Monnet plan" finally emerge into the light of day. This remarkable eleven-volume survey, compiled by the government's Planning Committee under the direction of the able businessman Jean Monnet, amounted to an inventory of what France possessed and needed. It proposed a four-year schedule of heavy capital investment, rising production, and integrated exports and imports which might conceivably make France a modern industrial state by 1951. Endorsement of the plan came from every quarter, ranging from the Communists to De Gaulle. Its fulfillment, however, promised more serious difficulties, since it involved at least four more years of austere living on the part of a people with little love for austerity. Furthermore, unlike the plans of the Soviet Union, it was not backed by the power of a totalitarian state; it would have to be carried through by the democratic methods of persuasion and consent. Its fate might be a test of France's claim to be a great power, and of the practicability of planning in peacetime within the democratic framework.

The "infinite possibilities" of liberation had been political and moral even more than economic, and here too it was disappointing to take stock. Where was the sense of unity which had bound together the anti-German underground? Where was the new generation of vigorous young leaders, precociously matured in the hothouse of the resistance movement? Two years of provisional government had seen unity disintegrate once more into deep political division. The new generation had arrived on the political scene, bringing a very respectable degree of ability and good will, but somehow falling short of the needs of a crisis period. None of the Fourth Republic's new leaders seemed capable of competing with De Gaulle as a national figure; most of them were overshadowed by a few surviving prewar politicians. As for the spiritual aspect of the new France, most Frenchmen sadly confessed that the nation was deep in a "crise de moralité." An ambitious slogan of the liberation era had been "De la résistance à la révolution." Two years later, a flippant foreign visitor proposed to substitute "De la résistance à la resquille" (for which the nearest American equivalent would be "scrounging").

True, the problems faced by liberated France had been immense. It had been necessary to nurse the nation back from economic paralysis, to shoulder part of the burden of finishing the German war, and to restore France to the ranks of the democracies, running the gantlet of dictatorship on the one hand and violent revolution on the other. "Seen in the perspective of centuries," concluded one French observer, "this liberation epoch which seems to us so bitter, so disappointing, may on the contrary appear as a success. It will have its explanation and its philosophy. . . . But let us recognize that everything remains to be done."

II. THE SPIRIT AND STRUCTURE
OF THE CONSTITUTION

Talleyrand once remarked that a constitution ought to be short and obscure. The Fourth Republic's fundamental law is neither. But it does possess another quality that is perhaps a virtue: it fits easily into the groove of French governmental tradition. For the average citizen, little effort at mental adjustment has been required. Some aspects of the new regime had become familiar during the 1945-46 provisional period; even more of its characteristics recalled the Third Republic.

There is something startling about this resemblance to a political mechanism which had been so bitterly vilified after its collapse. As recently as October 1945, eighteen million voters repudiated any return to the old constitution; yet just a year later nine million of them reluctantly accepted a new document of much the same type. Structurally, the only major changes are the shrunken role of the upper house and the reorganization of the empire. Functionally, the chief difference between the Third and the Fourth Republics will probably result from France's new system of monolithic parties rather than from the constitution.

This similarity has provoked the charge that the French people were cheated by the politicians; that the voters asked for bread in October 1945, and in October 1946 were given a stone. The argument would be irrefutable if all the Frenchmen who rejected the Third Republic had known just what they wanted in its place. Instead, most of them were moved only by a vague desire for a new deal within the democratic framework. To transpose such a collective ideal into concrete institutions was not simple. Between the partisans of a strong executive and the partisans of an omnipotent legislature, there was no common meeting ground except the ground on which the Third Republic had been built. It was not so much by choice as by force of circumstances that the politicians eventually found themselves back there.

The Fourth Republic, like the Third, does not fit nicely into

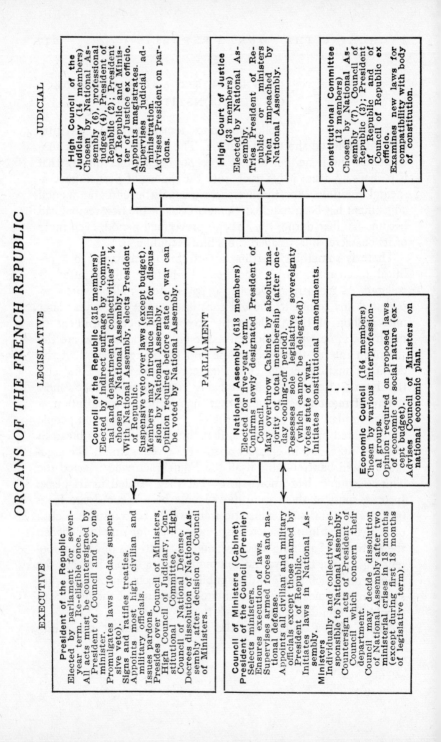

ORGANS OF THE FRENCH REPUBLIC

STRUCTURE OF THE FRENCH UNION

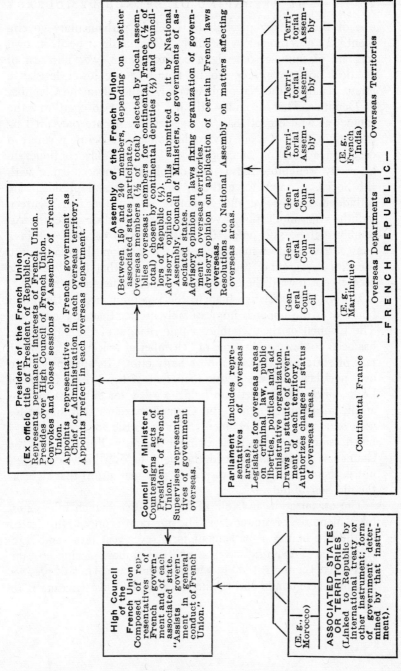

one of the ordinary pigeonholes labeled "parliamentary government" or "government by assembly." Once again it needs its own separate pigeonhole somewhere between those two. The seat of political power continues to be found in the lower legislative house, renamed the National Assembly rather than the Chamber of Deputies. That Assembly still has the right to overthrow the cabinet at will, except that "orange-peel" crises are prevented by the requirement of a one-day cooling-off period before a vote can occur on a question of confidence. The Assembly continues to be pretty well protected against dissolution. In accordance with the Socialists' safety-valve thesis, the cabinet and president are forbidden to dissolve the Assembly during the first eighteen months after an election. Even after that period of grace, the Assembly will be safe unless it overthrows two cabinets within a consecutive eighteen-month period. Dissolution thus fades into the dim background; there is little prospect that it will ever be used except toward the end of an Assembly's five-year term.

Within the legislative branch, the predominance of the lower house over the upper is immeasurably greater than it used to be. The Council of the Republic, a pale shadow of the old Senate, has been confined to the role of "chamber of reflection," with the task of correcting the Assembly's hasty errors. Its suspensive veto over new laws is less effective than that of the British House of Lords, since the Council can hold up a law for only two months at the maximum. Even if the Council exercises that suspensive veto and proposes amendments to a bill, the lower house may brush aside the changes by a simple majority. Furthermore, the Council is specifically denied the right to overthrow a cabinet, nor is there the slightest prospect that it may usurp that right as the old Senate did.

The organization and role of the executive branch brings nostalgic memories of prewar days. The president is once again elected by the two houses of parliament for a seven-year term, and is re-eligible once. Again he serves as political pinboy, picking up cabinets whenever the Assembly knocks them down. He still presides at public ceremonies and cabinet sessions, and his signature is required on most official decrees. He may send newly adopted bills back to the Assembly for a second reading, but such bills can be re-enacted by a mere majority in the Assembly. As in the past, the president's influence may be considerable at times, but it will have to be exerted through moral persuasion alone. Félix Faure or Albert Lebrun would no doubt feel perfectly at home in the job.

The premier and the cabinet likewise continue to be just about what they were in practice before 1940. Their effectiveness depends on the premier's strength of character, and on the solidity and coherence of the coalition which makes up the cabinet. The Third Republic's vice of cabinet instability may be corrected by two new developments. First, the upper house no longer has the right to overthrow a government, so that the cabinet is required to please only one house instead of two. Second, and far more important, the Fourth Republic's new system of large disciplined parties ought to permit more solid coalitions than in the past. The danger is that as the old evil disappears, a new one may be emerging to take its place. A coalition of ill-assorted monoliths may paralyze the cabinet even while making it more stable. Or, alternatively, a coalition which omits one powerful monolithic party may be hamstrung by the obstructionist tactics of the outsider—especially if that outsider can resort to the weapon of labor unrest.

One change in the premier's status is that he may no longer ask for "full powers" to issue decree-laws in emergency periods. Paul Reynaud was the only deputy who rose to the defense of the decree-law procedure; it was repudiated even by those parties which favored a stronger executive. The explanation lies in its prewar abuse by premiers like Laval. A less important change is the provision that a newly appointed premier must be confirmed by the Assembly before he forms his cabinet rather than afterward. The presumption is that the Assembly may feel more free to reject a new premier if he has not already gone through the painful process of constructing a cabinet. In fact, however, the new system shows no sign of differing very much from the old.

The judiciary in France has never possessed such independence or prestige as in Anglo-Saxon countries. This weakness resulted in part from the fact that the appointment and promotion of judges was vested in the Minister of Justice, whose stewardship was rarely free of political bias. The Communists proposed to substitute popular election of all judges, but this move was early headed off by the Socialists and the M.R.P. Philip and Coste-Floret pointed darkly to the example of the United States, where, they declared, "elected judges are often controlled by gangsters or the trusts." Instead, the new constitution sets up a High Council of the Judiciary with power to appoint judges, supervise judicial administration, and advise the president on pardons. Six of its fourteen members are chosen by the Assembly; four others are professional magistrates elected by their peers. The High Council thus avoids the dangers of either political or narrowly professional control. If the new system works successfully, it may give the judiciary a greater degree of independence than it has ever enjoyed in France.

Several other new organs, all of secondary significance, are added to the governmental structure by the constitution. One is a thirty-member High Court of Justice which has jurisdiction over cabinet ministers or over the president if accused of malfeasance in office. This Court, elected by the Assembly, is composed of twenty deputies and ten outsiders. It inherits the role which the Senate exercised ex officio during the Third Republic.

Another quasi-novelty is the Economic Council, which existed before the war but did not have constitutional status. The Assembly must secure its opinion on all bills of an economic nature prior to adopting such bills; and the cabinet must ask its advice in connection with economic planning. The Council includes representatives of the principal labor, employers', and agricultural organizations, plus a few from family associations and other broad-interest groups. Its makeup represents a clear victory for Communist-Socialist ideas over the "corporative" and regionalist concepts of the M.R.P. The latter party wanted to base representation on a long list of professional groups and on the various regions in France, rather than on the nationally organized interprofessional associations (such as the C.G.T. for labor and the C.G.A. for agriculture). The Left's victory meant that the Council would amount to little more than "an Academic Council of the French economy" rather than a potential economic sub-parliament with a corporative flavor.

Still another new organ is the Constitutional Committee, a body of twelve experts chosen by the Assembly or the Council of the Republic to act as watchdogs over new laws. If the Committee judges a measure to be incompatible with the body of the constitution, it will call on the Assembly either to revise the law or, if the Assembly prefers, to initiate a constitutional amendment in harmony with the law. In fact, the twelve watchdogs will rarely if ever have occasion to show their teeth. They will not be permitted to suspend laws on the ground of a conflict with the Declaration of Principles—the Socialists saw to that. Obsessed by the memory of Roosevelt's struggle with the Supreme Court, the Socialists were determined to avoid any mechanism which might obstruct future social and economic reforms. As a result, the Constitutional Committee cannot act to protect the individual's rights against the state, but only to prevent the legislature from infringing upon the main body of the constitution.

The new procedure for amending the constitution is relatively complex. Amendments will be initiated by the Assembly, but will ordinarily have to be approved by popular referendum. The referendum may be avoided, however, if the Assembly adopts the proposed amendment by a two-thirds majority, or if both houses of parliament approve it by a three-fifths margin.

One of the most obscure parts of the constitution is the chapter which deals with local government and administration. The Left's attempt to decentralize authority in a country which had long been the world's most centralized democracy ended in only partial success. In theory, each department (county) will run its own local affairs, with the president of the departmental council acting as executive. At the same time, agents of the central government will continue to be sent out from Paris, and will probably retain a considerable degree of authority even though the title "prefect" itself may disappear. Practice alone will determine the relationship between the prefect and the president of the local council.

There is some justice in Edouard Herriot's sarcastic comment that the constitution requires the two men to supervise each other.

Far and away the most important novelty of the Fourth Republic is the elaborate new structure of the French Union. This chapter amounts to a kind of constitution within the constitution. It defines the French Union as a group of "nations and peoples which pool or co-ordinate their resources and their efforts in order to develop their respective civilizations." Gone is the old concept of assimilating the natives to French culture; but gone also is the phrase in the Pierre Cot draft which based participation in the Union on free consent. Thanks to Bidault and the M.R.P. the pious gesture has been replaced by the *fait accompli*.

The French Union's mechanism is a curious blend of logic and realism. To begin with, all parts of the Union are classified into one of two broad categories: (a) the *French Republic*, including continental France, the assimilated overseas departments like Martinique and Guiana, and the overseas territories like Equatorial Africa or New Caledonia; (b) the *associated states*—Morocco, Tunisia, and the various segments of the projected Indo-Chinese Federation. The way is left open for the overseas territories to evolve either toward full assimilation as French departments or toward autonomy as associated states. Their status cannot be changed, however, without the consent of parliament in Paris.

The constitution provides for three new quasi-federal organs in Paris. The first will be the president of the French Union—ex *officio* title of the president of the republic. The second is the High Council of States, a consultative body composed of delegates of the associated states as well as of the French Republic. The High Council will resemble a collection of ambassadors from states linked together by international treaties. It represents a rather feeble attempt to co-ordinate the policies of the associated states with those of France. The third new organ, the Assembly of the French Union, will not include representatives of the associated states unless the latter voluntarily choose to participate. Half of its membership will come from the overseas areas, half from continental France. Its initial powers will be purely advisory;

it will have the right to vote resolutions and to express its opinion on proposed laws referred to it by the National Assembly or the cabinet. The constitution-makers presumed that all bills affecting the Union as a whole would be referred to the Assembly of the French Union.

For the immediate future, this commonwealth structure will amount to little more than a façade. Real power to legislate for the Union as a whole remains in the hands of the French parliament, which contains a small proportion of overseas representatives (at present, roughly ten per cent in the National Assembly and twenty per cent in the Council of the Republic). A limited degree of local self-government has been granted by setting up representative assemblies in all the overseas territories. One African deputy has rather unjustly stigmatized these assemblies as "caricatures of democracy." They possess relatively narrow powers to advise and control the governor, and most of them assure some representation to the white minority. Algeria has recently been granted an assembly with somewhat greater autonomy, but the federalist hopes of Ferhat Abbas are still unrealized. As of 1947, "progressive federalism" has not progressed very far. If that doctrine turns out to be more than a mere phrase, the day may come when the Assembly of the French Union will develop into the central organ of the whole system, with a federal cabinet responsible to it. At best, however, that day lies in the misty future.

Both in spirit and in structure, then, the Fourth Republic's constitution is familiar rather than revolutionary. Perhaps the times themselves are not revolutionary enough for any other type of mechanism. At any rate, the constitution offers a framework within which the nation can work out its problems, if only the divisions within France are not too deep to prevent a necessary minimum of common effort. Montaigne's dictum of four centuries ago holds good for the new constitution: *"Les choses ne sont de soy ni bien ni mal; elles sont la place du bien ou du mal, selon que vous la leur faictes."*

III. THE MACHINERY
IN SLOW MOTION

Three months after the adoption of the constitution, the essential parts of the Fourth Republic's machinery were in place and beginning to function. The new National Assembly, elected on November 10, was the first to convene; the Council of the Republic gathered in the old Senate chambers on the day before Christmas; and the two houses joined at Versailles on January 16 to name Vincent Auriol first president of the Fourth Republic. Auriol chose as premier his fellow Socialist Paul Ramadier, who had been one of the principal drafters of the new constitution. During the weeks that followed, the secondary cogs were fitted into place, so that by the summer of 1947 only the Assembly of the French Union and the High Council of States were still in the blueprint stage.

The constitution faced its first test even before it went formally into effect. Immediately after the October referendum, ardent Gaullists raised the cry of revision. Intoxicated by the fact that sixteen million Frenchmen had refused to vote for the constitution, they aimed to turn the November 10 elections into a revisionist plebiscite and to pack the new National Assembly with deputies pledged to carry out De Gaulle's program. All through France, Gaullist Union leaders put out feelers to Center and Right groups in an effort to form joint lists of candidates on a revisionist platform. One Gaullist Union official enthusiastically confided that he had a plan which would win over 90 per cent of the M.R.P. troops, leaving the party leadership high and dry.

This ambitious campaign quickly sputtered out. The only man capable of making it succeed was Charles de Gaulle himself, but De Gaulle still preferred a silent waiting game. His only public statement was a lofty recommendation that the voters choose deputies "truly resolved" to change their "absurd and outmoded constitution" at once. Without his personal leadership as a magnet to draw together dissident elements, revisionist coalitions simply did not materialize except in a few rare districts.

The second key to revisionism's success or failure was the attitude of the M.R.P. Many of its militants, disturbed by their shaky referendum victory, were strongly tempted, but the party's leadership once more held it in line. Francisque Gay announced that constitutional revision was a future M.R.P. objective but not an immediate one; that it would be wise to give the new machinery a trial before overhauling it. In place of revisionism, the M.R.P. built its campaign upon a more outspoken variety of anti-Communism than in the past. "Bidault without Thorez!" was their battle cry. It was the first time since liberation that a major party had openly urged the ousting of the Communists from the government.

De Gaulle's reserve and the M.R.P.'s resistance to temptation were enough to insure the constitution against immediate attack. The voters wearily trooped to the polls once more on November 10, and cut revisionism off at the roots. The Gaullist Union captured only ten seats, and none of the other groups which had opposed the constitution made any appreciable gains. Once again the three big parties swept more than seventy per cent of the total vote. The M.R.P., as a consequence of De Gaulle's almost-silent hostility, slipped back into second place behind the Communists; yet the wisdom of its strategy seemed to be confirmed. It won back three-fourths of the voters who had deserted in the referendum, and reaffirmed its permanence as a major political force. Even without De Gaulle's help, it was able to compete with the Communists on almost even terms. Nevertheless, the M.R.P. leadership still labored under the handicap of doubtful loyalty on the part of much of its following. One M.R.P. deputy remarked in disgust that of the 42,000 M.R.P. voters in his district, "there aren't 42 real militants." Therefore the same old specter remained to haunt M.R.P. dreams: what would happen if, some day, De Gaulle should finally choose to lead a rival party?

The M.R.P.'s partners in tripartism enjoyed varying fortunes. For the Socialists, it was the worst setback yet. They lost three-fourths of a million votes, some to the Communists in urban areas, even more to the M.R.P. or to the convalescing Radicals. The post-liberation trend toward two great blocs seemed to be gathering momentum in each election. The Communists were restored to the rank of "France's first party," although their margin over the M.R.P. was narrow. Their share of the popular vote grew to 28 per cent, thus equaling the M.R.P.'s June victory. This triumph confounded the analysts, most of whom had been proclaiming since June that the Communists had passed the peak of their strength and were on the downgrade. Almost everywhere in France, in city and country alike, they clung to their positions and even improved them slightly.

The election of the upper house in December further confirmed both the defeat of revisionism and the polarization of French political opinion around the Communists and the M.R.P. Those two parties ran neck and neck in continental France, with the M.R.P. winning a slight edge of sixty-two seats to the Communists' fifty-nine, and the Socialists trailing far behind with thirty-six. The overseas returns, however, tipped the balance toward the Left and gave the Communists a tiny margin of primacy. The Council of the Republic thus became a fairly faithful replica of the lower house, which meant that it would not be likely to act as a brake on the Assembly. Its membership suggested that the party machines meant to use it as a consolation prize for unsuccessful candidates for the lower house. The Leftists now felt safe enough to let the Council set up shop in the Senate's old quarters rather than in the less hallowed *Maison de la Chimie*, as some of them had suggested. True partisans of bicameralism, after watching the Council in action for several weeks, concluded in disgust that its "striking and total impotence" had already been proved. They might have added that a quasi-impotent body of more than two hundred men, with all the trappings of high rank, is a costly luxury in a poverty-stricken state. Their goal, however, was not to abolish it, but to aim at changing its mode of election in 1948.

One more barrier against revisionism was built when Vincent Auriol was made first president of the republic. The honor was well deserved for the man who had served as great compromiser all through 1946. There was a measure of irony in his election, though: Auriol, like Jules Grévy in 1879, took over a post which he himself had proposed to abolish. His elevation to the Elysée palace meant that no strong-executive precedents would be created during the first seven years of the Republic.

Far more important than the choice of a president was the question of a governing majority to operate the constitutional machinery and to lead the country back to economic stability. A year of bickering among the three big parties had worn tripartism thin; only the Socialists still clung in self-protection to the idea of a Communist-Socialist-M.R.P. coalition. Before the elections the M.R.P. had raised the cry "Bidault without Thorez!," to which the Communists had at once retorted "Thorez without Bidault!" The election results put a damper on both of these schemes, for neither the Communists nor the M.R.P. emerged quite strong enough to serve as anchor for a coherent majority. The M.R.P. and the Socialists could conceivably set up a cabinet by getting the aid of the Radicals; but this group of old-school liberals would not fit smoothly into a coalition dedicated to the Socialist-M.R.P. doctrine of democratic collectivism. Many Frenchmen concluded that the Fourth Republic was saddled with an "ungovernable" Assembly at the very start, and that the earliest possible dissolution was the only way out. Extremists of the Gaullist school, convinced that no compact and coherent majority could be found, sat back to await the arrival of anarchy and chaos.

The subsequent six months brought some surprises, but no conclusive proof that the Gaullist estimates were wrong. In a groping effort toward salvation, the Republic's leaders tried three successive experiments. The first, a purely interim affair, was a Blum cabinet without either Bidault or Thorez. The second was a return to the tripartite principle, broadened to quadripartism by the addition of the *Rassemblement des Gauches*. The third, and doubtless the most significant, came in May when the Communists were pushed out of the cabinet for the first time since liberation, leaving a Center bloc in control.

The Blum experiment in December and January was unpremeditated. It grew out of a two-week deadlock over the formation of a new three-party cabinet to replace that of Bidault. The crisis, which endangered the new regime at its very inception, was finally resolved by a *coup de théâtre*: seventy-four-year-old Léon Blum, acting against medical advice, emerged from retirement to set up the first one-party cabinet which France had known for sixty years. Blum was well aware, however, that his all-Socialist ministry was at the mercy of its larger neighbors, and that it could not be a permanent solution. Germany before Hitler and Italy before Mussolini had already gone through the experience of minority governments tolerated by two hostile blocs.

Blum's thirty days in power proved to be far more significant than any Frenchman had foreseen. For the first time in months the cabinet functioned as a harmonious team, proposed a set of vigorous and consistent measures designed to solve the country's problems, explained its aims to the people and called for their co-operation. Its program of economic stabilization through freezing wages and reducing prices met general skepticism at first. But to the general amazement of the country, Blum's call for an immediate five-per-cent price cut actually brought results.

When Blum left office in mid-January, his personal stock and that of the Socialist party had risen sharply. A public opinion poll indicated that sixty-two per cent of the people considered his cabinet the most successful one since liberation; De Gaulle and Bidault lagged far behind with ten and eight per cent respectively. Blum had achieved no miracle: he had barely nibbled at the edges of the nation's problems, and he had not brought together a dependable majority in support of his positive program. Besides, the success of that program depended on several uncertain contingencies, such as an increasing supply of foodstuffs and consumers' goods. But he had furnished France with an example of what could be done if the cabinet would offer leadership and could persuade the country to follow. There was some irony in the fact that the young Fourth Republic had been forced to save itself by calling on an elder statesman from the decadent old regime, and had been forced to learn from him that its problems might yet be solved by democratic methods within the framework of the new constitution.

Blum's very success made a return to coalition government more certain. The M.R.P., and still more the Communists, had no intention of letting the Socialists rebuild France and gain the credit for it. They were ready to accept a Socialist premier in Paul Ramadier, and to underwrite the Socialist plan for economic stabilization, but they also demanded and got a share of cabinet posts. From January to May, therefore, a broad four-party coalition sought to continue the program inaugurated by Blum.

Three months sufficed to wreck the quadripartite experiment. In quiet times a supple and resourceful politician like Ramadier might have managed to keep such an ill-assorted team in harness; but the Fourth Republic did not face quiet times. Positive problems had to be met with positive solutions, and at least one of those problems—that of colonial rebellion—seemed to have passed the stage of compromise. On December 19, only five days before the constitution went formally into effect, the uneasy truce in Indo-China had been swept away by a full-scale Viet Nam attack on French garrisons. In March a group of Hova rebels in Madagascar followed suit, led by the Malagasy deputies to the Assembly in Paris. Reports of mounting unrest came from Algeria, Morocco, and Tunisia; there were even rumors of separatist movements in Black Africa and Tahiti.

The question of French policy toward the rebels found the Ramadier cabinet split wide open from the start. All parties except the Communists were convinced that the empire was in grave peril. They believed that its loss might reduce France to the level of Portugal (as the M.R.P. put it), and that its fate would depend on the outcome of the Viet Nam revolt. These parties (even including most of the Socialists) felt that the government faced a choice of meeting force with force or else capitulating to such terms as Ho Chi Minh might offer—and those terms now would virtually eliminate the French from the most populous part of their empire. Some Frenchmen candidly admitted that there had been bad faith on both sides during 1946, and that France's record in Indo-China was scarcely a brilliant one. But, they argued, France was ready to offer a genuine new deal if the misguided native populations would only discard their leaders and agree to co-operate on French terms.

On this issue the Communists stood apart. In line with their policy of encouraging native nationalist movements, they insisted that the only way to maintain French influence overseas was to stop hostilities at once and to accept Ho Chi Minh's terms. It was the first time since liberation that they had openly run counter to French nationalist sentiment. Their stand was unpopular, and they knew it; but it grew naturally out of Leninist teachings. The cabinet almost broke up when the Communist deputies refused to vote special credits for the Indo-Chinese campaign; a fiction of solidarity was maintained, however, when the five Communist ministers agreed to cast token votes for the credits. The revolt in Madagascar shortly afterward brought the tension within the cabinet almost to the breaking point. Rather than leave the cabinet on that issue, however, the Communists seized upon a more popular cause which opportunely came their way.

That cause was higher wages. For three months the Ramadier cabinet had struggled to carry on Blum's stabilization policy, which required that wages remain frozen until midsummer at least. Some encouraging results began to appear; for example, the black market value of the dollar was cut almost in two. But while the program seemed to be effective in stabilizing the currency, it proved less successful in reducing the cost of living. A second five-per-cent price cut ran into serious technical difficulties, and food prices showed no sign of dropping. Besides, the future of the experiment was darkened by the prospect of a disastrous 1947 harvest, by the slackening of French production, and by the dwindling of dollar credits. As euphoria once more gave way to pessimism, labor began to feel that it was bearing the whole burden of the stabilization policy, and a series of wildcat strikes broke out in April. The Communists, with little hesitation, threw in their lot with the strikers and announced that they regarded the Blum policy as a failure.

Whether the Communists wrecked the Blum experiment or merely dealt it the *coup de grâce* is perhaps an academic question. In any case, their decision wrecked tripartism. For the first time since the restoration of the Republic, the Socialists decided to stay in a cabinet without the Communists, and to risk the experiment of government by a Center bloc. The Communist ministers refused to resign even after their party voted nonconfidence in the cabinet, and had to be pushed out of office by President Auriol in a "shotgun-resignation" procedure. Some enthusiastic Frenchmen welcomed the May crisis as "the most important political event since liberation," as "a turning point in postwar French history and even European history."

The future of the Center-bloc experiment, however, was by no means assured. Ramadier's new majority was fairly coherent as coalitions go, but it faced the constant threat of desertion by the *Rassemblement des Gauches*, already restless at the government's policy of economic controls. Meanwhile the left wing of Ramadier's own Socialist party watched suspiciously for any sign of truckling to bourgeois notions. This internal stress made it difficult to develop a positive policy as a substitute for the Blum stabilization program. Furthermore, there was the prospect that the Communists might sabotage any program by letting loose an epidemic of strikes.

In spite of all the omens, the cabinet managed to muddle through the summer. The strike threat was headed off by promises of new wage increases, and the *Rassemblement* went on muttering but chose to stay with the team. Meanwhile, two new factors arrived opportunely to bolster the coalition. The first was the Marshall plan, with its promise of financial salvation; the second was the growing tendency of the Communists to align themselves openly with Moscow, and thus to isolate themselves in French politics. It was the Marshall plan which smoked the Communists out from behind their façade of old-style patriotism. In 1946 they had sullenly approved an American loan (although *Humanité* had headlined the story "From Harpagon to Uncle Sam"). In 1947 they bluntly rejected further aid, describing the American offer as "an incredible humiliation" for France. If added evidence was needed, it came when Jacques Duclos and Etienne Fajon turned up in Warsaw to make their party a charter member of a new Moscow-sponsored Information Bureau. The "Cominform's" first manifesto branded Léon Blum and Paul Ramadier as "traitors," and thus slammed the door—for the time being at least—on any return to tripartism in France. French Socialism was left with no alternatives but outright schism or continued adherence to the Center bloc.

Neither the prospect of American aid nor the self-isolation of the Communists, however, could guarantee the success of the Center experiment. If it failed, few alternatives now remained. Tripartism could not be revived unless Moscow policy should zigzag sharply again. A purely Left-wing coalition of the Popular Front type was even more unlikely, for the Left lacked a clear parliamentary majority. There remained one last possibility which still hung dimly and disturbingly in the background. That possibility was the eventual return to power of Charles de Gaulle.

De Gaulle had already begun to prepare for the crisis which he believed must come. Late in March, while the tripartite cabinet was still feuding over colonial policy, he suddenly broke the silence which had enveloped him since the October referendum. "The day is coming," he declared, "when, rejecting sterile games and reforming the badly built framework of the country . . . , the immense mass of Frenchmen will rally to France." A few days later, proclaiming that the nation could no longer be allowed to "zigzag along the edge of an abyss," De Gaulle took a fateful step: he assumed the leadership of a new movement called the *Rassemblement du Peuple Français* (quickly abbreviated to R.P.F.) with the declared purpose of building up nationwide sentiment for constitutional revision. The R.P.F. was a new version of the discredited Gaullist Union, this time with De Gaulle's official blessing and with more carefully chosen leadership. The remnants of the Gaullist Union adhered en masse, but René Capitant was shunted into the ranks while the former anthropologist Jacques Soustelle became Secretary-General.

Although De Gaulle insisted that his movement was not a new party, he made it plain that all adherents would owe primary allegiance to the R.P.F. The party leaders had no choice but to pick up the gauntlet which the General had flung down. "From now on," declared Léon Blum, "the fight is in the open." The Communists, well aware that one of De Gaulle's purposes was to isolate them, were not surprised when De Gaulle followed up with a brutal indictment of "the party of separatists" and a call for all anti-Communists to rally to his standard. From that moment, the Communists were no longer satisfied with calling De Gaulle "Boulanger" or "Badinguet"; they dipped into their quiver of epithets for such names as De la Rocque, Laval, and Hitler.

The M.R.P., as usual, reacted more cautiously; but its leaders too ended by refusing to join De Gaulle's crusade. When the General announced that his R.P.F. would run candidates in the 1947 municipal elections, the M.R.P.'s old nightmare at last became real; even Maurice Schumann mildly reproved the General for undermining the Republic. The R.P.F., excommunicated by the organized Left and Left-Center, took on a predominantly Right-wing coloration from the start. The U.D.S.R. furnished a large share of its leadership, the Rightist parties and the M.R.P. rank and file most of its recruits. Within a month Soustelle claimed almost a million adherents. Inside the Assembly, about fifty deputies rallied to a new Gaullist intergroup, and several dozen more (notably Radicals and M.R.P.s) were restrained only by party discipline.

Until the R.P.F. could test its strength at the polls, the political importance of Gaullism was as misty as its program. De Gaulle continued to speak in high-flown generalities, to denounce the Center politicians as men whose sole concern was to cook "*leur petite soupe, à petit feu, dans un petit coin,*" to hint at a new semi-corporative system of capital-labor relations, and to imply that a strong man in a strong presidency could end division in France. As the October municipal elections approached, R.P.F. leaders set their sights on 20 per cent of the popular vote. Neither they nor their political rivals foresaw the landslide which was to give the

R.P.F. almost 40 per cent of the vote instead. Overnight, the whole balance of political power in France was altered.

The Gaullist success left the Fourth Republic teetering on its foundations, for the victory was won at the expense of the Republic's friends and not of its enemies. Just as in the constitutional referendum, more than half the M.R.P.'s voters deserted to the Gaullist camp. The Center bloc's narrow majority in parliament was not directly affected, but in the country at large the Center had obviously become a minority force. From Colombey came an imperious summons to the National Assembly to commit suicide, in order to clear the way for a new constitution and the return of De Gaulle to power.

Except for such an act of suicide or a stampede of M.R.P. deputies into the R.P.F., there was no apparent way for De Gaulle to achieve his aims save through a serious upheaval, perhaps accompanied by violence. The key to De Gaulle's whole strategy was that he had long expected such an upheaval, involving not only France but the entire world. The conflict, to him, was irrepressible and imminent. The rapid growth of tension between Moscow and Washington brought grist to his mill, and so did the new tactics of the French Communists. De Gaulle had no faith in the ability of the Center politicians to carry France and the empire through a major crisis. In his eyes, the Center bloc was only a desperate expedient which might delay but could not forestall a showdown. He remained persuaded that France without strong leadership was doomed; that in the long run, the choice would lie between himself and Thorez. Therefore he continued to preach the gospel of national unity and strength, to shape the minds of Frenchmen toward the approaching crisis, to await the rising ground swell of public opinion, and to prepare himself for another 1940.

VI. TOWARD A FIFTH REPUBLIC?

Prediction has no place in history. At most, the historian's role is to assess the meaning of the past with one eye on the future. The next generation will know whether the Fourth Republic was destined to be a stormy interlude like that of 1848 or an enduring framework like that of 1875. Perhaps that generation will wonder why we were ever in any doubt.

The record of France since 1940 proves that a large proportion of Frenchmen—probably a majority still—remains democratic by tradition and temperament. An alarming number of them are on the way to losing their faith, as discouragement and cynicism spread. Many have already deserted to the totalitarian or the authoritarian camp. Those who have not yet done so remain convinced that the Fourth Republic, with all its faults, is the best and perhaps the only vehicle for preserving democratic government in France. For three years that group of stubborn idealists has groped toward its goal, avoiding the threat of authoritarian rule by a minority of either the Right or the Left. It built the constitution with that purpose in mind; it tried to reorganize the French economy through democratic means and to democratic ends. It has worked inefficiently, haltingly, always against heavy odds. The Communists, through their control of organized labor, have held a heavy mortgage on the Republic's assets. De Gaulle, by his control over the emotions of many citizens, has held another.

To both the Communists and the Gaullists, the Fourth Republic in its present form is a mere interlude, and not a regime to be stabilized, strengthened, and gradually improved. Some Gaullists have already resorted to the phrase "Fifth Republic" to symbolize their hopes. They forget that in trying to trade a faulty republic for a more perfect one, France may find itself with no true republic at all; for a republic can hardly be the work of an aggressive minority, forced on the rest of the nation against its will. As for the Communists, their lip service to the Fourth Republic does not conceal their eventual goal: to convert the regime to their purposes, and to gain total control of the state. Like Communists everywhere, they are convinced that the current stage in the class struggle involves a dual polarization around communism and fascism, and that France like every other nation must move toward one or the other. De Gaulle to them symbolizes the fascist threat; their strategy must be to make sure that all Leftist elements will choose the proper side when a choice becomes inevitable.

De Gaulle thus far has played into the Communists' hands, just as they have increasingly played into his. Caught between these two irreconcilable rivals, the Fourth Republic appears almost hopelessly fragile. Its defenders, both Catholic and anticlerical, heirs of a democratic socialist tradition, have a long and wishy-washy record of division and weakness to live down. Not even four years of common resistance to the Germans could wipe out the memory of their ancient quarrels. Unfortunately, the crucial post-liberation period found them without a great political leader —a Jaurès, a Masaryk—who could ignite their enthusiasm and could rally the country to their support. History offered Charles de Gaulle a chance to be that kind of leader, but only if he would accept the democratic method of give-and-take. Inflexible, he viewed compromise as a synonym for weakness, and gradualism as intolerable. If De Gaulle's prestige and high purpose could have been lent to the democratic socialist leaders without requiring that the latter abdicate before him, the alliance would have been well-nigh unbeatable.

The success of the Fourth Republic has a critical importance for this whole era, for the fate of France and of the world society are closely intertwined. French survival and recovery depend on both the Soviet Union and the United States, and on the preservation of peace between them. Conversely, world peace depends in considerable part on the steady return of Western Europe to stability. A France split into two warring blocs can only hasten a world split along the same lines. But a France which uses democratic methods to muddle its way toward social justice can help to divert history from the "inevitable" course marked out by the Communists. By thus disproving Marxist-Leninist-Stalinist predictions, it may open the way to an eventual revision of Moscow policy, and to a relaxation of world tension.

The years since V-E Day have proved that it is not easy for Western-style democracy to survive in a world which contains a powerful Communist state, or in a nation which contains a powerful Communist party. Perhaps such coexistence has already been proved impossible. If any hope still remains for an alternative to violence, that hope is tied up with such groups as the Center bloc in France and with such regimes as the Fourth Republic. At best it involves a long armed truce, the slow erosion of the barriers which separate the proponents of Western democracy, and the success of a middle way in the social-economic sphere.

The Fourth Republic's fate depends on its enemies as much as on its friends. So long as the Communists choose to wait for history to do its work without trying to help history along too much, hope will remain. If the Gaullists do not push too hard and too soon for a showdown, the Republic's chances rise. Finally, the Republic's democratic leaders will need a combination of courage, luck, and determination to stick together on essential issues if they are to save the regime. They may even need a temporary alliance with the Republic's enemies on the Left or the Right, provided that they can get it without handcuffing themselves. So far the Fourth Republic has lived by compromises and coalitions. If the day of compromise is over, then the Republic is as good as dead.

An effort to bring history up to the brink of tomorrow sometimes leads one perilously close to crystal-gazing. For the moment, then, let it suffice to conclude that democracy in France still has a hand grip after seven of the hardest years in the nation's history. It is wiser not to ask whether the Fourth Republic deserves to be saved on the basis of either faith or works. Perhaps, in the modern world, the bare fact of survival alone is a sufficient virtue to justify salvation.

Appendix

I. Distribution of popular vote in continental France in the elections of October 21, 1945, June 2, 1946, and November 10, 1946:

	October 1945	June 1946	November 1946
Trotskyites	10,817	44,915	59,824
	(0.07%)	(0.23%)	(0.3%)
Communists (and M.U.R.F.)	5,004,121	5,145,325	5,475,955
	(25.1%)	(25.98%)	(28.0%)
Socialists	*4,491,152	4,187,747	3,454,080
	(23.4%)	(21.14%)	(17.5%)
MRP	4,580,222	5,589,213	5,033,430
	(23.9%)	(28.22%)	(26.3%)
Rassemblement des Gauches (Radicals, U.D.S.R., etc.)	**2,018,665	2,299,963	1,971,660
	(10.6%)	(11.6%)	(10.3%)
Right-wing groups	3,001,063	2,438,167	3,136,630
	(15.83%)	(12.83%)	(16.4%)

* The Socialist total in October 1945 included most of the U.D.S.R. vote, since the two groups generally followed coalition tactics in that election.

** The Rassemblement des Gauches was not organized until 1946. This total includes the vote polled by the Radical Socialists and by independent lists of the same general character.

259

II. Statistical results of referenda held since liberation (figures include the vote cast in overseas areas as well as in continental France; figures given for the October 1946 referendum are tentative and approximate rather than final):

Referendum of October 21, 1945, to determine nature and powers of new Assembly:

Eligible voters	25,717,551
First question:	
For a Constituent Assembly	18,584,746
For a Chamber and Senate to revise the 1875 Constitution	699,136

Second question:	
For the Provisional Government's plan restricting powers and tenure of Assembly	12,795,213
For an unrestricted Assembly	6,449,206

Referendum of May 5, 1946, on first constitutional draft:

Eligible voters	25,827,377
For approval	9,453,675
Against approval	10,583,724

Referendum of October 13, 1946, on second constitutional draft:

Eligible voters	25,800,000
For approval	9,257,432
Against approval	8,125,295

III. Distribution of seats in the two Constituent Assemblies, and in the first National Assembly chosen under the new constitution (the groups are listed as they sat from left to right, with their strength as it stood late in each session. For the National Assembly, figures are given as of July 1947):

	First Constituent Assembly	Second Constituent Assembly	National Assembly
Communists	152	146	168
Union of Republicans and Resisters (M.U.R.F.)	9	7	15
Triumph of Democratic Liberties in Algeria (Messali)	—	—	5
Algerian Manifesto (Abbas)	—	11	—
Socialists	143	129	105
U.D.S.R.	29	21	27
Radical Socialists	28	32	43
Algerian Moslems (Bendjelloul)	7*	—	6
M.R.P.	150	169	167
Peasant group	10	9	8
Independent Republicans	19	23	28
P.R.L.	35	35	35
Madagascar Nationalists**	2	2	3
Unaffiliated	2	2	8
	586	586	618

* Three of the seven Algerian Moslem deputies in the First Constituent were finally unseated for election irregularities, and were not replaced.

** During the Second Constituent Assembly, the Madagascar deputies moved from the far Right to the Left benches adjoining those of the Algerian Manifesto group. In the spring of 1947, all three Madagascar native deputies were deprived of their parliamentary immunity and arrested for their part in the Madagascar revolt.

Bibliographical Note

The source materials for contemporary history are always spotty, usually inadequate, and often unreliable. I have used a combination of oral, privately circulated, and published sources of information, all of which I have tried to sift and verify according to accepted standards of historical research. I have violated academic tradition, however, by avoiding the use of footnote references. To cite the origin of information which I received orally might in some cases embarrass my informants; and to cite the printed sources alone would produce a kind of unbalance.

Among the published materials used, I have drawn most heavily upon French government documents and upon the French press. The constitutional debates, and the legislative achievements of the four different Assemblies which have succeeded one another since liberation, may be found in the *Journal Officiel de la République Française* (two series, *Débats* and *Lois et Décrets*). Bills, amendments, and preliminary versions of the two constitutional drafts were published currently as *Documents de l'Assemblée Nationale Constituante*. The text of the Fourth Republic's new constitution (together with four subsidiary "organic laws") appeared in the *Journal Officiel (Lois et Décrets)* of October 28, 1946; a series of cabinet decrees setting up the new territorial assemblies overseas was published in the October 27 issue. The ill-fated April constitution never reached the sacrosanct pages of the *Journal Officiel*, but it was circulated by the Ministry of Information as a special newspaper supplement.

The minutes of the first and second Constitutional Committees have been issued in condensed form in two bulky volumes called *Séances de la Commission de la Constitution: Comptes Rendus Analytiques* (Paris, 1946). Unofficial minutes of these Committee sessions were also taken by representatives of at least two of the major parties, and were circulated daily in mimeographed form to fellow deputies. I had access to these unofficial accounts, which add some color to the official version.

Other government publications of value were the Ministry of Information's series of brochures on a wide variety of subjects, and the weekly (later biweekly) *Bulletin d'Information* of the Ministry of Overseas France.

Two useful reference works for the early post-liberation period were issued privately. André Siegfried, Roger Seydoux and others edited *L'année politique: revue chronologique des principaux faits politiques, économiques, et sociaux de la France de la libération de Paris au 30 décembre 1945* (Paris, 1946); and Raoul Husson produced a statistical compilation called *Elections et referendums des 21 octóbre 1945, 5 mai et 2 juin 1946* (Paris, 1946). Surveys of public opinion were conducted by two private groups: the *Institut Français d'Opinion Publique* and the *Service de Sondages et Statistiques*. Both groups issued biweekly reports of indifferent accuracy.

French newspapers and periodicals offer a kaleidoscopic variety of information and misinformation on current politics, and sometimes throw light on past events as well. The following daily newspapers were extensively used:

Communist or pro-Communist: *L'Humanité* (official party organ); *Ce Soir* (evening paper controlled by party); *Front National* (outgrowth of Communist-controlled resistance movement of the same name; ceased publication 1946); *Libération* (organ of M.U.R.F.).

Socialist: *Le Populaire* (official party organ); *Cité-Soir* (frequent editorials by André Philip; ceased publication 1946); *Franc-Tireur* (left-wing Socialist, following consistent fellow-traveler line).

M.R.P.: *L'Aube* (official party organ).

Center: *Résistance* (U.D.S.R. tinged with Christian Socialist

views of *Jeune République* party); *Parisien Libéré* (U.D.S.R.,
founded by the more conservative O.C.M. element); *Combat* (independent, critical, allegedly reflecting the pessimism of existen-
tialist philosophy); *L'Ordre* (independent, organ of Emile Buré;
a relic of prewar personal journalism); *Le Monde* (Right-Center,
linked with business and industrial interests); *Le Figaro* (Right-
Center, directed to *bien-pensant* bourgeoisie, increasingly sym-
pathetic toward M.R.P.).

Radical Socialist: *L'Aurore* (edited by Paul Bastid); *La Dépêche
de Paris*; *La Voix de Paris* (organ of the maverick "Radical-Com-
munists" like Pierre Cot and Albert Bayet who left the party in
1946; ceased publication 1946).

Right wing: *L'Epoque* (ties with big business; strongly Gaullist); *L'Etoile du Soir* (violently Gaullist); *France Libre* (outgrowth of Rightist resistance movement *Ceux de la Libération*
headed by André Mutter); *La Nation* (independent Rightist,
organ of Louis Marin; ceased publication 1946).

The following weeklies were used most frequently: *Action*
(M.U.R.F.-Communist); *La Marseillaise* (pro-Communist, organ
of *Front National*); *Libertés* (left-wing Socialist); *La Vérité*
(Trotskyite); *Climats* (Gaullist, specializes in problems of the em-
pire); *La Bataille* (Gaullist, edited by Rightist deputy François
Quilici); *Carrefour* (M.R.P.).

Monthly periodicals: *Les Cahiers Politiques* (editors mostly Socialist, M.R.P., or U.D.S.R.; published underground during Vichy
period as organ of *Comité Général d'Etudes*; suspended publication 1946); *Renaissances* (board of editors likewise drawn from
various Center parties); *Politique* (M.R.P.); *Esprit* (left-wing
Catholic); *Les Cahiers du Communisme* (official party publication); *La Revue Socialiste* (sponsored by Socialist party); *Res
Publica* (organ of old-school Radical Socialists); *Le Socialiste* (ir-
regularly published private organ of Paul Faure's ex-Socialists).

Few studies of post-liberation France have yet appeared. Doro-
thy M. Pickles's *France Between the Republics* (London, 1946)
stands almost alone; it covers the period from June 1940 to November 1945. The eminent constitutional lawyer Boris Mirkine-

Guetzevich has produced a kind of preliminary study entitled *La quatrième république* (New York, 1946). Two recent articles analyze the new constitution: "Pertinax" [André Géraud], "The New French Constitution," *Foreign Affairs*, April 1947; and R. K. Gooch, "Recent Constitution-Making in France," *American Political Science Review*, June 1947. There is a good brief study of the Fourth Republic's trend toward state ownership in *The World Today* (London) for August 1946 (J. C. B., "Nationalization in France"). Aspects of the labor movement are discussed in Henry W. Ehrmann's "French Labor Goes Left," *Foreign Affairs*, April 1947.

The best recent reappraisal of the Third Republic is David Thomson's *Democracy in France* (London, 1946). François Goguel has examined the weaknesses of the prewar regime from a left-wing Catholic viewpoint in *La politique des partis sous la IIIe république* (2 vol., Paris, 1946). The standard history of the Third Republic is D. W. Brogan, *The Development of Modern France* (London, 1940); two excellent analyses by American scholars are W. R. Sharp, *The Government of the French Republic* (New York, 1938), and R. K. Gooch, *The Government and Politics of France* (in J. T. Shotwell, *Governments of Continental Europe*, New York, 1940). An up-to-date constitutional history is Marcel Sibert's *La constitution de la France du 4 septembre 1870 au 9 août 1944* (Paris, 1946).

Among the books on constitutional reform which appeared during the last years of the Third Republic, the following may be mentioned: René Capitant, *La réforme du parlementarisme* (Paris, 1934); André Tardieu, *La réforme de l'état* (Paris, 1934); Léon Blum, *La réforme gouvernemental* (Paris, 1936); Jacques Bardoux, *La France de demain* (Paris, 1937); A. Soulier, *L'instabilité ministerielle sous la troisième république* (Paris, 1939). A survey of reform proposals advanced before 1940 was published in *Politique* for August-September 1945. A bulky documentation on party attitudes toward constitutional reform in 1934 may be found in the *Documents Parlementaires, Chambre des Députés*, for that year.

Details on the demise of the Third Republic at Vichy in 1940 are contained in Vincent Auriol's *Hier . . . Demain* (2 vol., Paris, 1945); Joseph Paul-Boncour's *Entre deux guerres* (vol. III, Paris, 1946); Jean Montigny's *Toute la vérité* (Clermont-Ferrand, 1940; by one of Laval's henchmen); Louis Gros's *République toujours* (Avignon, 1945; Socialist view); René Cassin's *Un coup d'état: la soi-disant constitution de Vichy* (London, 1941); and Jean Castagnez' *Précisions oubliées* (Sancerre, 1945; by a lieutenant of Paul Faure).

On the Vichy regime, the best governmental analysis is Pierre Tissier, *The Government of Vichy* (London, 1942); see also the reminiscences of a Vichy official, H. du Moulin de Labarthète, *Le temps des illusions* (Geneva, 1946). The best brief survey of the anti-Vichy resistance movement may be found in a Ministry of Information bulletin: [Odette Merlat], *Esquisse d'une histoire de la résistance française* (Paris, 1946). The Ministry of Information has also published the National Resistance Council's program for liberated France.

General de Gaulle's views on the problem of government are more or less dimly apparent in his books *Le fil de l'épée* (Paris, 1932); *Vers l'armée de métier* (Paris, 1934); and *Discours aux Français* (2 vol., Paris, 1945). De Gaulle's public statements since 1945 have been collected in various leaflets by the Ministry of Information.

A number of books written during the occupation or after liberation dealt directly or incidentally with the problem of government: e.g., Léon Blum, *A l'échelle humaine* (Paris, 1945; written in 1941); Jean Zay, *Souvenirs et solitude* (Paris, 1946; also written in captivity); Vincent Auriol, *Hier . . . Demain*; Maxime Blocq-Mascart, *Chroniques de la résistance* (Paris, 1945; studies made during the Vichy period by the O.C.M.); Jules Basdevant *et al*, *Refaites une constitution* (Paris, 1946); "Indomitus" [Philippe Viannay], *Nous sommes les rebelles* (Paris, 1945); Pierre Hervé, *La libération trahie* (Paris, 1945). The text of the C.G.E.'s constitutional project of 1943 was reprinted in *Les Cahiers Politiques* for October 1945; the Communist reaction to it appeared clandestinely in *Les Cahiers* [*du Communisme*], 1er trimestre 1944.

The final report of André Philip's Committee on State Reform, which functioned at Algiers in 1943, may be found in the periodical *Etudes et Documents*, July-August 1945. A sampling of the clandestine press of 1940-44 revealed only sparse references to the constitutional problem.

Index